THE ETERNAL TIGHTROPE

Jarl Jørstad

MINERVA PRESS
LONDON
MIAMI DELHI SYDNEY

THE ETERNAL TIGHTROPE
Copyright © Jarl Jørstad 2000

All Rights Reserved

No part of this book may be reproduced in any form,
by photocopying or by any electronic or mechanical means,
including information storage or retrieval systems,
without permission in writing from both the copyright
owner and the publisher of this book.

ISBN 0 75411 062 1

First Published 2000 by
MINERVA PRESS
315–317 Regent Street
London W1R 7YB

Printed in Great Britain for Minerva Press

THE ETERNAL TIGHTROPE

Original title: Balanseganger
Translated from the Norwegian by Susi Enderud

To my children and grandchildren

Incidit in Scyllam qui vult vitare Charybdim

The story is told in the *Odyssey* that during their sea voyage from Troy, after Odysseus and his men had escaped many dangers, they were about to pass through a narrow strait between high rocky shores. There the two monsters Scylla and Charybdis were lying in wait for all passing seafarers. As the ship entered the strait, the monster Scylla, with six heads on six long necks, came out of its cave, snatched six men from the deck and devoured them with a snapping sound. Immediately Odysseus altered his course. But then he came dangerously close to the maelstrom caused by Charybdis. Charybdis swallowed inconceivably great masses of water several times a day, only then to spit them out again. The result was that the entire passage between the rocks boiled and churned, so that even the largest ships were dragged down. The wind was strong and the crew rowed for their very lives, but they noticed how the stern of the ship was being pulled around, and for minutes it seemed as if they would be dragged down into the deep sea. However, they succeeded in passing by safely.

Contents

Preface		9
I	In solitary confinement *Loss, loneliness and anxiety*	13
II	Prisoner in Germany *Fellowship and leadership*	26
III	What are we doing to each other? *Projective phenomena in a small group*	38
IV	What goes on in large groups? *Community meetings and Tavistock Conferences*	45
V	What turns me into a bully or into a victim of bullying? *The Dynamics of Bullying*	57
VI	Why do we not tolerate those who are different? *Discrimination, xenophobia and racism*	72
VII	We are all murderers *The Roots of Aggression*	90
VIII	What causes us to kill others? *Circumstances which influence the boundaries between fantasy and reality*	103
IX	Why are men more violent than women? *Some ideas about the male role*	116
X	Sexual child abuse – fantasy or reality? *How reliable is our childhood memory?*	134

XI	Homosexuality – do we know anything about its causes?	
	The balance between male and female	154
XII	Body and soul, muscles and feelings	
	A hypothesis about fibromyalgia	172
XIII	The body tells us something that reason does not understand	
	Some psychsomatic fragments	189
XIV	The invisible traumas	
	Loss, narcissistic injuries and generational narcissism	207
XV	Words and lack of words – opportunities and limitations	
	On communication in psychotherapy	224
Epilogue		243

Preface

Life is a balancing act.

From the very first moment of birth, we are faced with apparent contradictions within ourselves and in relation to our surroundings. At first, as a tension between something that is good and something that hurts, and later, between what is me and what is not me. In the course of our development, we attempt to extricate ourselves from our total dependence on the 'almighty' mother, gradually achieving relative independence. We are going to be dependent on other people all our lives, and we must try to find a balance between these two extremes of our existence. This dilemma is most dramatically displayed in the two deepest causes of our anxiety: the fear of loss, of separation and loneliness (Chapter I), and the fear of losing oneself in the group (Chapters III and IV). However, sometimes life confronts us with terrible, deadly threats. This I have illustrated by describing my experiences as a prisoner in Germany (Chapter II). It is in situations like these that the sense of fellowship can help us to survive.

We are confronted with similar problems in several areas, when that which provokes us in others, unconsciously activates in us what we do not accept in ourselves – a balance between the known, and the unknown or alien (Chapters V and VI). A related perspective is the perpetual balance between fantasy and reality, impulse and action, love and hate (Chapters VII, VIII and X). The necessity for keeping the balance also presents itself in the way in which we manage to reconcile ourselves to both weakness and strength (Chapters V and IX), the female and the male in us (Chapter XI), and body and soul (Chapters XII and XIII).

We realise that in most areas, it is not a question of contradictions ruling each other out, but of pairs complementary to one another, which together stand a greater chance of achieving wholeness and harmony. However, in all areas dangers lie in wait, like Scylla and Charybdis: too much or too little of the one or the other, may have catastrophic consequences for the individual.

In Chapter XIV, I have attempted to gather and condense some of the experiences I gained from working from more than forty years with people. I mention some severe traumas or defects, which very often lie at the root of psychic and psychosomatic illness. Here too, we can recognise the tightrope walk between too much and too little, often running like a scarlet thread through several generations.

In Chapter XV, I try to show that in the psychotherapeutic relationship, many of the polarities which I have touched upon in this book, are put to the test, and even reinforced. This is evident, among other things, in the balance between closeness and distance, and in the understanding of another person by becoming aware of something in oneself. At the same time, we, the therapists, have to be ourselves and different from the other. Psychotherapy will also continually have to be a balancing act between speech and silence, between communication with words and without words, between fantasy and reality. In fact, some of the most important changes come about when we test and recognise our own limits, and when we interact with others.

The aim of this book is to try to share some of my most important experiences, from my personal life, as well as my work as a physician, psychotherapist and psychoanalyst.

The reason why I have used personal experiences as a starting point in several chapters, or to shed light on something by describing my own symptoms, is primarily to show that personal and self-experienced issues may become a gateway to understanding areas which are problematic for most people. My two training analyses and my work with people have taught me the importance of recognising that I count nothing human alien from me. *Homo sum, humani nil a me alienum puto*; I am tarred with the same brush as regards everything that is considered alien, different, frightening or pathological.

In many ways, I have considered myself fortunate and privileged in having had a lucky start in life with a loving family that gave me emotional security. Also, because I survived, literally and metaphorically, the threats and dangers I encountered.

Basically, I was just as blind during my voyage between Scylla and Charybdis as others had been. It was only when I was in obvious and imminent danger that I tried to change my course. Visibility was often poor and my awareness of a conceivably more correct course was limited. Hindsight makes it easier to realise that some of the most serious crises in my life led to significant experiences which contributed to my personal development.

In addition to being very lucky indeed in many situations, I have had the privilege in my professional life of being able, most of the time, to work with people 'in depth', and over a long period of time. Apart from my training analyses with Harald Schjelderup and Astri Brun, this work made my life more exciting and meaningful. Over the years, it has also afforded me a wider overall perspective of life's many aspects, some of which I would like to impart in this book.

It may perhaps seem naive and uncritical to deal with these complex areas in some brief chapters. Needless to say, it is not my ambition to present a comprehensive or lengthy study of each topic, but rather to convey some *partial perspectives* which I also consider important for other people.

Some of my readers will have difficulties understanding why I alternate in many chapters between subjective experiences and scientific studies. The point of this book is, however, to try to bridge the gulf between a hermeneutic, empathetic and interpretative attitude towards the feelings and experiences of my patients and myself, and research, which seeks to find general connections and regular patterns applying to many people. In my opinion, there need not be a contrast between these two approaches. On the contrary, there should be interaction if we are to understand more about people and their problems. A casuistic approach has its strength and weakness in the individual, subjective and situational area. The strength of traditional research which operates with large numbers and statistics lies in regularity and the possibility for comparison. Its weakness lies in the likelihood that the individual may get lost in statistics. There is so much in each individual and in life that cannot be expressed in numbers and statistics. We need both. Here, too, I perceive a balancing act.

I have attempted to avoid technical terms and a more scientific presentation, in the hope that as many people as possible who are interested in this subject, may benefit from the book. Where I have used technical terms which cannot be translated, an explanation will be given in the text. Those who wish to study certain areas in depth will find a reference number to the index at the end of each chapter.

I wish to thank those of my earlier patients who consented to let me use material from their treatments, with the changes necessary to conceal their true identity. I wish especially to thank Jørgen Rygh for his thorough perusal of the manuscript, and for his wise comments and suggestions for changes. During the process of writing, Stig Jørstad's constructive and critical comments have been useful. I am grateful to Susi Enderud for working a translation into English.

Sandvika,
February 1999

Chapter I

IN SOLITARY CONFINEMENT
Loss, loneliness and anxiety

In prison

Man's worst experience is presumably to lose contact with other people – to be totally isolated from the environment. This experience is the chief cause of our anxiety and has its roots in our earliest childhood. We attempt to protect ourselves consciously and unconsciously against this anxiety throughout all our lives.

My own recollections go back to July 1943 when I was locked up in a small cell in hut E of the Bredtveit prison in Groruddalen, in the northern part of Oslo. I sat on a wooden stool in a tiny cell measuring one and a half by three metres, containing a bunk which could be put up against one of the walls, a slop pail and a small table with a wash basin. High up on the wall there was a minute window for ventilation, not more than thirty centimetres square, which just about gave me a glimpse of the outside world if I stood on the stool. From there I could discern some fields and high, double barbed wire fences which enclosed the whole prison compound. To the left I could see the big three-storeyed brick prison building with its rows of large barred windows facing the hut in which I sat. It was very quiet, I heard no signs of other prisoners being in the hut, at least not in my vicinity.

My worst fears had come true. Three men from the Nazi state police suddenly appeared at my home in Snarøya in Bærum. They ransacked the whole house, my room in particular. Afterwards they took me in for questioning at the Victoria Terrace, the centre for the Gestapo and the state police in Oslo, and later drove me to Bredtveit.

The state police suspected me of having distributed illegal newspapers. However they disclosed nothing about what had caused them to suspect me, nor was I told which newspaper it concerned. It was, however, quite obvious that they knew something. I flatly denied everything, but was on tenterhooks while they were searching my room. They found neither copies of the illegal newspapers *XYZ* and *London News*, nor the small amount of coloured posters with pictures of all the bombers produced in the United States which I had been foolish enough to hide.

I sat and pondered over the whole situation and my thoughts went out to my family. I was frightened and desperate. Certainly my parents and my sister were also. They had no idea what I had been up to. What was going to happen now? There was a death penalty for producing and distributing illegal newspapers and anti-German propaganda. But the state police had found no evidence. Someone must have been forced to divulge my name – under torture perhaps? Who could it be? Some of the people with whom I collaborated knew me only under my cover name 'Arne'. What could they have said? My mind was full of unanswered questions, and a gnawing anxiety and fear of the future.

The twenty years of my life passed before my inner eye. I thought about how privileged I had been and how much I cared for my family. My thoughts went to my friends and classmates in the third form of my high school, and to the girl I was in love with. The team spirit of this form had been excellent. We had anticipated the official *russetid* (period of graduation celebrations) with many unbelievably enjoyable private parties throughout the winter and spring, I had just about managed to achieve the required seventy-five points in my A-levels to enable me to study medicine, and I was to start in the autumn. Having lacked a few points in my A-levels at Stabekk the year before, I had made a fresh attempt with good results. But what would happen now?

The man I first became acquainted with was the prison officer, a man from Stavanger, more than two metres tall, who hurled abuse at me at the slightest opportunity. He would suddenly fling open the door to the cell in order to disclose me doing something against the rules. There was little food and I was almost always hungry. My weight went down by six kilos during the first month, but it helped when my mother left some boiled potatoes for me during two visits. During the three months of my stay at the Bredtveit prison I never got out into fresh air, nor did I get any exercise. I left the cell only when I was taken out for an interrogation and on the two occasions of my mother's visits.

The two officers interrogating me used abusive language and threatened me with their fists against my face but I was never tortured physically. (Both officers were liquidated by the Milorg Resistance organisation before the end of the war.) I denied everything for two months but then I was confronted with my classmate who ran one of the illegal newspaper printing offices. He bore distinct marks of physical torture – he was pale, thin and broken down, and repeated in my presence what he had said about me. Luckily it was not much and limited to only a few episodes. Seeing him and realising what he must have gone through deeply affected me. At the same time I was relieved and grateful to him for not having said more, I now started making admissions and the officers were furious because I had refused to do so for such a long time. Afterwards I was removed to a relatively large cell in the main building which strangely enough somewhat improved my situation.

I am, naturally, perfectly aware of the fact that many other prisoners during the war had been far worse off. I have not described these external circumstances in order to emphasise my particular situation, but because they may serve as a background for my feelings and experiences while sitting in solitary confinement. They contain perspectives beyond my own situation and point to important phenomena and problematic areas in lives of all people.

Fear and anxiety

During the first few weeks I had a quivering and unpleasant feeling in my chest, combined with a feeling of not getting sufficient air. This understandable fear became especially strong when I started thinking about my situation. I had been torn away from my home and separated from those nearest to me. Apart from the prison officer, the two men who interrogated me, and my mother's two visits, I had been totally isolated from other people and left to myself in the tiny, narrow cell. The future seemed totally unpredictable, with all the terrifying possibilities implied by wartime imprisonment. We were given little to eat and, in addition, our sleep was disrupted every night by the barking of dogs roving around the barbed wire fences of the prison compound.

Now, more than fifty years later, I understand that – apart from the natural fear caused by my situation – I was in touch with an anxiety with deeper roots, associated with being separated from those nearest to me and isolated from all other people. This type of anxiety, 'separation anxiety', which we all carry within us from the first three to four years of our lives[1] is the central core of all human anxiety. It is a feeling of being totally alone in the world, of lacking the security, warmth and caring which is so vital to a small child, and which is as a rule connected to the person of the mother. None of us can totally avoid experiencing this anxiety because no mother can ever be continually present and accessible to her child. However, every 'loss' of contact with a mother may have consequences later in life.

Loss may induce anxiety

When looking back at this period of solitary confinement, countless memories of patients with whom I have worked as a psychiatrist throughout the years come to my mind. I recall people with an anxiety similar to that which I had experienced at the Bredtveit prison even though my anxiety had been reinforced by a realistic fear.

I remember a great number of patients with anxiety neuroses who suffered their first panic attack after a significant person in their lives had died, fallen ill or deserted them for someone else.

This happened to a thirty year old single woman who had her first panic attack when her father became seriously ill. She subsequently suffered from anxiety for long periods until she was helped by psychotherapy. The loss of her father had activated many unconscious traumas and losses dating back to her childhood. It had undermined the character-neurotic defences she had unconsciously developed to protect herself against her underlying strong feelings of abandonment, loneliness and helplessness towards all people and in almost all social contexts.

A married, female academic had her first anxiety attack when her father, who had been divorced from her mother for many years, married a woman of her own age. Her emerging anxiety also had many other causes. She had been a neglected child, left to maids by parents who were only concerned about themselves and their own interests. As a child she had always felt lonely and abandoned, and had cried a great deal. She had survived by identifying herself with her remote yet dominating father, and by developing exaggerated feelings of care and responsibility for other people, but at her own expense.

Both these women had had very bad relationships with their mothers. So their fathers had become the only safe, fixed points in their lives.

I remember the successful and active businessman who had his first anxiety attack a short time after the death of his boss. This man had been a good father figure for him whom he could – in contrast to his own father – oppose without being punished or rejected.

It seemed to him as though he had lost an important anchor in his life. During his panic attacks the ground literally seemed to give way under his feet. He also became impotent and gradually developed a phobia of going out alone (agoraphobia) and of being shut up in small spaces, such as lifts and aeroplanes (claustrophobia). In his childhood his extremely busy parents had often left the children to their own devices, while at the same time applying rigorous moral standards in their upbringing. The reason for his anxiety neurosis was partly due to the fact that his own conscience had accepted a great deal of his parents' morality.

A twenty-eight year old gifted and competent married woman with children began to feel anxiety and had symptoms of depression after losing three of her relatives during the course of one year. She also had lost an extremely challenging and stimulating job when the family had had to move on account of her husband's career. Also in this case there were traces going back to her childhood, to her difficult relationship with her mother, and the feelings of loss, disappointment and longing connected with her father. To crown it all, this patient now had difficulties relating to one of her own daughters who unconsciously provoked some of these feelings of loss and longings in her. These cases illustrate that anxiety and depression often make their first appearance after several losses have occurred during a short period of time. (Chapter XIV, p.212)

Loss and depression

The question of whether loss induces anxiety, depression or both depends on the person concerned, and on what this loss represents emotionally and unconsciously. As yet we have too little knowledge about the factors predisposing people to one thing or the other, but we do know that loss often rips open old wounds from childhood. We also know that depressions may reflect diminished self-esteem. Most of us need close relationships with other people in order to feel self-esteem. This may explain why the loss of persons may cause depressions.[2,3,4,5,6]

It is easy to understand why all elderly women and men develop depression after losing their spouses through death following a long life together. Sometimes the survivor dies after a short interval – life no longer has any meaning. Loss through divorce may cause a similar reaction, but here the picture will often be complicated by feelings of having been wronged by bitterness or open aggression, and this may conceal the actual depression, at least in the initial phase.

However, the loss of the spouse may lead to more losses. I am thinking of a widow whose social status, life and social activities had depended primarily on her husband's position. When he died after a prolonged illness during which she had nursed him, her situation changed radically. Not only did she feel lonely and abandoned by her husband, she also lost many of the social contacts which had given purpose and meaning to her life. At the same time she also lost a small job which had given her the opportunity to keep in contact with other people and which gave her a feeling of achievement. Nor could she accept her physical decline and her changed appearance as a result of ageing. All her life she had thought of herself as a beautiful and youthful woman. This was a matter of great importance to herself. Now she had lost this as well. She went into a deep depression imagining that her brain was damaged and that she was slightly mad. She had to be hospitalised in a psychiatric clinic.

Social isolation and psychosis

In the psychiatric departments where I worked, one saw that the causes for many depressive and paranoid reactions in single elderly women were often prolonged social isolation, and lack of contact with family, neighbours and the local environment. These are problems typical of large cities.

I also remember all the patients who had more or less withdrawn into their own world, away from contact with other people. This was their final defence against a world with which they could no longer cope. The term for this mental state is 'autism' and we see it in children and adults who have become psychotic, especially in patients with schizophrenic psychoses. Their internal world has taken over. They populate their external world with their internal experiences of persecutors, with voices or with physical perceptions when others are present. These phenomena are called paranoid delusions, auditive hallucinations and ideas of reference.[7]

In a certain sense they have placed themselves in a prison; not by conscious choice, but as a defence and a means of survival. Even in this withdrawn 'prison' they cannot survive without the presence of others. These they recreate with the help of their 'inner objects' or 'images' which populate their internal world. The fact that these projections are mostly evil and persecutory, the voices critical and judgmental, may reflect painful and frightening experiences from early childhood. In spite of everything it must be better to have some persecutors than to live in total isolation, without any human contact. None of us can survive that.

For a child it is a catastrophe to lose its closeness to its mother

The Swiss psychoanalyst Rene Spitz became known worldwide after the war when he published his observations of infants who, after first having had a good relationship with their mothers, were separated from them for a period of three to six months.[8] Even though the children had been placed in a children's home where they were given sufficient nourishment and care by professional children's nurses, they developed a severe depression after several months. He termed it 'anaclitic depression'. The symptoms are growing apathy, and a halt in the child's physical and mental development which in a number of cases ended with the child's death. If the separation lasted for more than five months, the prognosis for the child was bad even if the mother returned.

Anaclitic means 'to lean against', that is to say that the child is totally dependent on a nourishing and a caring mother-person without whom the child cannot survive.

In the 1960s the American psychologist H F Harlow described his experiments with rhesus monkeys. In some experiments newly born rhesus monkeys were taken away from their mothers and put into a cage in which feeding bottles were suspended from which they could take nourishment. Even if they did take the nourishment, they became deeply mentally disturbed and totally lacking in social skills. This was heartbreakingly demonstrated on films. In another experiment the rhesus young were given an artificial monkey-mother, a piece of fur covering a steel-wire contraption. When frightened, the baby monkeys clung to the fur and were seen to be less impaired in their development.[9, 10]

For the human child the piece of fur – that is to say, the skin contact with the mother – is absolutely vital. However, emotional warmth and mutual contact, closeness and caring, is just as important. Experience shows that we are more vulnerable to the loss of mother-contact (mother-deprivation) than monkeys and other animal species, partly because our dependence on the mother lasts so much longer (Chapter XIII).

Many of my patients have told me that they have no memories of sitting on their mother's or father's lap, or any other indications of tenderness or warmth. Even though we do not usually remember a great deal from the first five years of our lives, these impressions can be confirmed by the fact that these parents even today lack the ability to be close to their adult children and even to their grandchildren. No wonder, therefore, that children with this type of background may have problems later in their lives. They simply lack some of the most important foundations.

An English documentary by Joyce Robertson made a deep impression on me.[11] It showed a two-and-a-half year old boy who was placed in a children's home for eleven days because his mother had to be hospitalised for an operation. He was a healthy, happy boy from a perfectly normal family. His father visited him every day at the children's home. The place was adequately staffed but operated with rotating shifts as is usual in these types of institutions for children and adults.

The boy went through the typical stages of loss of mother contact. At first a period of protesting, weeping, despair, and clinging to his father each time he was about to leave. Then a phase in which the child attached itself to one of the nurses, but when she did not turn up on account of the rotation system, the boy went into depressive despair and completely withdrew from the other children and the staff, he became quiet and distant. When, after eleven days, the mother came to take him home, it was as though he did not know her. He rejected her.

I have presented a few glimpses into the enormous material which demonstrates the vital importance of the mother–child relationship during the first three to four years. It shows how vulnerable we are when this contact is broken during the separation–individuation phase, as it is called. We all carry within us the injuries from this 'forgotten' period in our lives; some people more so than others. This explains why all our lives we are most vulnerable when faced with loss and separation from those nearest to us. We cannot ever totally escape from separation anxiety.

I do not know much about the times of separation during my own childhood except that my parents went abroad for a couple of months when I was three years old. I was then sent to a relative in the country who was a widow. She had two sons, one of them being of my own age. The only thing I remember from that period is that I was downright miserable. There is a photo of me taken when my father came to collect me. I am standing on a road, skinny and barefoot, and with an expression of sadness on my face. I know that I was greatly loved as a child but my parents – like most parents at that time – were not aware of a child's vulnerability, and the 'upbringing' was often influenced by the idea that the child should not be spoiled.

What helped me to survive?

Returning to my predicament in the cell at Bredtveit, another important reflection comes to my mind. What was it that actually helped me to survive, to cope with my anxiety and my fear?

I was totally convinced that I was in the right, that 'the others' were Nazis and therefore 'evil'. I also felt sustained by the certainty that my family cared about me and loved me.

In those days I also had Christian faith. This was the result of my parents' influence and did not represent a considered opinion on my part or an integrated philosophy of life. But it gave me a ray of hope in my state of loneliness, anxiety and uncertainty. It also gave me a sense of purpose in the apparent meaninglessness of the situation, a belief that there was a god who heard my prayers and those of my family. It freed me from the iron grip of fear and anxiety, and gave me a feeling of being connected with God and those nearest to me. This faith helped to restore my sense of reality and counteracted my feelings of isolation, helplessness and anxiety. Throughout the ages man has recognised the important function of possessing a religious faith, especially in difficult or dangerous situations. I do not pretend to explain with this all the reasons for religion and faith in God, but it may be considered as one perspective.

Another beneficial factor was that I was able to use my intellect and divert my attention by reading books sent by my family. I set great store by the Bible and the collected works of Ibsen which I read from cover to cover. The Bible deepened my faith, and Ibsen engaged me both intellectually and emotionally. *Peer Gynt* and *Brand* had been required reading in the sixth form in grammar school and I had acted the part of Brand when we performed the play. Reading it again at that time fascinated me and gave me a deeper understanding of this play.

My third strategy was making vigorous attempts to contact other prisoners. One day, while standing on my stool and looking at the big prison building, I realised that only inventiveness would enable me to reach my goal. I saw another prisoner in one of the windows on the second floor of the building and waved to him. Then I took a piece of toilet paper and tore out a small circle which I fastened onto the tip of my forefinger with spit. With this primitive equipment I began to write large inverted letters against my windowpane. Soon he began to follow suit. Thus, for many weeks we were able to exchange information about ourselves by communicating in this 'wireless' manner. His name was Arne Holst and in 1952 during the Winter Olympic Games in Oslo he won a medal in bobsleigh. Our communications were abruptly interrupted when the prison officer one day searched through the lining of my jacket and found a scrap of paper on which I had jotted down the name of Arne Holst – another example of my naivety. He was moved to another cell which could not be observed from my small window. However, while it lasted, I was greatly encouraged by this episode.

There is another episode which I cannot easily forget. One day when I was desperately hungry, I shouted in an unguarded moment to another male prisoner working beneath my window: 'Can you get hold of some food for me?' He was an ungainly, slightly bent man with glasses who pretended not to hear me. An hour or two later the slit in my door suddenly opened, and into my cell slid two salt herrings and a few boiled potatoes wrapped in newspaper. Never before or after have salt herrings and potatoes tasted so delicious! More important, however, was that I had reached another human being with my cry for help and he had shown compassion by reacting positively.

I met this man later in the group of students arrested by the Germans, first in the camp near Stavern and later in Germany under the most dramatic circumstances. His fearless and hazardous behaviour on several occasions helped many of us to keep up our courage and our spirits. His behaviour demonstrated moral courage, 'civil courage'. His name is Michael Sars.

Isolation – punishment or challenge?

At all times isolation in solitary confinement has been used as a frequent method of punishment for criminals and political prisoners. Legislators and authorities have doubtlessly been aware of its devastating effect on the individual. Isolation was used to give the prisoner time for reflection and remorse, which should make him more motivated to confess to his crimes or heretical ideas. Whether this goal was actually achieved depended greatly on the individual. For young people like myself, who had lived a relatively protected life, and who – apart from holidays – had not been away from home for any length of time, solitary confinement was a shocking experience – indeed, the most harrowing experience in all my life. This was true, even though I found myself in far more dramatic and dangerous circumstances in the following eighteen months in Germany. But there I was not alone. I was together with other Norwegian students.

Perhaps the days in solitary confinement had in some way been a preparation, had made me a little more mature and independent, thus enabling me better to bear the subsequent strains? Today I believe so. We know that being alone and isolated from others can sometimes turn into a positive challenge, a possibility for growth and development. A moderate degree of anxiety can also be an advantage.

But it is always a balancing act between the degree and the duration of the strain, and our sensibilities and tolerance. It is a balancing act between anxiety caused by loneliness and factors that may constitute a defence against this anxiety. Too much anxiety has a paralysing effect, while too much defence may put us into a state of deadlock and impede our development. We all strive to find a solution to this eternal dilemma, a middle course between too much anxiety and too much defence – between Scylla and Charybdis.

What helped *me* most to get through the days of solitary confinement was faith, hope, and the contact with others and their caring, as well as the salutary effect of reading. This is covered by the words: Faith, Hope and Charity.

NOTES TO THE TEXT

[1] Bowlby, J, *Maternal Care and Mental Health*, Schocken Books, New York, 1966.

[2] Freud, S, *Mourning and Melancholia*, S.E., Vol. XIV, Hogarth Press, London 1917.

[3] Bowlby, J, *Attachment and Loss*, Vol. III, Loss, Sadness and Depression, Hogarth Press, London, 1980.

[4] Brown, G W, & Harris, T, *Social Origin of Depression: A Study of Psychiatric Disorders in Women*, Tavistock, London, 1978.

[5] Jørstad, J, Psykodynamiske synspunkter på depresjoner, *Depresjonshåndboka*, Organon, Oslo, 1988, pp.39–49.

[6] Jørstad, J, *Sånn er livet, sånn er du og jeg,* Aschehoug, Oslo, 1986, 1987, 1989, pp.197–213.

[7] Green, H, *I Never Promised You a Rose Garden*, a Signet book, The New American Library, New York, 1964.

[8] Spitz, R A, *The First Year of Life*, Int. Univ. Press, New York, 1965.

[9] Harlow, H F, 'The Nature of Love', *The American Psychologist*, 13, 1958, pp.673–685.

[10] Harlow, H F and Zimmermann, R R, Affectional Response in the Infant Monkey, Science, 130, 1959, 421.

[11] Robertson J, and Robertson, J, Film: Young Children in Brief Separation, London, Tavistock Institute of Human Relations; New York, New York University Film Library, 1967.

Chapter II
PRISONER IN GERMANY
Fellowship and leadership

The Beauty of the Earth

In the early morning hours of 11 December 1943 we stood on the quay in Stettin. Two hundred and ninety Norwegian students and four hundred other prisoners from the Grini prison in Norway. It was cold and dark. Damp fog concealed the landscape and the prison transport boat *Donau*, from which we had just disembarked. The atmosphere was sinister, and we felt anxious – what awaited us here in the 'Third Reich'? After arresting one thousand one hundred students on 30 November, of which I was one, Wilhelm Rediess, chief of the German security police, addressed us in the university's aula. He informed us that we would be sent to a '*Sonderlager*' in Germany as a result of our 'national hostility towards Germany and our international propaganda activities'. But what did this imply, and where was the '*Sonderlager*'? The nine days spent so far in the camp at Stavern, south of Oslo, had been a foretaste of the future which did not augur well. We met a small group on board the *Donau* who had spent three weeks in the Berg labour camp after having been arrested as 'agitators'. To put it mildly, our future seemed most uncertain.

We had to line up in long columns while SS guards armed with guns and machine pistols ran around shouting commands and insults at us: '*Los, los, aber schnell!*' They kept on counting us to see if anyone was missing. We stood there in the dark, trembling with cold, feeling completely lost.

Suddenly we heard the voice of someone starting to sing. Seconds later the hymn *Deilig er Jorden* (The Beauty of the Earth) resounded from seven hundred voices on the quay. In spite of our anxiety and the enveloping fog, the singing united us in fellowship, and gave us hope for peace on earth. Never shall I forget this amazing and paradoxical moment.

Inferno

The scene changes. That same evening, after having spent the whole day waiting on the quayside, we were transported by train to Pölitz, the concentration camp twenty kilometres north of Stettin. The four hundred prisoners from Grini had been sent ahead by train to an unknown destination. Marching from the station through the bleak, flat landscape, I noticed the outlines of watchtowers, floodlights and high barbed wire fences looming up out of the fog. Once inside the gate, we came across a huddled crowd of emaciated, tattered, ghost-like creatures who looked at us with mute helplessness in their eyes. Never before had we come across 'Mussulmans'. We had not even known of their existence, but here they were actually in their thousands. Dogs barked, and SS men roared and shouted at us: '*Los, los.*' These words I had had in my ears for some weeks now, but this place was worse than anything I had ever imagined in my wildest nightmares. Surely this was Dante's inferno – real hell on earth.

After a short and threatening speech by an SS man, I and three hundred other prisoners were packed together into barracks, each with two rooms containing a coal bin, but no furniture, no toilet or any ventilation. The doors were locked and the windows boarded up. We were told that the commandant was about to address us. We sat huddled tightly together on the floor, waiting. Suddenly the door was burst open and we heard renewed shouting. A uniformed guard with riding boots and a pistol yelled: '*Austreten! Ausgehen! Bald kommt der Lagerkommandant!*' ('Step out, go out! The camp commandant will soon be here!') Outside on the parade ground there was another roll call and more shouted orders: '*Augen links!*' ('Eyes left!') and '*Stillstehen!*' ('Stand at attention!') Not only were the prisoners tense, but the soldiers also showed signs of nervousness as we all stood waiting for his lordship: '*Der Lagerkommandant!*' ('The camp commandant!').

Then all at once he was there, in the centre of the beam from a searchlight. It was a strange apparition that we saw: bull-necked, with a huge belly, and a florid face with fisheyes. A thick cigar stuck out of his crooked mouth. 'Heil Hitler! Who can interpret?' He was, of course, completely unaware that we all understood German. A tall and ungainly student wearing glasses came forward, with hands in his pockets. I recognised him immediately. It was Michael Sars, the man who had smuggled food into my cell at the Bredtveit prison.

And now a strange and macabre play ensued. The commandant roared and shouted threats and curses at us in the hoarse voice of a drunkard. We would be shot at the least sign of disobeying orders. We would be shot if we did this or that, we had to take off our caps each time we passed a German, we must not laugh or whistle, and so, on and on in the same vein. To put it mildly, neither the man nor his words helped to keep up our spirits.

A common destiny – once more!

After each sentence he waited to let the interpreter 'translate' his words. But what we heard in Norwegian was definitely not a translation: 'As you can see, fellows, this chap has obviously gone completely off his rocker. So it will be better for us not to get him steamed up more than necessary because then there will be shooting from all directions. It is probably a good idea then for us to salute these idiots since it seems to mean so much to them. I don't believe any of this will actually have a decisive influence on the outcome of the war... and, on the whole, we can expect very little goodwill in this madhouse.' He nodded towards the commandant signalling that he had finished translating these first warm words of welcome. The commandant then went on yelling and screaming, cursing and threatening, gesticulating with his arms and trotting forwards and backwards in front of us, all the while chewing his cigar to pieces. In between, he paused in order to let the interpreter carry on with the translation. This he did, with a humorous and ironical running commentary to the outpourings of this personification of evil and meanness.

I did not know whether to laugh or cry over this grotesque spectacle but I saw that no one around me moved so much as a single facial muscle. I sent up a silent prayer of thanks that none of the Germans seemed to understand Norwegian, while at the same time I was full of admiration for Michael Sars, for his cool courage and calm behaviour in this truly desperate and critical situation. He gave us hope and a feeling of standing together, of being united in a common destiny.

In this first roll call of Norwegian students in Hitler's Germany, there was a meeting of two cultures. One, none of us who were present will ever be able to forget.

Nor can we ever forget the three days and nights spent in the inferno of the commandant. The nights were the worst. We were locked up inside the same barracks as before where we had hardly any room to sit down on the floor. The lack of oxygen made most of us feel that we were suffocating, and gradually the air became so moist that a trail of condensation ran down the walls. I sat leaning against a wall and discovered a knot hole in the wood through which some air was able to trickle in. It felt like being rescued. The men who needed to urinate had to let go into their trousers or into some cracks in the floor. Those with diarrhoea had no other options.

Psychological influence, pressure and threats

After a train journey of several days, we came to St Andreas outside Sennheim (Cernay) in Elsass, a former 'Idiotenanstalt' (lunatic asylum) which had been transformed into a training camp for the SS. Materially we were far better off than we had been during the first few months, but we were subjected to a psychological pressure of a quite different kind. It was planned that we were now to be re-educated and indoctrinated with the 'correct ideology' which would finally make us realise that it was our duty to fight together with our 'Germanic brothers' for the 'Greater German Reich'. This plan, allegedly hatched by Himmler, was based on the fantastic notion that if only one single group of fair-haired, blue-eyed Norwegian students were brought under the right influence, then all would volunteer within a short time for service at the front together with the Waffen SS.

I will not enumerate here all the occasions on which attempts were made, both individually and collectively, to entice, force or threaten us into obedience. Detailed accounts of this have been supplied by others. However, since not one of us succumbed to the pressure, even in the most dramatic situations when the risk of being shot was enormous, the Germans soon understood that their plan had misfired. Consequently they tried to call us out as a workforce, first as slave labourers in a small armament factory in Bitschweiler near Thann in the Vogeses. When the Americans were approaching Elsass after the D-Day landings in 1944, this factory was evacuated, and we were made to dig tank traps outside Sennheim. In both instances we sabotaged, referring to the Geneva Convention and our rights as civilian internees. But the Germans only ridiculed, or raged at us. A particularly dramatic situation arose when we were evacuated by foot, to the north and to the east, out of Elsass, and across the Rhine near Breisach over a bridge which was still intact. The Americans had broken through near Belfort and were rapidly approaching. We were divided into several groups of which the two largest were billeted in Burkheim and Bischofingen, two small villages east of the Rhine. There the Germans tried to force us to work with a ferry landing which they had built for the transport of German troops who were now being withdrawn across the Rhine. There were several dramatic scenes where the SS leaders and guards lost control and became raging mad. This indicated that they were absolutely at their wits' end and capable of doing anything. In spite of this, we had enough strength remaining to stand together, and to refuse to carry out this type of work which could clearly be classified as 'war effort'. Again we claimed that this was a violation of the Geneva Convention.

We all felt that we were balancing on a knife's edge. What probably saved us was the fact that the SS had not received orders from Berlin confirming that they could shoot us. Instead, we were transported to the concentration camp Buchenwald, in Thüringen, a somewhat longer, more drawn out form of *Vernichtung*, (annihilation).

A group of three hundred and fifty students had arrived earlier in Buchenwald, directly from Norway. It was not until the summer of 1944, shortly before we were to be evacuated, that this group, with the exception of a few students who had returned to Norway before the evacuation, joined us in Elsass. There were also a few medical students who were allowed to continue their studies at German universities. The lives of these men would be totally different from what lay ahead of us.

Buchenwald

After several weeks of long and strenuous day's marches with little to eat and a great deal of verbal abuse, we came to Alpirsbach in the Black Forest. Here we were tightly packed together into cattle trucks, fifty men to each truck. We spent the next four days and nights without food and almost without water. It is no exaggeration to say that we were in dreadful physical shape as we staggered in through the gates of Buchenwald, the concentration camp outside Weimar in Thüringen. Through a mist I saw SS-Obersturmführer Wilde, our 'boss' from Elsass. He greeted us with a triumphant and malicious grin as we passed through the portal bearing the ominous inscription: *'Jedem das Seine'* – ('Everyone his due').

Three hundred and fifty of the students had been there before and knew what was in store for us. The rest of us would not remain ignorant for long. The Mussulmans, and the corpses piled up outside the crematorium, which was in use around the clock, gave the revolting smell of charred meat over the whole area. Because of the Russian advance the number of transports of starved prisoners arriving from Poland increased steadily. These men often ended their lives in the crematorium. Fleas and lice, hunger and cold, sickness and death, all this became part of our daily life.

We were removed to Block 51 in the 'Kleinlager', one of the worst areas, with wretched sanitary conditions and more mud than could be found anywhere else in the camp. The barrack, which was fifty metres long, consisted of one single room with three tiers of bunks along one of the walls. There were a few benches and tables, but no windows and only one single door. High up below the ceiling there were a few tiny hatchways. Moisture was continuously dripping from the ceiling and running down the walls due to the lack of ventilation. At first we were five hundred men in this barrack, later the number increased to six hundred. It was hopelessly crowded. We had to lie, head to toe, like sardines on the bunks. Two small ovens were supposed to warm up the whole barrack.

The worst, however, was that after fourteen days of 'quarantine' we were made to work. Getting up at 5 a.m., marching off at 6.15 a.m. and then working from 6.30 a.m. to 5 p.m. in bitterly cold winds and drifting snow. The temperature was down to minus twenty degrees. We were thinly dressed, our footwear was insufficient and we felt terribly cold. The job consisted of 'Ziegelputzen'. In the vicinity of the camp were the ruins of the Gustloff-Werke which had been bombed and totally destroyed in August 1944. We were made to hammer used bricks to clean them of their plaster. With only a small amount of black bread for breakfast and turnip soup for supper, our output did not come up to scratch. Our parole was still to sabotage everything, *'sich drücken'*, which we had learnt to perfection in Elsass.

However, amid all the fear, starvation and misery which we witnessed all around us, there were rays of hope. The group's team spirit was excellent and together we had survived the most unbelievable pressures. Thanks to good leadership we had managed to keep up our courage in spite of all the odds being against us most of the time.

We were very fortunate to have two thousand Danish police officers living in the block next to us. They shared many of the food parcels which they received from the Red Cross with us. Yet, in spite of the abundance of food, the Danes were troubled by great difficulties. Finding themselves in these circumstances seemed to be a far greater problem for them than it was for us, as many of them were elderly. During the first four months after their arrival there were forty-five deaths in this group. Later on there were even more.

During the first days after our arrival the unbelievable kindness and generosity of these Danes saved the lives of many men in our group. Unfortunately it was not long before they were sent away to an unknown destination.

The group of students who had previously been in Buchenwald had already made contact with many other prisoners, some of whom held important positions in the camp. This proved to be a great advantage. We had many good friends among Czech and Russian prisoners. Originally, Buchenwald was a fairly well-organised camp. German criminal prisoners held the post of block-chief, they were camp police and also administrated other areas of the daily life of the camp.

As the East front was drawing closer, there came an endless flow of thousands of new prisoners from the camps in Poland. Most of them were starving and ill. One of the transports from Auschwitz included the tiny number of Norwegian Jews who had escaped the gas chambers. One of these was Leo Eitinger, who was later to hold the chair of psychiatry in the University of Oslo.

Once more we had a run of good luck. After only a few weeks we were let off work. We were moved to slightly better barracks and gradually began receiving Red Cross parcels which were a most welcome supplement to the food in the camp. Our optimism rose.

A night of bombs in Erfurt

In March 1945, we were once more loaded into cattle trucks and transported from Buchenwald to Neuengamme, near Hamburg. We had no idea of our destination, nor did we know that this transport was part of a plan of Count Folke Bernadotte. He had succeeded in getting Himmler to agree to this: in this chaotic final phase of the war all Norwegian and Danish prisoners were to be rounded up from all the camps and prisons throughout Germany, and transported in Danish and Swedish Red Cross buses via Denmark to Sweden.

The five days and nights spent in the cattle truck during the transport from Weimar were most dramatic. I shall never forget the first night. It started with an air raid carried out by American planes. The target was the large goods station in Erfurt where our truck was stationary between rows of goods wagons containing petrol and ammunition. At the first whining sound of the bombs falling on us and exploding in the station area, the SS guards who had been placed in twos in each truck, opened the doors and ran for dear life. I remember the air pressure from the first bomb lifting the ceiling of the truck in which I sat, and then hearing a heart-rending scream from one of our students: 'Dear Jesus!' We scrambled out through the door and tried to take cover under the trucks while all around fires were starting and bombs were exploding everywhere.

In the midst of this highly dangerous situation, there was Michael Sars, standing upright in one of the door openings and shouting encouraging words to us. We were all truly terrified. He shouted advice about where he believed it would be safest to take cover and how we might find our way out of the large station area. Again, here was 'Mikkel' showing his amazing courage! Although this had not been a major air raid, it seems incomprehensible even today that none of us were injured or killed. When, after much confusion, a few of us had succeeded in escaping from the station area, we ran head on into a group of policemen armed with guns who promptly chased us back into the inferno. The following day we were once again crammed into trucks and the journey continued.

There were two more air raids during this transportation. If a coupling between two wagons had not accidentally broken, leaving our wagon standing outside Hildesheim for twenty-four hours, we would probably all have been annihilated on the night on which the whole station area was bombed. The following night we stopped outside Bremen and witnessed a major attack by 'flying fortresses' on this city. But we had arrived and had hopes of surviving.

'The bloodhound from Lublin'

Neuengamme was one of the worst camps in Germany. The SS men there were even worse than those in Buchenwald. The camp commandant was Obersturmführer Thumann, nicknamed 'the bloodhound from Lublin'. He had – just for the fun of it – personally killed twenty thousand Russian prisoners with his machine gun. All the prisoners in this camp were in a terrible state, and so were the barracks and the sanitary conditions. The diet was far below subsistence level.

Transports of Norwegian and Danish prisoners from camps and jails all over Germany continued arriving until we were about four thousand men in the Scandinavian sector of the camp. A great number of those who came from other camps were terribly emaciated and ill. Although food parcels from the Red Cross began arriving, several of them died after just a short period. There were rumours about the Swedish rescue scheme but no one knew anything for certain. Meanwhile we were hearing the thunder of guns and canons, and realised that both fronts were closing in on us.

The rescue

One day we were suddenly ordered to line up outside on the parade ground. We were left standing there for several hours without anything happening. Then the entrance gate to the camp opened and the first to enter was a man in the uniform of the Swedish Red Cross. He was recognised by someone who whispered: 'Count Folke Bernadotte!' Behind him, with a gloomy expression, shuffled the 'bloodhound'. This was not at all to his liking. Folke Bernadotte walked down in between our ranks saying encouraging words: 'This is going to work, fellows, you will be all right!' For us this was a wonderful moment. Quite unbelievable, to see a representative of the Swedish royal family exercising his authority over the SS executioner in a German concentration camp! I was moved to tears. Later Folke Bernadotte toured the barracks and greeted all the people who were lying sick in the bunks. Now our optimism knew no bounds!

In the days which followed sick prisoners began to be transported back to Sweden. On 20 April 1945 all the remaining Scandinavian prisoners were collected by white Red Cross buses and driven to Frøslev and Horsens, two camps in Denmark. After ten days we were driven in triumph through Denmark. Schoolchildren lined the streets of every town we passed through. They were waving flags and singing *'Ja, vi elsker'* – the Norwegian national anthem. It was only when we boarded the ferry that the Gestapo guards left. It was with unspeakable relief and gratitude that we came ashore in Sweden on 1 May 1945, one week before peace was declared in Norway.

Afterthoughts

I have included these glimpses and episodes from my time in captivity in order to bear witness to a demonic system which brought out the worst in many of Hitler's henchmen, and caused inconceivable suffering and millions of deaths.

I have often wondered what made people commit the atrocities we witnessed in the camps and I have marvelled at the phenomenon of national socialism which, under Hitler, had evolved into a well-oiled lethal machine. Sometimes I speculated about what it would take to turn *me* into a Gestapo or SS man, or a torturer. What are the hidden forces which drive mankind? I realise now that during those days in German captivity, the first seeds of my subsequent choice of profession as a psychiatrist and psychoanalyst were sown.

There were many more episodes which were dramatic and important to those experiencing them, and which in part have also been described by others.[1,2,3] The story I have told illustrates a fact which, I have since realised, is of great significance: the critical importance of solidarity in a group in case of emergency. Our survival at that time had depended in the main on this team spirit, as well as the leader's attitude and his exemplary moral courage.

The other students and I were certainly no more courageous than most people, and we often felt defenceless and afraid. I believe that separately some of us would have given up. But we were not alone in our fight for survival; we were a group with a strong feeling of community and solidarity. In critical situations where basic values and ethical attitudes were at stake, we stood together.

This group feeling was enhanced by a core of leaders, practising moral leadership, who helped us not to lose faith. One of these was Michael Sars. Perhaps it is precisely under extreme conditions like these that these qualities manifest themselves.

The solidarity we felt and the help we received from the Danish policemen, from other prisoners and from the Red Cross, saved many a life. Again I had seen compassion put into practice, in the relationships between individuals and on an international level by the Red Cross.

However, one must not forget one important individual mechanism: our fantastic ability to adapt ourselves to heavy physical and mental stress. If the changes do not come about too rapidly we are given time to develop our defence mechanisms. It was first after my return to Norway in June 1945 that I recognised one of these mechanisms in myself. It was a kind of insensibility, my protection against all the deaths and evil which I had witnessed.

I also felt the need to get away from all people I dealt with by going up into the mountains to live in a cabin in Vestfjellet in Gausdal. There in these surroundings, nature, solitude and my fishing rod helped to melt down the ice within me so that once again I could feel normal. But the inner protection had been necessary.

These experiences can be summarised as follows: the human degradation, evil, anxiety and suffering I experienced and witnessed during my wartime imprisonment in Germany taught me the importance of belonging to a group which sticks together and has a moral leadership. The individual will then derive strength from this group. It helped me and many of us to find a road between hope and hopelessness, and thus a way of surviving.

Notes to the Text

[1] Sars, M and Tranøy, K E, *Tysklandsstudenter*, Cappelen, Oslo, 1946.

[2] Eidem, K, *Aulaen brenner! Norske studenter under hakekorset*, Gyldendal, Oslo, 1980.

[3] Dahl, H K, Politisk fange I Norge og Tyskland 1943–45. En medisinstudents opplevelser, T.n. Lægeforening 11, 115, pp.1397–1401, 1995.

Chapter III
WHAT ARE WE DOING TO EACH OTHER?
Projective phenomena in a small group

The Group Consultant

At a conference on group relations in Sigtuna, Sweden, I am one of a group of ten participants. Garret O'Connor, an Irish-American, is the consultant. According to the information received in advance, his task will be to help us to understand what goes on in the group as a whole. Garret is a tough type who is totally impervious to all niceties and social conventions. As soon as we are seated on the ten chairs placed in a circle in the room, he pulls out a cigarette. Before he has time to light it, a female participant next to him takes out her own lighter to light his cigarette, but he demonstratively turns his head away and lights the cigarette with his own lighter.

We are all unknown to each other; women and men from different professions, many holding leading positions. The special focus of the course is to be on authority and leadership. I am the only Norwegian in this group. Some of us have participated in other types of groups, but this one is different. While we make the rounds on the first day introducing ourselves to each other, the consultant keeps quiet. He makes no reply to our direct questions. This makes us feel frustrated, angry and confused. What sort of a rude bastard is he?

Gradually as the group develops during the six days we spend together, we begin to get an inkling of Garret's role. He is not the type of group leader we had expected, the type we had been used to from other groups. Garret's provocative behaviour has a purpose; which is to intensify our initial reactions towards him as a figure of authority and thus to get the group process moving. When he does say something, it is obviously to make us aware of what is going on under the surface of this group in the here and now. Neither the remarks made by individuals nor their reactions are interpreted on a personal level, but are seen only as undercurrents in the group as a whole. We, as participants cannot understand this at first. Through his interpretations the consultant attempts to make us aware of the unconscious tendencies in the group.

The group's crucified Christ

Gradually, during the course of time we became better acquainted with each other. The topic drawing subtly closer was that of homosexuality. At one of the group meetings where the members displayed a high degree of involvement, candour and strong emotions, the atmosphere gradually became charged with anxiety. Several members of the group reported feeling devoid of any emotion. With a certain degree of surprise I registered this in myself. I had become empty of thought and felt totally uninvolved. This was in striking contrast to my earlier mood.

After a long interval during which one participant in particular – Anders – had remained quiet for a long time, Garret exploded. Pointing at Anders, he cried out with great emotion: 'Don't you realise what you are doing to him? He has become the group's crucified Christ!' Saying this, Garret got up and quickly left the room, in the same second as the group's allotted time, one hour and a half, was up.

So, there we were sitting with the crucified Christ Anders who was unable to move or to say a single word. He sat there like a statue, petrified. We were terrified and felt totally unable to help this group member who we now believed had turned mad. Anders reminded me of the typical catatonic schizophrenic patient with catalepsia, muscle rigidity, whom in former times one used to see in psychiatric hospitals. However, it took only a few minutes before most of us returned to our senses. One of us put an arm around Anders, saying soothing words to him. Another lit a cigarette and placed it in his mouth. Gradually his ability to move returned and after eight to ten minutes he was his usual self again. For us this had been a truly unsettling experience.

To 'thrust' one's feelings onto others

How are we to explain what actually happened? One explanatory model is based on the phenomenon called *projective identification* – an unconscious defence mechanism which dates back to our childhood. It might be said that our reaction to the anxiety-provoking topic was to get rid of the feelings and effects which the topic of homosexuality aroused in us, and to transfer them onto Anders. We were then totally drained of feelings. Anders, on the other hand, became so 'filled up' with our concerns, that he was literally immobilised, his will paralysed and his muscles rigid. The group made him into its scapegoat, or, as it is termed in technical language, he was made into a *container*, a 'carrier' of all the feelings and effects which we did not want to admit to ourselves. The expression the 'group's crucified Christ' was here used as a metaphor: our unconscious projections had 'crucified' Anders. Consultants sometimes use similar mythical images and symbols in order to reveal what goes on in the group.

Why was it precisely that *he* of all people became the 'crucified' victim of the group's anxiety? We can only speculate. I have no reason to believe that Anders was gay. We know that different people are predisposed to be the recipients of different projections from others. The English psychoanalyst Wilfred Bion's explanation is that we all have different *valencies*, a concept taken from chemistry indicating our different abilities to bind to us – or take up in us – that which others unconsciously thrust onto us. Why does one person become the scapegoat in a family or at work? Perhaps this person sends out some signals which are caught and then trigger off projective mechanisms in others. (See Chapter V.)

All this may sound mystical and supernatural to many readers, but perhaps it will be easier to understand this phenomenon of projective identification if we return to the early mother–child relationship. The interaction between mother and child is currently described as an ongoing process where something is expelled (projected) and something is taken in (introjected). For example, when as a child we feel discomfort or pain, we get rid of these painful feelings by figuratively 'spitting them out' and placing them onto the environment. At first we place them onto the mother's breast, then gradually onto the whole mother, for example by screaming. The infant's effects have a great impact on the mother. The outcome of this interaction will differ, according to the mother's personality and her condition. She may react calmly and reassuringly to the baby's desperation or rage, 'digest' its pain and give back bodily contact, reassurance and care, which is 'taken in' by the child who then calms down.

However, if the mother herself is provoked by the child's painful feelings and screams, either because she is afraid, insecure or worn out, or if she has hateful feelings towards her child, then it will be more difficult for her to bear or to 'contain' the child's psychic pain. She may then perhaps give back some of her own bad feelings, and these are again 'taken in' by the child whose pain will increase. The outcome may be that the child continues feeling bad and may scream even more. It is in these situations that the image of the 'witch' is created in the child's fantasy. Or in technical language: 'the bad breast' or 'the bad mother' – even though the mother herself is far from being either a witch or bad.[1]

On the other hand, when both infant and mother are in harmony, feeling well and content, then the good feelings will be projected from the child onto the mother, and back again from the mother onto the child, thus creating a good circle. They both become 'containers' for good feelings. This may be the origin of well known concepts in psychiatry, the internal images of 'the good breast' and 'the good mother', the good fairy in the fairy-tales, 'the Garden of Eden' or 'lost paradise'.

The secret behind our ability to be 'containers' for others may be found in these early interactions between the mother and the child. Our 'valency', the tendency to attract particular projective identifications, will also be dependent on the quality of our good and bad experiences in early childhood.

Boundaries and boundlessness

Projective identification has also many other important consequences for us. Again, taking the early mother–child relationship as our point of departure, we know that in this first symbiotic phase the boundaries between the mother and the child are diffuse. A mother often feels her child's feelings, she is filled with them and reacts intuitively – at best by satisfying the child's needs. The child then takes in the image of the breast, or of the mother, and also the feelings conveyed by the mother. In this almost boundless condition lies the basis for empathy, the ability for empathic understanding of other people. By letting ourselves become aware of our own feelings, we can understand a little of what the other person may feel. We are able to identify with the other because we feel something similar. This is the positive aspect of the saying: 'It takes one to know one'. However, we cannot really be certain of this until the other person has confirmed what we believe to be his or her feelings. Therefore, we ought to be careful not to insist that we know what the other person feels, since it is often difficult to distinguish between our own feelings and those of others.

This early symbiosis may contain a certain element of risk in that we may later in life 'lose our boundaries' in relation to other people. We can observe this in psychiatry, particularly in people who are in a regressed state, that is to say, a state where there is a re-emergence of tendencies from earlier developmental phases, such as the symbiotic phase. Even though we all have some traces of this condition, it is particularly pronounced in people with personality disorders, and even more pronounced in those who develop a schizophrenic psychosis. Since these individuals make extensive use of projective defence mechanisms, they may greatly influence other people. They themselves and others may have doubts about who is the one and who is the other – are those my feelings or are they the other's feelings? Many individuals who are psychotic or near-psychotic are extremely anxious about coming into close contact with others due to the fact that they feel their boundaries dissolving. For this reason they have a strong need to withdraw. During psychotic crises, people often imagine themselves to be directly influenced by the thoughts of others, or that they are exposed to 'radiation' or 'forces' emanating from others. Thus their identity will be under constant threat.[2]

We know that having boundaries in relation to others is an important part of our identity. These give us a feeling of being a whole person, deeply rooted in ourselves with stability over time. However, these boundaries should not become too rigid or too impenetrable, such as those we can see in stubborn and opinionated individuals. The ones who always know best and have no, or scarcely any, ability to listen to others or to learn from their experiences. Of course, stubbornness may also derive from an exaggerated need for self-assertion, which is often a defence against insecurity or an acquired strategy for coping with life. As so often in life, it is a question of a balancing act between too little and too much.

Summary

Projective identifications are normal and important tendencies in the early interaction between the mother and the child. Later on in life, they will continue to play a crucial role in our relationships with other people, and form the background for our ability to feel empathy, that is to say, develop an empathic understanding of others. But here too there is a balancing act. If the projective tendencies in individuals are too strong, they may lead to a lack of contact with reality. This refers particularly to psychotic and paranoid patients. The opposite, weak projective tendencies, may explain a certain lack of interest in the environment as is demonstrated by patients with deep depressions such as melancholia.

In this chapter, I have attempted to illustrate how this tendency to project may be employed by a group of people, in *group dynamics*, as it is called, signifying the unconscious tendencies which may influence each group member to a greater or lesser degree. We may 'thrust' our feelings and effects onto other people without even being aware of it. The recipients of such projected feelings may be greatly influenced by what has been 'thrust' onto them. They may be 'filled up' with these feelings, and – in extreme cases – this may cause a situation such as we witnessed with Anders. However, in everyday life, some of this may happen without such dramatic consequences, as for instance when someone is turned into a scapegoat. In Chapters Five and Six I elaborate on some other aspects of projection.

When we are in a group of people like the one I have described, a certain regression will sometimes take place. We may begin to react rather like children, unconsciously using the same mechanisms as we did when we were small, including projective identification. A collective fusion of the projective mechanisms of several group members may then take place, whose impact is even greater than in a two-person relationship. There seems to be a connection between the number of participants in a group, the depth of the regression and the strength of the projected feelings. Needless to say, the dynamic processes I have presented here are not the only ones at work in small groups. A small group may also be effective as a therapeutic method – as group psychotherapy.

Individuals who become the recipients of many projected feelings will soon find it difficult to maintain their own identity. They may literally become dumbfounded, as in the case of Anders in our group. In large groups it appears that this mechanism is even more evident. It seems to be even more difficult to maintain one's identity and the feeling of being a person in a large group than in a small group.

---

[1] Klein, M, *Love, Guilt and Reparation*, The Melanie Klein Trustees, London, 1948, 1952, 1975.

[2] Jørstad, J, Utfordinger I schizofrenibehandling. I: *Livslinjer, psykiatri og humanisme. Festskrift til Endre Ugelstad*, Eds: Gilbert, Haugsgjerd og Hjort. Tano, Oslo, 1989, pp.145–165.

Chapter IV
WHAT GOES ON IN LARGE GROUPS?
Community meetings and Tavistock Conferences

A conference discussion

Let me give you another example of an incident which left a deep impression on all present. This took place during a group-relation conference, many years after the incident with Anders in the small group, as described earlier. As a member of the conference staff I had to act as a consultant in one of the small groups. A participant in my group, Hans, had a marked tendency to attract the projections of others. His reactions to the group process were hypersensitive and quite different from those of other group members.

We had arrived at the concluding conference discussion on the final day of the conference. The sixty participants were free to address questions to the staff, or to make comments on the conference as a whole, or on any single incident which had occurred during the six days we had spent together. The staff of ten sat alongside one of the walls with the participants sitting in rows of chairs facing them. The only door in the room was in the corner, to the left of the staff.

A number of questions had already been answered, partly by Lars, the leader of the conference, and partly by other members of the staff. The general mood was irritable and tense. It was obvious that a number of people were dissatisfied with the answers they had received. All of a sudden, Hans got up from his chair and remained standing there in the middle of the hall without saying a word. Then he sat down again. Nobody said a word. After a while he got up again and slowly began to move between the rows of chairs, heading for the door. Before he reached it, Lars said in a loud voice: 'It is evident that *one* person here in this meeting is demonstrating by his action what many people in this room are feeling: the fact that they would really prefer to get up and leave the room.' On hearing this, Hans turned, went back to his seat and sat down again. After a while, a number of people got up and began speaking about their own ambivalence, admitting that they had aggressive thoughts and feelings towards Lars and the conference as a whole. The atmosphere had totally changed. The participants were relaxed. They initiated constructive discussions and felt that they had acquired new knowledge.

This event clearly demonstrates how a large group can turn an individual into a 'container' of thoughts and feelings which have not as yet surfaced in the group. It also demonstrates the impact of a correct interpretation: a number of people 'took back' their projections by freely admitting their feelings. And Hans, the 'container', was let off.

This episode with Hans during the conference discussion was unique, as it took place in a group situation where the aim was *not* to interpret the process here and now. The object was merely to clarify the various elements of the conference by answering concrete questions put forward by the participants. And yet, by his behaviour, Hans had demonstrated the potency of underlying group dynamic forces. The ensuing interpretation by Lars had then clarified what had actually taken place.

As staff members we often run the risk of becoming 'containers' of collective projections. I have learned from my own experience that for reasons unknown to me, my ability to think and to speak is sometimes paralysed when I find myself in a similar situation. The most likely explanation is that anxiety plays a role. The only way to 'survive' in very large groups is therefore to speak up about one's feelings. Then one's ability to think clearly will promptly return. This applies to members of the staff as well as to ordinary group participants. These mechanisms are partly due to the impact made on individual members of a large group. Many readers may recognise their own fear of speaking up in large assemblies.

Experiences in community meetings in the therapeutic community

The community meeting in a psychiatric ward is an important element of the 'therapeutic community', a model for hospital treatment which was applied in several wards in Norwegian hospitals. There were therapeutic communities both at Lien, the Dikemark hospital, where I was the chief physician for twelve years. Also in the psychiatric ward 6B, Ullevål Hospital, where I spent fourteen and a half years in the same capacity.

I shall limit myself here to a short description of what I experienced at these community meetings, where forty to seventy people, both staff and patients, took part. At Lien there were three community meetings per week. At Ullevål there were daily meetings for many years, at which the day's work always started with a community meeting. Later, when the ward was transformed into an emergency ward mostly for psychotic patients, both the content and the form of the community meetings underwent a decisive change.[1]

I remember feeling very insecure at my first community meetings, probably because all at once I had to relate to many people. Even to people whom I could not even see because they were sitting behind me, or behind others. I remember I felt that I was at the mercy of this large group. Everything I said or did would be noticed. At times I had a definite feeling of anxiety in my chest, especially during those periods when no one said a word and the atmosphere grew increasingly oppressive. For a short while I would be involved in what was going on, but then I lost interest, I 'flipped out', daydreamed or let my thoughts wander aimlessly. Also, at times it was difficult to hear what was being said, and to understand what was going on. I soon realised that there was a great difference between sitting in the inner or the outer circle. It was easier to become involved and participate in the inner circle than when sitting in the outer circle of chairs where 'flipping out' was one of the options.

I was struck by how many patients and staff members remained silent, afraid to say anything during the first part of these unstructured community meetings. If they did venture a few words, it was often in such a low voice that it was difficult to hear what they were saying. There was a general atmosphere of watchfulness, and anonymity, also anxiety about being noticed. At first I wondered why these initial fifteen to twenty minutes of the community meetings were such heavy going, until I gradually discovered that a higher level of structure and leadership would have decreased the level of anxiety.

On the other hand, if meetings were filled with agendas, long reports and discussions about practical issues, as was initially the case at Ullevål, it would soon lead to a lack of involvement and boredom in the participants.

In subsequent years, I developed – as everyone else did – an increasing ability to 'survive' at these meetings by taking a more active part. At Lien, in the years between 1971 and 1973, I actually looked forward to these community meetings which were mostly lively and meaningful, although at times they could be both difficult, exciting and unpredictable. These meetings represented a valuable resource in the therapeutic work with forty young patients, ten of whom were drug abusers. The others suffered from grave personality disorders or schizophrenic psychoses.

There was a fairly long tradition of the therapeutic community in psychiatric ward B at the Ullevål hospital. In 1976, the chief physician Herulf Thomstad retired and I took charge. The ward contained many neurotic and relatively resourceful patients. Initially the structure of the community meetings was far more formal than I had been used to at Lien. The meetings were filled with formal procedures, administrative issues, minutes and reports. There was hardly ever any time for spontaneous personal remarks. Not only the patients, but also the staff, showed very little tolerance for silence during these meetings. With hindsight I believe that there were both conscious and unconscious motives at work to avoid possible controversial topics and anxiety-laden material. Gradually we changed the structure of the community meetings and found that they functioned optimally as long as we kept a certain balance between the formal part and the informal part when everyone was free to speak. Also it was important that the staff, instead of questioning the patients, should come out with their own personal views and genuine feelings.

At these community meetings it was easy to recognise certain phenomena from the small groups, for example, that some of the members became the informal leaders, spokesmen or scapegoats. We often found that the most outspoken people in the group were the seriously ill patients. The most direct and honest statements would come from the most 'schizophrenic' patients. At times, these utterances could be both critical and revealing, or they could express empathy, and be supportive of both patients and staff members. A few times these patients even articulated what several of the staff were thinking, but did not dare to communicate. On other occasions, patients and members of staff acted out feelings and conflicts which had not been verbally expressed in the ward. Thus, the community meetings sometimes functioned as a barometer for the situation in the ward, or as a safety valve when other channels of communication had failed.

Due to our traditional role of authority, there was always the risk that we the doctors would influence these meetings too much. Often we were encouraged or obliged to be active, to talk a great deal or to take more charge than the other participants, even though this was not always intentional or even desirable.

Even after many years of experience as chief physician, I was still not spared from sometimes feeling insecure, embarrassed, in a dead end or confused at the community meetings. At other times I was angry and filled with a rage, the strength of which seemed inexplicable in view of the actual situation.

The Tavistock conferences

My experiences at the community meetings in the psychiatric wards reflect universal phenomena which manifest themselves in most groups of more than fifteen to twenty persons, and in most organisations where, however, they are more concealed, and far more difficult to comprehend.

I came to this realisation after I had participated in a number of group relations conferences in Sweden (AGSLO – working group for leadership and organisation) in the years after 1975, and after 1983 in Norway (NORSTIG – Norwegian trust for studies in group leadership and organisation). It is a model developed at the Tavistock Institute of Human Relations in London, and each year conferences are arranged in a number of European countries and the United States.

The aim of these conferences is to offer the participants a deeper understanding of what goes on in groups and between groups, in all social systems and organisations. The focus is especially on the latent and unconscious processes which influence the interaction between individuals and organisations: on how these processes may either promote or hinder the rational exercise of leadership, and the teamwork in a working group or an organisation with regard to its stated objectives.[2]

A leader will be able to function more effectively when the boundaries between the role of the leader and those he leads have been clearly defined and accepted by both parties. The conference therefore tries to examine the functions of the boundaries, and what the lack of boundaries may lead to. The boundaries in question are those between the person and the role, between individual members and the group, between the leader and those he leads, and between one group and another.

It is emphasised that participation in these conferences constitutes a form of learning, and not therapy. The conference concentrates on the group as a dynamic field and on the role of the staff in the group, e.g. on how authority influences both ourselves and others. The private affairs of the participants or their individual characteristics are not included in the study.

At this point the method clearly deviates from sensitivity training and encounter techniques, that is to say, from more confrontational methods. The task of the participants here is to gain knowledge through experience; partly in 'here-and-now' situations, and partly when there is time for reflection on what has been going on. One of the purposes is an attempt to connect feelings and intellect, experience and thought, without neglecting one or the other. It is up to each participant to get the most out of this learning situation. He will not be told beforehand what to learn. However, by attending these groups, many individuals have found that they have become more capable of fulfilling their role, of working more effectively and with a deeper understanding.

This conference is intended specifically for persons in leading positions. All sectors of society are represented: industry and business, municipal and public administration, public health service, political economy, schools, universities, the church, national defence, etc. The participants learn about group processes by taking part in small groups with eight to twelve participants, large groups with fifty to seventy participants, and in inter-groups which study the ways in which the groups cooperate. I would like to draw special attention to some tendencies which often develop in large groups, since these are the least known factors of all.

The dynamics of large groups

The example of Hans in the conference discussion illustrates the dramatic effect collective projections can have on a group member of a large group. Hans had become the container of the projections of many individuals, even though this occurred at a meeting that had aims which differed from those of regular large group meetings. This can be seen even more frequently in daily large group meetings in conferences which also last for one and a half hours. As a participant in many similar groups, and later as a member of the staff, I realised that this is an exciting but as yet little explored area of inter-personal dynamics.[3]

What fascinated me most each time was the speed in which deeply regressive tendencies surfaced in these large groups of healthy, well functioning individuals. Relatively soon there was an emergence of strong effects and projections, as well as primitive fantasies and myth-formations. These were revealed when the individuals began expressing their feelings and fantasies. As in the case of Hans, some of them felt themselves to be 'driven' to express, or to act out, what the others were feeling or thinking, but did not talk about. This proves that regression and collective projections are usually more pronounced in large groups. I cannot help thinking that these observations may throw a light upon well known phenomena which occur in other group situations, such as in religious confessions, speaking in tongues, in group séances between psychics and trance conditions, possessions, etc.

As mentioned above, one may have greater difficulties in preserving one's personal identity and the feeling of being a whole person in large groups than in small ones. There are several reasons for this. It is, for instance, not possible to remain in contact with a great number of people at the same time. Also, the individual may feel lost in the group which is experienced as something huge, impersonal and overwhelming. This may be one of the causes of regression. If the projective processes become massive, then one's self-esteem and one's ability for rational thinking may become impaired. One may then have bizarre and magical fantasies about oneself and the others, especially about those who have roles of authority, in particular the conference leader who represents 'the supreme authority'.

Getting unconsciously rid of something frightening or painful through the mechanism of projective identification is no guarantee that one can escape from what one has projected onto the others.

Getting rid of aggressive feelings, for example, leaves one weak and unaggressive, while the person or persons onto whom the aggression has been projected, may then be seen as more dangerous and threatening than previously. In large groups it is the very 'group' from which one cannot escape. In one's fantasy, the internal danger is then transformed into an external menace, a monster which must either be calmed down at all costs, or surrendered to.

Pierre Turquet is one of a number of scientists who has conducted a study of the factors which may threaten the identity of individuals in large groups.[4] He describes the centrifugal and centripetal forces which often cause individuals to oscillate between participating in the group, or withdrawing from the group and into their own internal world. Both situations can be frightening. If one enters into the group process of a large group, one may easily feel the boundaries between oneself and the group dissolving, and that one is swallowed up or annihilated by the group. As described in connection with the community meetings, in a large group one may often feel small, changed, squeezed together or at a standstill.

Faced with such unpleasant feelings or menaces, it is tempting to seek refuge in one's own internal world which is not corrected by reality. We may 'flip out' at this point. But it will make us feel lonely, isolated from others and out of contact with what is going on. Nor will it make us feel good. The fantasies which arise in this mental state may soon become bizarre and frightening.

The large number of participants in this type of group makes it easy for the participant to project several parts of him/herself onto others in the group. This facilitates the release of destructive forces until then held in check. Occasionally someone will express this in words and report that it feels as if he/she had an atom bomb inside. When such fearful fantasies about violence and destructive forces are given free rein, they may become undercurrents in the dynamics of the group. Often, this is revealed by utterances such as: 'I am scared'; 'What will happen now?' On other, occasions, the fantasies may be of a more mystical nature such as that someone will be 'sacrificed' or 'executed'.

The distance in the room and its size may also cause people to raise their voices in order to be heard. This may raise the level of anxiety. Some people may believe that the speakers are angry, critical or judgmental, especially when members of the staff are speaking up. The result may be a centripetal and regressive movement towards fusion, dissolution of individuality, as well as homogenising and anonymising.

Perspectives from the large group

The question naturally arising is whether these large groups at Tavistock conferences are artificial and therefore do not reflect processes inherent in other situations. It is true that when organising the conferences, heavy emphasis is put on the professional roles of the staff, the time limits and the use of interpretation in both large and small group meetings. This will inevitably intensify some of the group processes thus making them more discernible for the participants.

At these conferences one will easily recognise several phenomena one sometimes observes in completely different circumstances, as, for instance, in some of the community meetings already described. This recognition greatly helped me to understand, and to cope more successfully with certain irrational reactions sometimes encountered in my work as head of psychiatric wards. Later, when working as a consultant for other institutions and organisations, I had many confirmations as regards similar processes which I previously had not understood and which many leaders still do not understand.[5]

One may ask why all this does not emerge in ordinary group gatherings, when teaching school classes of up to thirty pupils, for example, or when lecturing and speaking to even larger audiences. Or at general assemblies and large public meetings of different types, not to mention in political and religious settings.

My experiences in the community meetings in psychiatric wards may provide an answer. The formal structures of large meetings, which include chairmen, agendas, minutes, reports, traditions and rituals, have an anxiety-reducing effect. We see that in these group gatherings structures of this kind usually take up a great deal of time. Therefore very little room is left for silences or for spontaneous reactions from the participants. This is a predicament which most chairmen fear because it may easily turn into an unpredictable situation, with emotional and irrational reactions by the participants.

If the formalities are too numerous or the programme is too full, the involvement and the interest of the audience will diminish. One obviously associates the soporific effect of long sermons, formal lectures and detailed accounts. In education, at lectures and sermons it is customary for a person to speak at great length, while the audience sits and listens passively. This furthers regression in the entire group. The risk of falling asleep is great, and many of the audience do not catch what is said. This may be explained as a weakening of the ability to concentrate and to comprehend. Here too the processes at work are similar to those at the large group meetings at conferences, except that they are less potent and less overt. We know from school that those sitting at the back of the class do not benefit as much from the teaching as those sitting in front. Positioning in the room plays an important part. There is a great difference between sitting in the inner circle, as compared to the outer circle.

Throughout the ages political and religious leaders have consciously or unconsciously played upon the irrational processes in large groups. I shall return to this later (see Chapter VIII). It is important to realise that these regressive and irrational processes do not only take place where many people are gathered in one room. They also manifest themselves in all large organisations and systems where many people work together without actually being present at the same time and place. This is one of the most important reasons why problems concerning teamwork and leadership have a tendency to grow in accordance with the size of the organisation. This could be fully observed at the two large hospitals, Dikemark and Ullevål. It is therefore not accidental that in small hospitals – as compared to large ones – there is as a rule a far better atmosphere, better teamwork and better treatment and care of patients.

This actual fact is often ignored or not understood in today's society where economic considerations and rationalising lead to constantly expanding units, to large concerns and fusions. Considering the current knowledge of the dynamics of large groups, a great deal may be said for the title of E.F. Schumacher's book *Small is Beautiful*.

However, large groups do not only represent something fearful and menacing. They also offer creative possibilities for jointly thinking out aloud, thus clarifying many aspects of life and human interaction which we are unable to see or understand by ourselves. I first learned this at the community meetings together with extremely 'sick' patients, as well as in the large groups at the Tavistock conferences.

The experiences in large groups has also taught me that we all strive to find a path between two types of anxiety: *on the one hand, we have a longing for closeness and belonging to a group, though also a fear of fusion and dissolution. On the other hand, we strive for our independence, but are also afraid of loneliness.* This dilemma is inherent in all human relationships, and most evident in individuals with weak or insecure identities. The centrifugal and centripetal forces which influence the individual in large groups point to the universality of this human dilemma – the balance between Scylla and Charybdis.

NOTES TO THE TEXT

[1] Jørstad, J, Fellesmøtet I lys av nyere synspunkter på storgruppedynamikk. Nord. Psykiatr. Tidskr., 1984, pp.265–275.

[2] Karterud, S and Jørstad, J, Tavistock-konferanser om grupperelasjoner. En annerledes læring om lederskap og organisasjoner. Tidsk. Nor. Lægeforen, 1986, pp.35–37, 106, 3004–7.

[3] Main, T, Some Psychodynamics of Large Groups, *The Large Group*, Constable, London, 1975.

[4] Turquet, P, Threats to Identity in the Large Group, *The Large Group*, Constable, London, 1975.

[5] Jørstad, J, Gruppeprosesser som influerer på teamsamarbeid og lederskap i våre psykiatriske institusjoner. Nord. Psykiatr. Tidskr., 1974, pp.38, 4, 277–286.

Chapter V
WHAT TURNS ME INTO A BULLY OR INTO A VICTIM OF BULLYING?
The dynamics of bullying

My first day at school ended tragically: I came home to my mother crying and with a bleeding nose! I do not remember much about this first encounter with life's harsh realities except that a small, sturdy fellow called Reidar had – without provocation – given me such a sock in my face that blood spurted. Never before had I been exposed to physical attacks by children of my own age. Nor had I learnt to defend myself, or to fight. In those days I was such a good boy and far too well behaved to hit back. On that particular day when everything around me seemed new and strange, I believe I must have looked rather helpless and unsure of myself. Besides, I was only six years old then – one year younger than the rest of the class.

Only much later on I realised that my parents' high ambitions for me had been the reason for my premature school debut. With their unrealistic expectations they believed me to be both precocious and unusually gifted. Later, they allowed me to skip one more class, to go into the fifth class at the Halling private school, which had five preparatory classes and four secondary classes. A year later, I started in the first secondary class aged only ten. Understandably, I came under too much pressure and became nervous. My parents realised then that something was wrong. Most likely they put most of the blame on the school, and therefore I was transferred to another private school, the Adelaide Stangs Forskole, which was situated in Parkveien and had six preparatory classes. I took the fifth and the sixth class, before starting in high school at Stabekk, at the age of twelve, still one year younger than my classmates.

The private school

My schooling was therefore extremely irregular and always being younger than my classmates, I was under a constant strain. One thing was absolutely certain: physically I was not in the least precocious. I was slender-limbed and anything but tough. Around the age of ten or eleven, I suddenly shot up and became quite skinny. But still I was no fighter. Moreover, I was the only pupil at Stangs' school wearing glasses, so that nicknaming me 'flagpole' and 'four-eyes' soon became very popular.

There is much to be said for Stangs' private school, but it was definitely a typical school for snobs. The pupils came almost exclusively from affluent families with well known names. Between my classmates and myself there was a division of class distinction. My father was a mere municipal engineer, which placed me in the lowest social stratum. This must have been one of the reasons why Jon Peder, who was tall and strong, and the son of a shipowner, took such pleasure in bullying me. On one occasion when he clouted me, my glasses flew across the street where they finally smashed into smithereens. I was more angry than scared, and it infuriated me that this rich boy did not even for one moment consider compensating me for the loss of my glasses. However, I was not the only victim of bullying in the class. Bernhard and I shared this role and we found some solace in our common predicament.

Parents often believe that they know best what is good for their children. But parents may also be easily misled by their own fantasies and prejudices, attributing to their children certain qualities and degrees of maturity which have very little to do with reality. However, most parents mean so well! Today I do not believe that my experiences as a victim of bullying at school left me with deep wounds to my soul, but I did learn something. There are, of course, others who have had far worse experiences than I.

Serious consequences

Maria is a twenty-four year old woman with Asiatic looks, who comes for treatment because she feels that she hates her own body. She is depressed and does not feel that life has any meaning. She suffers particularly in connection with her menstruation which started when she was eleven years old. The week prior to menstruation and the week after, she feels absolutely desperate. She has hateful fantasies about herself and everything connected with being a woman. Her hatred is also directed against other people. Sometimes she has murderous fantasies about them.

Maria tells me that when she was six months old, she was adopted by Norwegian parents who did their very best to give her a good home. She does not know anything about her origins except that her biological father was probably an American. Maria believes that her problems first began when she started school and was gradually exposed to systematic bullying by both girls and boys. One reason for this was that she looked different from the other pupils. The first few years had not been too bad because Maria had a good friend in her class. However, when this friend was moved to a different class, she lost touch with her and began to feel lonely and frozen out by the other girls. At the age of eleven, she was physically more developed than the other girls and started growing breasts. One day, a group of boys grabbed her and forcibly undressed her while pawing her genitals and breasts. This happened several times more and each time Maria felt shattered and terribly humiliated. She felt completely powerless and unable to defend herself. No one on the staff knew about this and she did not tell her parents.

In Maria's mind, all her years at school were one long nightmare, especially in seventh and eighth class. In secondary school she often played truant, and spent her time in groups where she felt accepted among the outcasts. She was unable to adjust either to schooling or to steady work. She felt she had to be free; she could not bear feeling bound to anybody or to anything. Most frequently she felt different from everybody else, an outsider. Maria was often depressed and anxious. When she was about thirteen or fourteen years old, she began having eating disorders. The treatment projects she attempted were mostly unsuccessful.

During Maria's therapy it soon became clear that the bullying she had been subjected to had left deep marks on her which were the main cause of her present problems. Her hatred against her own body and her femininity reflected her hatred against the girls in her class. Also that it had been precisely her body which had provoked the boys' abusive behaviour. In order to protect herself she also had to learn to 'push away' all her feelings.

This particular form of bullying had both racial and sexual elements. The typical pattern in cases like these was that the girls 'froze her out', while the boys behaved more violently using their superior physical strength.

What is bullying?

The word bullying means to oppress or to tease another person physically or mentally. A little more specifically, we can say that bullying is an interaction between two or several people. In this interaction one person or a small number of persons become the victims of one or several persons' devaluation, scorn, contempt or violence, the precondition being that this goes on for some time and is repeated a number of times. It is therefore quite different from random teasing. A distinction is also made between direct bullying with overt assaults on the victim, and indirect bullying in the form of social isolation and exclusion from the group.

Basically, there have to be at least two persons for a bullying situation to arise, although there are often more people involved. The victim often plays a passive role and is quite unaware of the fact that there is something in his or her behaviour that triggers off the bullying. Bullying is therefore an expression of an interaction between individuals, played out on both conscious and unconscious levels. In many cases there is also a third party just looking on, without either taking sides or becoming involved. This is for fear of also being bullied. For the same reason the third party may just remain a passive hanger-on.

The least complicated and perhaps the most common bullying situation arises when one person bullies another person. For instance, bullying taking place in a marriage or other couple relationships, or between parents and children when a son or a daughter is bullied by the mother or the father. However, we use the word more often when it concerns a group, at school or at work, where unfortunately bullying is a very common occurrence. Without being aware of it, most of us may have a tendency to bully others. At times we may have a need for a scapegoat in order to rid ourselves of something which disturbs us so that we may again feel well.

The significance of projections

When you point at another person, there are three fingers pointing at yourself. It is the same image as in the Bible's analogy about observing the splinter in your brother's eye and never noticing the plank in your own. The deepest reason for bullying is your own hypersensitivity to unaccepted aspects in yourself when you see them in others. By unconsciously thrusting these unaccepted aspects onto others, you ascribe to them the feelings and qualities of which you are afraid, or which you hate in yourself. And, to top it all, you may then feel certain that your indignation is perfectly 'justified', and gives you the right to attack the other person. We call this projection. It is a defence mechanism which we all use to a certain degree. If we constantly use projections, it is often a sign of immaturity and that we are unable to see ourselves realistically. When something goes wrong, then it is always the 'fault' of the other or the others. This is a fundamental cause of bullying, and also the reason for many of our prejudices. The same applies to all forms of fanaticism where we fight our own unconscious tendencies by fighting them in others. It is also the source of most conflicts which arise between individuals, in groups, in political parties and in nations, and which are the cause of so much suffering and violence (Chapters III, IV, and VIII).

Bullying in couple relationships

In order to explain some of the unconscious causes of bullying, it is best to look at the interaction between two people. For example, between the man and the woman in a couple relationship. The traditional pattern of sex roles usually ascribes the 'strong' and dominating role to the man, while the woman represents the 'weak' and submissive party in the couple. It often becomes important for the man to maintain this feeling of being the 'strong' one. Hence he attacks and represses everything that might threaten this self-image, either from within or from outside. The woman may play at being 'weak' in their mutual interaction in order to enable the man to preserve his self-image. Yet she may, surreptitiously, develop her own strength and superiority in relation to her children, her ability for giving care, her greater sensitivity to human needs, in her sexuality and in regard to the practical and economical issues of homemaking. The wife's competence in these areas will often greatly increase the husband's dependency on her and she will become the 'stronger' of the two.

The overt or the concealed balance in a couple relationship may be threatened if the man begins to feel weak or inferior, or if the woman becomes more openly self-assertive, stronger and more independent. This may induce the man to bully his female partner. We call this oppression of women or marital violence. The bullying is here due to an illusion of strength, a self-delusion in the man who does not accept his 'weak' sides, but 'places' them onto his partner. The man's false self-image becomes a weakness in itself, an 'Achilles' heel'. He who believes himself to be strong, can be revealed as being weak, and he who has the power may feel powerless. The road to aggression and violence can be very short (see also Chapter IX).

Parents who bully their children

The most disastrous spheres where bullying can take place are in the relationship between parents and children. What is it that can make mother or father bully their child by taking advantage of their own superior strength and their child's dependence? As psychiatrists we have gained a great deal of knowledge about the suffering, anxiety and desperation which parents sometimes inflict on their small children. The parents may, for example, laugh at them, ridicule them, humiliate them by meting out unjust punishments, or they may tease, frighten or abuse them.

A close study of child abusers shows that it is frequently the very helplessness of the child, or its prolonged crying which may provoke the adult. Most of us are very frightened about feeling helpless. We protect ourselves against this feeling by becoming angry – men more often than women. The less we are in contact with our own helplessness, the more we have to attack in others what unconsciously reminds us of it in ourselves. Another important point is that individuals who have themselves been bullied or misused by their parents, will tend to do the same to their own children. We identify unconsciously with our parents, regardless of their personality, and in spite of the suffering they may have caused us. This is one of numerous indications about the power of the subconscious in our lives, which runs its own course irrespective of rationality, knowledge or willpower.

Black Jack and the scapegoat

The card game of Black Jack which we played as children, symbolised the role of the scapegoat in a group: one child got a black nose and had to endure the shame of being singled out as the scapegoat in the group. We can all recognise this situation from family life: the two year old starts saying 'no', refuses to do what the mother or father asks it to do; the three year old cries all the time because it has a pain or is afraid; the four year old makes a mess on the table or knocks down a vase. These are all situations which may provoke parents who are already worn out, anxious or irritable. Or who may still have problems dating back to the same period in their own childhood.

It may be even more provoking when a teenager in strong opposition to his parents, criticises them for their lifestyle, their values or their double standards. Or, if the teenager allows himself to do things which would have been unthinkable for the parents to have done as teenagers. These are normal situations in the lives of children and adolescents. However, immature parents may often be provoked if they feel narcissistically hurt, or if their self-confidence is threatened. By way of defence they may then use projections and bullying. The teenager may even be excluded and 'thrown out' as the family's scapegoat. Some of the young drug abusers who roam the streets of large cities, have been victims of bullying and have been thrown out by their families. Typically, their self-esteem is low, they are lonely and feel hatred towards their parents, adults in general, and themselves.[1,2]

Bullying at school

My own experiences, as well those described by Maria, are in no way extraordinary. Mutual bullying at school is a widespread phenomenon, manifesting itself at all levels. In recent years there has been an increase in violence with pupils using knives and other weapons. A Norwegian study shows that nine to ten per cent of all school children are bullied, and six to seven per cent are bullies themselves. In former times, teachers did very little to prevent bullying. Today, they are more aware of the problem but they often feel helpless because the victims are afraid to complain about it for fear of revenge. In most cases parents also are kept in ignorance.

Even though girls have their own particular methods of bullying, for instance 'freezing out' or excluding one member of their group, it is the boys who more often feel the need to assert themselves by teasing or harassing weaker, anxious or younger pupils. Or else they need to start a fight in order to demonstrate their physical superiority.

On the basis of my previous statements, one might presume that teenage boys often feel unsure of themselves and therefore use this type of 'masculine' and aggressive bullying of someone who is 'weaker' as a defence against their own anxiety. However, several studies indicate that this is not as common as one might think, and that, on the contrary, some bullies are less anxious than others.

But as a rule, the bullies come from dysfunctional families where children are given severe physical punishment, are humiliated and hurt by their parents or older siblings. They may also come from broken homes where the parents are engrossed in their own personal problems and where there is little contact, particularly with the father. The most important fact, however, is the absence of caring and the lack of love in these homes, and the non-existence of firm boundaries.

In circumstances such as these, children become both angry and frightened. Bullying will then become a means of acting out their anger, of revenging themselves. This will make them feel superior and help them gain control over their own anxiety (Chapter VII). Studies made on bullies show that these are often not only aggressive towards their own comrades, but also towards adults in general. They are impulsive, they feel the need to dominate and they are adherents of violence. As a rule, they are unable to empathise and feel sympathy for their victims. They are good at talking themselves out of trouble and often show anti-social behaviour, for example, by committing criminal acts. Some of them turn into adult criminals. All this is characteristic of individuals who are strongly narcissistic (egocentric) with psychopathic tendencies (Chapter XIV).

Corresponding studies on victims of bullying reveal that compared to other children they are more anxious and insecure, and as a rule cautious, sensitive and quiet. Their self-esteem is low and they regard themselves as stupid, unsuccessful and unattractive. They feel lonely at school and seldom have a close friend in the class. Boys who are bullied are usually physically weaker than their comrades.[3]

Bullying at work

Unfortunately bullying is also fairly common among adults. It seems that we humans are subject to the same 'pecking order' as was discovered among hens by the animal psychologist Schjelderup-Ebbe. The strongest hens peck at weaker ones, and these in turn peck at the ones who are even weaker. Those at the bottom of the hierarchy in the poultry yard, are pecked at by all: these are the proverbial 'hens at the bottom of the pecking order'.

A hospital ward with a hierarchical organisation may serve here as an example. In some wards the person on top of the hierarchy, the chief physician, may bully a senior registrar or a nurse, and the nurse may then in turn retaliate by bullying the nursing assistant or the cleaner. However, there is now less of this type of bullying because an increasing number of people refuse to be bullied by their superiors. Also, because it has become possible to file complaints with staff representatives, trade unions with reference to the work environment law. And yet, one can still today find authoritarian leaders in the public health service and in other areas.

Most of us sometimes need to take out our stress and frustration on someone. People working in the social services and the public health sector are regularly exposed to stress of all kinds which affects them both consciously and unconsciously. This may create a need to find a 'chopping block', particularly if there is no one at home to take it out on. Someone at work, preferably on the same level, may then be chosen for this role. As in school, some individuals may have a need to assert themselves at the expense of others, or they may feel superior to, and better than others. They demonstrate their 'superiority' by letting the weakest in the system become the target of unreasonable criticism, devaluation or slander. For example, the newcomers, most junior or those who are anxious and have difficulties asserting or defending themselves. We suspect that these individuals may have narcissistic tendencies to compensate for their own low self-esteem. This assumption is corroborated if they never admit to their own faults.

Sibling rivalry and jealousy in relation to parents is another source of bullying at the same level, and it is probably most pronounced in women. No one is permitted to be popular or clever, and if they are, they are 'punished', sometimes in rather devious ways. The underlying issue can also be rivalry for men. Coming from a man, this statement will probably irritate many readers. But it is no use denying the fact that if, for example, the newly arrived female employee is prettier and more sexy than the other women and therefore more appealing to men, it may trigger off bullying by the 'sisters'. If a stable relationship develops between two employees at a workplace it may cause real trouble if it arouses feelings of jealousy and insecurity in the others. The loyalty created between a couple is much stronger than the loyalty towards the workplace or within an occupational group.

The fear of being different

In his book *En Flykning Krysser Sitt Spor* (A Fugitive Crosses His Own Tracks), the Norwegian author Axel Sandemose describes the 'Janteloven', the law of the fear of being different, which we see applied here and which contains the following articles:

> 'You shall not believe that you are any good. You shall not believe that you can compare yourself to us. You shall not believe that you are more clever than we are. You shall not believe that you are capable of anything. You shall not believe that anyone cares about you...'

And so forth. These tendencies do not only manifest themselves in the small town of Jante, but can actually be seen in almost all groups of people and at all workplaces. Why then are they so common?

Today we know a great deal about unconscious tendencies in working groups and organisations, especially through the studies carried out on group relations at Tavistock conferences (Chapter IV). In all large groups there is an unconscious and growing pressure towards uniformity. Anyone making himself or herself conspicuous will become the target of collective projections. The individual who is the recipient of many projections from the group members comes under great strain. This is the origin of Jante.

The bullying of leaders

In large groups we can observe that individuals in positions of authority often become the target of collective projections. These projections are either idealising or devaluating. In the latter case, the leader may be exposed to bullying because the group ascribes qualities to this leader which are far more dangerous, threatening or authoritarian than he or she is in reality. Another reason can be that the leader is unable to live up to the magical and unrealistic expectations created by an idealising projection. He or she will then be considered weak and useless.

In a group the leader may easily fall down from an idealising pedestal. We only have to look at today's political leaders. There is a quote by Mirabeau which expresses this very well: 'It is only one step from the Capitol to the Tarpeian Rock' (place of execution). Or, as Bjørnson (a Norwegian author) says about Napoleon in his poem 'My Company': 'With victories from Moscow to Cartagena, he dies yet lonely on St Helena.' Sometimes a leader is bullied openly. But more often it is done in an underhand way, by maligning or by talking 'bullshit' in corners and circulating disrespectful, idle rumours which undermine his authority. The same object is achieved by sabotaging the leader's messages and resolutions, by 'forgetting' what has been decided, or by arriving too late at the meetings convened by the leader. Many readers will recognise these situations.

However, there may also be rivalry about leadership, rivalry and fighting between the sexes. For example, doctors and nurses often compete about who should be in charge of the wards and the hospitals. Women's lib and the change in sex roles have played a significant role in this connection. Perhaps the younger generation of nurses feels that it has to make up for what earlier generations suffered by having to maintain submissive attitudes towards authoritarian chief physicians.

How do patients affect us?

I have already mentioned that the work in caring professions and health services exposes one to special strains and stresses. We see a great deal of human pain, suffering, anxiety and death. This affects us deeply and may cause anxiety, perhaps disguised as physical aches and pains, as tiredness or irritability. Or we may become what is called 'burnt-out'. This may result in conflicts and bullying at our workplace.[4]

We, who are working in psychiatry, are familiar with one particular knock-on effect from the psychiatric patients which may lead to bullying: namely, the ability of very sick patients to divide the world and other people into angels and devils. These patients unconsciously project their experiences from early childhood onto the therapists and the care personnel. As we have seen in the large groups, this splitting will have a strong impact on the persons who becomes the carriers of these 'good' or 'bad' projections. The persons who are idealised will begin to feel somewhat superior to the others, while the ones who are devaluated will begin to question their own skills and lose self-confidence. This may lead to great differences of opinion about how to treat these patients, since one or several therapists will be convinced about the efficacy of their own methods of treatment, while the others are merely 'mistaken'. In the heat of the battle, none of the contending parties realise that by disagreeing and fighting each other, they are in fact acting out some of the patient's internal drama. It is only when they become aware of this and stop bullying each other, that the patient shows signs of improvement. The 'good' and the 'bad' aspects of his internal world will make contact, initiating a process which will lead to better integration and wholeness.[5]

Also in this scenario, our narcissism plays a part in the interaction. We all wish to be 'clever' helpers and to see the result of our work. This makes us very susceptible to idealising projections. We tend to become very vulnerable when others are sceptical about our knowledge and views, and we defend ourselves by attacking and bullying them.

We are not always aware of why we have chosen a career in one of the caring professions. Perhaps we can agree with the words of a student nurse who came into therapy because she was in a crisis. Being suddenly aware of her own motivation, she said: 'It is easier to be strong among the weak, than weak among the strong'.[6]

What can we do to counteract bullying?

As in so many other areas, the foundation is laid in the family. If we were brought up by parents who had a reasonably sound relationship and gave us sufficient love and security, and if they moreover set clear limits, then most likely we will not turn into bullies or become victims of bullying. The child's relationship to its father is particularly important (Chapter IX). It seems, however, that an increasing number of families fail in their task.

This may be due to the change in social conditions. There are now more broken homes, less contact and nurturing between parents and children, more single parents, and a general lack of firm boundaries.

Because of this, schools today have to deal with a series of problems which in fact originate in the family. This is becoming a growing challenge for teachers, especially in secondary school. Many teachers come under pressure due to the attitudes of their pupils: their lack of respect and pity for others, their lack of impulse control, their egocentricity and materialism. They have no knowledge of clear limits and no experience of having to take the consequences for their own actions.

However, schools can do something. Preventative measures, such as better supervision and the presence of more teachers during the breaks, have had positive results. Clear rules against bullying are essential, as well as parent-teacher conferences held in school and in the classes. Serious talks with bullies and the victims of bullying in the presence of their parents have also proved successful. Anyone who is bullied has a right to be protected from further harassment.

Perhaps the most important issue is to establish a close co-operation between the school and the home. Parents need to be observant and take action if their child does not thrive at school, if it starts playing truant, comes home with torn clothes, bruises or other injuries on the body. It may also be significant if the child has lost its clothes, or books, or has no friends at school.

We can all do our best to learn to understand the factors which create the preconditions for bullying. For example, the 'Jante' tendencies which are inherent in all groups and are active at all workplaces, as well as at places where many people congregate. It may be helpful to understand the irrational interactions between leaders and those who are led, between the 'strong' and the 'weak', between women and men, the elderly and the young, and between 'in-groups' and 'out-groups'.

What is even more important, but far more difficult, is to change the conditions for bullying which we harbour in ourselves: our need to thrust onto others feelings and qualities which we refuse to acknowledge in ourselves, either by projecting them downwards in a hierarchy, sideways onto work colleagues, or upwards onto the leader. The greatest challenge, therefore, is to work with ourselves, to come into contact with our own feelings, and to acknowledge them to ourselves and to others. This applies to anger and rage, but just as much to feelings of helplessness, insecurity and anxiety, of which we are most afraid. This is the reason why supervision is so important in all the caring professions and for therapists. We may gradually discover that a great deal of what seems to be strength, in reality is weakness. And what is traditionally looked upon as weakness, may often prove to be – or may become – a sign of strength. This applies first and foremost to ourselves, but will have automatic consequences in our relationships with others. We all try to find the balance between strength and weakness, and between self-deception and self-knowledge. My own experience is that the only strength that really holds is the one that acknowledges its weakness.

NOTES TO THE TEXT

[1] Vaglum, P, *Unge stoffmisbrukere I et terapeutisk samfunn*, Universitetsforlaget, 1979, pp.60–74.

[2] Jørstad, J, Unge stoffmisbrukere I Oslo – erfaringer med sykenusbehandling, Nordisk Medisin, 1975, 90, pp.116–121.

[3] Olweus, D, *Mobbing I skolen*, Univeritetsforlaget, Oslo, 1992.

[4] Jørstad, J, 'Utbrenthet – et økende problem I helsearbeid', Nordisk Medisin, 1988, 103, pp.102–105.

[5] Main, T, 'The Ailment', Brit. J. Med. Psychol. 1957, 30, pp.127–145.

[6] Jørstad, J Wenn die krise des patienten auch die des Therapeuten wird. Uber risiken und Möglichkeiten psychiatrisher und psychotherapeutisher Arbeit. In Battegay (ed.), *Herausforderung und Begegnung in der Psychiatrie*, Huber, Bern, Stuttgart, Wien, 1981.

Chapter VI
WHY DO WE NOT TOLERATE THOSE WHO ARE DIFFERENT?
Discrimination, xenophobia and racism

The fat lady and other aberrations

My mother often told an amusing story about me as a three or four year old. One day when she and I were travelling in the tramcar, an extremely fat lady came and took a seat opposite us. Turning to my mother I said in a loud voice: 'Why is that lady so fat, Mother? Do you think she will burst?' I had never seen anyone like her before and my reaction was therefore quite natural. I just wanted an explanation of the phenomenon of the 'fat lady'. My mother was not particularly amused by the situation which I had created. Instead of giving me an answer, she got both of us off at the next stop. She never told me what she had said to me afterwards, but I presume I was given a lecture about not asking that type of question in the presence of others.

During my childhood in Oslo, I very rarely saw people of other races or from other cultures. I remember feeling surprised and a little scared when I first encountered black people. I suppose I imagined that Negroes were probably wild and dangerous people. My father was a very tolerant man, but I recall him speaking of Russians and Bolsheviks with fear in his voice, and also of 'the Yellow Peril'. In his imagination, he saw the Chinese inundating the whole earth with their beliefs in the near future. My mother also had her prejudices. For example there was the one about farmers and country people speaking in dialect. I believe that she looked down upon them as slightly inferior, this may have been due to her own Swedish background. She had actually grown up in the Swedish countryside, but had been convinced from an early age that she was 'from a different species'.

In the Thirties both my parents became Christians through their involvement with the Oxford movement. I believe it made them more tolerant. As I myself experienced it before the war, this movement represented a cheerful and liberal form of Christianity. My childhood home was always open to all types of people, both 'publicans and sinners'. Initially the Oxford group, as it was also called at the time, practised an ecumenical, open and tolerant form of Christianity. After the war, when it changed into the moral rearmament movement, it became – to my mind – far more moralistic and intolerant.

After the war my mother worked as a foot therapist for the elderly, with a charitable organisation, the Slum-sisters. Later on, for many years in collaboration with the psychiatrist Gordon Johnsen, she took in psychiatric patients as boarders, anticipating today's system of sheltered homes. I was therefore quite accustomed to having people about the house or for meals who had many problems, and who often behaved very strangely. I still remember a number of dramatic situations from these years. I do not know if these experiences were responsible for my subsequent choice of profession, but I do believe that they contributed towards making me more tolerant of human aberrations and diversities.

The stranger

Why do we so often look down on people, fearing or hating them because they are different from us? Is it because their appearance is different, they talk differently, or have a different religion? Do we know what causes prejudice, antagonism and conflicts among people? Physical and mental suffering and violence? Why have there been wars since the beginning of time? Needless to say, there can be no precise or complete answers to these questions, but I believe that the knowledge we have today may throw some light on these issues (see also Chapters V and VII).

To discriminate means to distinguish between different categories. In this particular context, it means between different categories of people. However, it is hardly accidental that the word also signifies the devaluation of others, when these are experienced as both different and inferior.

Why do people's appearances provoke us? It is primarily because this represents something alien, something unknown. It seems that physical aspects also, such as the colour of the skin, the appearance, face and eyes, also movements, sounds and smells are important determining factors.

These physical aspects are among the child's very earliest perceptions. Thus our fear of strangers, of the unknown, can be traced back to these very early roots. This begins already during the first year of life when the child is learning slowly to distinguish between its mother and other people. At that stage it is the mother who represents security for the child, gradually, also the father. Other persons, however, are unfamiliar and therefore somewhat frightening.[1]

We know that skin colour plays a key role in racial prejudices. Dark-skinned people, 'blackies', 'niggers', are not only discriminated against in the United States and South Africa, but also in many other countries, including our own. There are various reasons for this: historical roots from the days of slave-trading, and seeing 'the natives' in Africa as primitive and inferior races in contrast to 'the white man'. In the United States in particular, the fact that even today the blacks belong mostly to the poorest section of the population, reinforces this derogatory attitude.

Moreover, at a deeper level, the fact that black people have a greater capacity for surrendering to physical and sensuous emotions may be provocative for white people. It is seen in the way they move, in their sense of rhythm, in their dancing, music and songs. Also, the fact that they are the top athletes, especially in running events. Could this be a form of envy? Is this not how we would like to be ourselves! Men may also feel sexually provoked and jealous because it is precisely the sensuality of black men which attracts white women. This represents a latent threat to the white man's self-image and hegemony. At the deepest level, is the Ku Klux Klan perhaps, a reaction to this threat? It organises the collective hatred by justifying the lynch law, and especially by sowing suspicions about black men's rape of white women.[2]

That which is alike but rejected

Charles A. Pinderhughes, a well known black American psychoanalyst linked the reason for the discrimination against blacks to an unconscious association with faeces.[3] Most white children are taught by their parents to look upon their faeces as something nasty and disgusting with which one should have nothing to do. This reasoning may seem far-fetched, but unconscious connections of this type are far more common than we are aware of.

Black or brown skin colour may also, at an unconscious level, awaken the 'dark' side in us – all that we do not want to admit to, or that we wish to get rid of, either consciously or unconsciously. We project it onto the 'Black Man' in the card game, in reality it is projected onto the 'nigger' (Chapter III). Black means something dark, which prevents us from seeing, which hides the unknown in ourselves. It is the symbol of the unconscious, the 'shadow', as Jung called it. Our unconscious often conceals hateful and aggressive feelings, sexual fantasies and impulses. These may sometimes be guilt and anxiety-laden remnants from our childhood (Chapter X). These 'dark' sides in us are easily projected onto others, and in particular onto those with black skin.

Paranoid fantasies

There is a certain disposition for paranoid reactions in all of us which has its roots in our earliest childhood (Chapter VII). The degree to which we use projection as a defence will depend on our proneness to feel threatened or persecuted. The more we project our aggressive and hateful fantasies onto others, the more we will experience these individuals as aggressive and hateful. In our fantasies, they may become threatening persecutors. In large groups the scope for paranoid projections increases. The impact on group members who are exposed to these paranoid projections may be so strong that they actually begin to live up to the fantasies of others.

A typical example of a circular escalation of collective paranoid fantasies of this kind took place between the Civil Rights Movement (CRM) with Martin Luther King on the one side, and Malcolm X and the Black Panthers on the other. Initially, the CRM was an idealistic and highly ethical movement which united blacks and whites in their efforts to fight against race discrimination. They believed in change. Malcolm X and his movement, on the other hand, lacked all confidence in whites. He fought militantly for black segregation, while at the same time building up a self-assertive, provocative and menacing self-image in the blacks. This image was exploited and reinforced by the media, while far less attention was given to the Civil Rights Movement. The only publicity it got in the media was when there were large demonstrations. Consequently the white Americans were reinforced in their collective prejudices about blacks being evil, menacing and dangerous. An informal but powerful 'White Power' movement was started which prevented the implementation of the civil rights laws by sabotaging them. This again had a boomerang effect: not only Black Power, but also the blacks were confirmed in the prejudices they held against the whites. The CRM was slowly forced into a militant direction.[4]

This example demonstrates how quickly a process of discrimination may escalate when both sides confirm each other's prejudices. It also shows how the media may enhance this type of process by unilaterally focusing on its alarming or negative aspects – the aspects which are sensational and therefore guarantee large bold-faced headlines in the press – and 'sell'.

In the tragic conflict between Jews and Arabs, fanatical militant groups on both sides continue inciting each other to acts of violence. It is a well known fact that violence, both individual and collective violence, spreads from the perpetrator to the victim, 'violence breeds violence'.

For years Norwegians were intensely engaged in morally denouncing all racial discrimination, and in particular that in South Africa. This has perhaps led us to believe that as far as discrimination is concerned, we are a nation morally superior to others. This collective delusion received its deathblow when, twenty years ago, black immigrants began to enter the country in steadily increasing numbers. To our surprise, we discovered that in this country racism also flourished in the disparaging attitudes taken by many people towards the so-called 'Pakis' and 'niggers'. An opinion poll held in 1995 showed that twenty-five per cent of the Norwegian people are negative towards immigrants. However, very few people will remain unaffected if their own child chooses a friend or a lover from immigrants of different cultures. Even the strange smells coming from the kitchens of immigrants can cause negative reactions. We are no better than any others. It is worth considering the old adage, 'Pride goes before a fall'.

Distance gives rise to fantasies and myths

The greater the distance, the more we resort to fantasies about 'the others'. This applies to normal relationships between individuals, and even more to the interaction between large groups. Geographical distances may therefore give rise to prejudices and nationalism. We all live in different areas, with borders around us and distances between us. Those living within our borders are our compatriots and are therefore like us. The others, those living outside our borders are different. Even though the world and distances are 'shrinking', we still have very strong feelings about our right for self-determination.

We can recognise similar discriminating tendencies within the frontiers of any country: between southerners and northerners or the inhabitants of other regions – indeed, even between urban and rural dwellers. These tendencies may also surface in relation to a neighbour living on the other side of the fence, or across the landing in a block of flats. It is the distance between people that gives rise to fantasies, myths and prejudices. The greater the distance between people, the greater the possibility for alienation and hostility.

Psychotherapeutic work offers a profound insight into the factors which have formed the individual. This makes it more difficult to maintain judgmental attitudes.

Religious discrimination

Different religions often embody racial and cultural differences. This generally gives rise to antagonism. History has given us many horrifying examples of persecutions and pogroms carried out for religious reasons, not least in the name of Christianity. Proclaiming that they represented 'the God of Love', the crusaders slaughtered millions of so-called heathens, people who adhered to other creeds. There are many examples of religious discrimination: the crusades in the Middle Ages. The havoc wrought by the extermination of the Indians in Central and South America by the Conquistadors. The witch burnings by the Jesuits and the Thirty Years' War. In recent years we have seen the rise of Khomeini's Islamic fundamentalism which justifies the use of violence and mass executions. Fundamentalism is still flourishing today in a number of religions.

We also have examples in this country of the religious fanaticism inherent in religious sects and revivals. These sects exalt themselves by claiming that they have a monopoly of the 'one and only truth', or that they are 'God's chosen people'. In all charismatic movements where a group of people feel that they have been 'chosen' or 'saved', there is a corresponding contempt for those who are 'beyond redemption', the 'heathens', who do not share the true faith and will therefore land in hell. Some are inside, the others are outside. Jesus himself warned against the Pharisees who elevated themselves on the grounds of their orthodoxy and sacred lives. In spite of this, collective Pharisaism is still practised in some Christian groups even though it is contrary to Christian doctrine.

Political discrimination

There are many examples of political discrimination, both historically and internationally. Authoritarian regimes, tyrants and dictators have always abused their power to suppress those 'who think differently'. Propaganda, indoctrination, prisons, slave camps, torture and executions are well known politically legitimised methods. Today's disclosures of what went on in the former Soviet Union and in Eastern Europe, the current suppression of the democratic movement in China and Saddam Hussein's terror regime in Iraq, all prove that political discrimination is still very much in existence all over the world. It not only proves that there is a certain type of personality who can gain total power over the masses, but also that the irrational layers in people often can be 'played on' by these characters (Chapter VIII).

What we term extreme nationalism, is often at the root of the various forms of discrimination which are mentioned. Basically, nationalism is not negative. On the contrary, it strengthens people's sense of their own identity, and intensifies their feelings of solidarity and community spirit. But there is always a risk that nationalism may lead to an over-estimation of one's own country and national interests, and hence to a devaluation of other countries. Nationalism may therefore induce a large country to intimidate or occupy a small neighbouring country.

The former Soviet Union and Yugoslavia are both examples of how strongly centralised and oppressive regimes – by placing the enemy outside its own borders – were able to hold many different nationalities together and partly control them. With the decline in governmental power and subsequent loss of control, the enemy 'out there' ceased to exist. Ethnic, national and religious conflicts exploded into civil wars, with inhuman cruelty and 'ethnic cleansing' in their wake.

The gas chambers

One of the most horrific examples of a combination of racial, religious and cultural discrimination was the persecution and extermination of six millions Jews in the gas chambers by the Nazis during the Second World War. Witnessing some of these atrocities myself in Buchenwald and Neuengamme (Chapter II), I began to wonder at that time what it was that made people commit such terrible acts.

One cannot merely interpret the persecution of the Jews as a manifestation of Hitler's psychopathic personality and of his uncanny ability to sway the masses. He was able also to play on the collective prejudices of the German people. Many Germans took an active part in pogroms against the Jews, or else they closed their eyes and passively accepted the crimes which were perpetrated. And this actually took place in one of Europe's great cultural nations. But, however, not only there. The Allies were also prejudiced against the Jews. This was reflected in the attitudes and actions of leading English and American politicians and officials before, during and after the war. In the Soviet Union anti-Semitic attitudes were even more widespread. Pogroms against Jews were a common occurrence in many parts of the country.

Jews have been persecuted for almost two thousand years. There are many reasons why they in particular have been the target of discrimination and hatred. The conviction within certain Christian communities that the Jews crucified Christ is offered as a partial explanation. But they forget that Christ himself was a Jew. Basically, the Jews cannot be distinguished from other Europeans by the colour of their skin or by any other racial characteristics. However, they often stand out because of their great skills and talents in many spheres. Not only are they successful traders, but they also excel as artists, scientists and politicians. How can one explain their extraordinary abilities?

Every time I meet a Jewish family, I am struck by one particular fact. Their remarkably strong family ties, and their deep loyalty to their own ethnic group. It seems that many Jews are more secure in their personal and ethnic identity than the other citizens of the countries in which they have lived. This may constitute a threat to the possibly already low self-esteem of others. Is it on account of these particular qualities and because of their talents, that the Jews have always aroused envy and hatred in non-Jews? Or have two thousand years of persecution generated this deep solidarity and these special qualities? Perhaps the answer is both.[5]

Children, adolescents and the elderly – a provocation

Politicians often declare that the most vulnerable groups in society ought to be given priority. But in practice and in terms of a budget, there is a constant down-grading of children, adolescents and elderly people in need of care.

Invariably one of the most important groups discriminated against, also in this country, is the children. This assertion may elicit some scepticism, but after forty years of experience in psychiatric and psychotherapeutic work, I believe this to be one of the gravest problems in today's society. In what way does Norwegian society qualify as a society hostile towards children?

There are many different ways in which children are misused and oppressed. This is often concealed from society. Children are weak, helpless and totally dependent on adults. At first they are mostly unable to verbalise their own needs. What parents cannot 'take out' on their own parents or on each other, they often take out on their children: their need for power, their need to own, to control. Many parents have a need to form another human being in their own image. Or they have a need for a scapegoat onto whom they can project their own unacceptable parts, a chopping block for venting their feelings of frustration and anger. Another reason may be that they feel powerless and helpless in their parental roles. Some parents use the child for satisfying their own sexual needs (Chapter X).

The child's smallness and its helplessness may provoke the helpless child in the parent. This often lies behind the abuse of children. Women are often maltreated by men who cannot tolerate their own weakness, and are thus provoked to perform violent acts. This is particularly true in situations where they lose some of their self-control under the influence of drink (Chapter IX).

The second group discriminated against are young people in their teens. There are many reasons for the conflicts and antagonism arising between adults and adolescents. These are partly due to the gradually growing generation gap, and partly to the normal need of young people to rebel and to free themselves. I learned a great deal about these issues when my own four children became teenagers. It was a useful experience for my work with young patients suffering from various mental illnesses, including drug addiction, at the Dikemark Hospital, Lien. These young people not only had a normal need to free themselves, they were also beset with great family problems.

If adolescent children provoke their parents beyond their limit of tolerance, the response may be rejection and even expulsion from the family. The adolescents may then continue to rebel against other 'authorities', such as teachers, politicians or the police – whoever represents 'law and order'. By catering to the needs of these types of adolescents, the Blitz-group in Oslo strengthens the already existing prejudices against youth, especially by wearing provocative clothes, acting aggressively or using narcotics.[6]

A third group discriminated against are the elderly people who are in need of care. They remind us of our own mortality, and that one day we may all become weak and helpless. These thoughts are best not dwelt upon. The elderly are no longer 'productive', and they do not represent a political pressure group. Although much has been achieved in this country regarding welfare for old people, especially in the minor counties, it is a disgrace to see how fundamental human needs are still being neglected in some of the nursing homes. There are still not enough vacancies in nursing homes for old people in Oslo, although many of them are without any family support, totally helpless and in dire need of nursing.

Other low-status groups which today are often discriminated against and rejected in Norwegian society are psychiatric patients ('the crazy ones'), the mentally retarded ('the idiots') and the physically handicapped ('the cripples'). Criminals are in a different category. By placing themselves 'outside society' through their criminal behaviour, they become the target of strong discrimination. They often feel that they have been 'unfairly' treated. Punishment will in many cases increase their hatred and their need for revenge on 'the others' who represent law and order. Especially the police and those implementing the punishment – the prison administration.

I could name many other areas, where one group despises and devaluates other groups, thereby risking an escalation of open conflicts, of physical violence or war.

What is the common denominator in discrimination?

As already mentioned, we discover very early that someone is different. In this way, outer and inner premises for the experience of an in-group and an out-group are created. The group we belong to will normally seem important and more secure than 'the others'. It will therefore be upgraded both consciously and unconsciously, while the out-group will be devalued. 'We are the best!'

In addition, there is a need in all of us, just as in animals, for a 'territory' which belongs to us, either connected geographically to a tract of land, to our workplace or to the family. This is a fundamental human need. If strangers come too near, or if in our fantasies or in reality they threaten any of these territories, then this will trigger aggression. 'Don't trespass!'

These processes, common to all mankind, have certain individual and group-dynamic aspects which may reinforce them. Let us first look at the individual perspective.

Let us begin with normal development in infancy, the first year of life, when the baby attempts to get rid of its bad feelings, its pain, rage and anxiety by projecting these feelings onto its mother.

If, for example, the infant is angry, it will experience its mother as being angry, indeed, as an evil witch. Since the mother is of such vital importance to the infant, an opposite process will take place: the image of the mother, perhaps of the witch, is taken in, internalised, with the help of introjection. Possibly in order to gain control over the mother by 'swallowing' her in the psychological sense[7] (Chapter XV).

In this to-and-fro process of projecting and introjecting between the mother and the infant, the 'inner images' of the mother are created in the child. These images are filled with strong effects, with good and bad feelings. These have to be kept separate in the child's inner world, because otherwise the bad images could destroy the good ones, and then the world would become unbearable.

Thus our inner world, the image of ourselves, and the outer world with the perception of others, is divided into two – into good and bad. To put it differently, initially we experience the good mother and the bad mother as two totally separate persons, just as we experience the 'good me' and the 'bad me' as two different persons.

In normal development, during our first three years of life, most of us will gradually have achieved a fusion of the good and the bad parts of our inner world. Around the age of three, we may become aware that one and the same person can be both good and bad – and that we too – can be both good and bad. This is a decisive step in our development and maturation.

We also know that in some individuals this fusion of good and bad images does not come about. In psychiatric terminology, these individuals suffer from personality disorders or borderline states. Unconsciously they use the combination of projection and introjection as a defence mechanism. In order to protect themselves against their own anxiety and a feeling of perishing, the world for them is split up into good and bad projections, into 'angels and devils'. These individuals have weak identities and very little self-esteem. They find it difficult to tolerate frustrations, and they have a tendency to act out their inner conflicts.

They are not the only ones who divide the world and others into black and white. We all share this tendency and especially the inclination to project our unacceptable feelings and qualities onto other people. In special circumstances and under particularly trying conditions, most of us will make use of these defence mechanisms far more than we normally would.

Group processes

We can learn a great deal from studies dealing with interactions in large groups of people (Chapter IV). In these groups there is no tolerance for people who make themselves 'conspicuous'. Either by making a remark, asserting a personal viewpoint, or stating something at variance with the opinions of the group's majority. These people risk becoming the targets of the group's devaluating and scornful projections. Here we are at the source of the law of

Jante (Chapter V).

However, Jante is not merely a small town of Jylland. It can be found everywhere where people are gathered together or organised into groups. In a block of flats in Oslo, in the workplace, in a political party, or in a church congregation – even in a psychiatric clinic. Within these groups there is a tacit agreement, which is partly unconscious, that everyone has to be identical. No one must deviate from the norm or from the piecework contract. Preferably everyone should look alike, dress alike, talk alike and behave alike. Deviation is not tolerated. The regressive forces propel the group in the direction of conformity.

Whether the regressive group processes are reinforced or weakened, will depend on the style of the leader.

Authoritarian, paranoid and weak leaders will strengthen the regression. The same applies to typically narcissistic leaders who only focus on themselves, their prestige and their jealousy. They also lack the ability to understand others and to show them consideration.[8]

In large groups both centripetal and centrifugal forces are at work. The drive of the first-mentioned force is towards fusion, towards a dissolution of the boundaries between the individuals and towards their fusion with the group. The centrifugal force goes in the opposite direction, creating fantasies about resigning or distancing oneself from the group. Both tendencies may cause anxiety. It may be a fear of losing oneself in the group, or of being excluded, expelled and lonely. Different people react differently to these contrasting tendencies in the group. Some will join the group and become totally involved, while others will move away from the group. This may be the model on which in-groups and out-groups are formed.

As already mentioned, it is a well known fact that the team spirit in a group intensifies when its members have found a common enemy outside the group. By placing the 'bad' projections and splitting onto the enemy out there, the latent tensions and conflicts between the group members are automatically lessened. This is analogous to the individual who avoids inner splitting and anxiety by keeping his good inner objects to himself and projecting the bad objects onto the other person.

If we succeed in finding other groups, parties, races or nations whom we can devaluate, despise or hate, the group's feeling of unity, strength and solidarity will be heightened. The members may even believe that they have been specially chosen by their leader or by God. Under special conditions this type of group may become a willing tool for a religious fanatic, a commander of an army or a dictator. This is an important part of the psychology of hatred (Chapter VII).

Some years ago there was a film called *The Wave* which brilliantly illustrated the dynamics in such groups. A teacher wanted to use his class for an experiment to prove to them the potency of group processes. He divided the class into two halves – those with blue eyes and those with brown eyes. The blue-eyed pupils were favoured, while the brown-eyed ones were devaluated. Slowly he brainwashed the preferred group into feeling superior to all the others. They were furnished with a special logo for their group, and they greeted each other in a special way. Soon the members of this group began a typical up-grading of their own 'in-group', while showing an increasing degree of contempt for the other group. All people, who were not among the 'chosen', were bullied. Only two pupils in the group managed to maintain their own powers of discernment and their critical senses. When they spoke their mind about the behaviour of the others, they at once became the target of collective bullying by both groups. The experiment was discontinued at a critical point which left one with the feeling that it could all have ended in catastrophe. The pupils were 'roused' from this group seduction by being shown a film with an enormous close-up of Adolf Hitler addressing the masses on 'The Party Day' in Nürnberg.

How can we counteract discrimination?

It is not easy, either on an individual or on a collective level, to prevent discriminating attitudes because they are mostly founded on unconscious tendencies which are not directly accessible to common sense, knowledge or willpower. We know that more knowledge about other races, religions and cultures reduces the prejudices which are based upon ignorance. Therefore, travelling in other countries will make us more tolerant, providing we keep an open mind. The 'distance' between people and nations will shrink, both in terms of world economy and culture.

We are all now dependent on each other. The issue of poverty in the developing countries is of great concern to all of us and should therefore be addressed on an international level. The same applies to environmental problems. It does not help speaking to hungry people about the problems of pollution. But we hope that the days of narrow-minded nationalism are over. Personally I see a ray of hope for the future in the work carried out by the United Nations, and the regional alliances of independent states which are ceding part of their sovereignty to the international community. I believe that in the long run this will pay off.

The Bulgarian-French psychoanalyst Julia Kristeva believes that there may be a solution in what she calls the 'Transitional Nation'. It represents a 'space' which allows for identity, confirmation, candour and creativity. 'In it, strong individuals, sensitive fellow citizens and forceful cosmopolitans are created'.[9] As yet we have not gone very far down this road.

Authoritarian regimes will also present a problem in the future. We had hoped, however, that Europe would be spared from tragedies such as the war in Bosnia. In numerous countries in the Third World, there are still many opportunities for despotic dictators and tyrants to play on the masses by singling out enemies within or outside the frontiers of their countries. Democracies keep an equilibrium between legislative, executive and judiciary authority. It counteracts abuse of power, projections and splitting, but only if each part respects the other's sphere of authority. Majority rule is not representative of democratic leadership in organisations and industry. In a democracy everyone should be given the opportunity both to be heard and to participate in decision-making.

Openness on all levels counteracts the fantasies and myths which are often created through lack of candour. Religious pluralism, tolerance and ecumenical efforts prevent the spread of religious fanaticism and fundamentalism which has today become a truly global problem. It is of crucial importance that with teachers as role models, schools create attitudes which will counteract prejudices, discrimination and racism.

Many of these ideas have been the ideal aims for this country, and to a certain extent, they have been realised politically. However, there is a fourth power of the state: the media which has an alarming ability to upset the balance, often by unduly influencing public opinion. The tabloids, in particular, cater for the primitive and irrational emotions in people. On the other hand, a free press is one of the pre-conditions for democracy and a guarantee against the abuse of power and excessive irrationality. The media, therefore, is in a crucially important position of power. It can either reinforce or diminish the discriminating processes in a society.

Collective prejudices and delusions are deeply rooted. For this reason it is important that as many people as possible learn about the origins of these phenomena. Also, about the group dynamic forces which have an impact on the way in which people relate to their leaders, their colleagues and subordinates. Participation in a conference on group relations will offer a valuable experience and give knowledge about these matters (Chapter IV).

It is far more difficult, however, to change the individual and the unconscious parts in us which cause us to discriminate against others. The attitudes of parents towards people who are different are crucial to the attitudes of their children. Parents are models for their children, both regarding tolerance or intolerance. Contact between Norwegians and immigrants will counteract the prejudices and myths about 'the others'. Even more important is the way in which parents either use or abuse their children, as this pattern is transferred from one generation to the next. Or to quote the Bible: 'For I the Lord thy God am a jealous God, and visit the sins of the fathers upon the children unto the third and fourth generation.' I believe the mothers should also be included!

Another reason for our prejudices is our fear of the unknown. We are all afraid of taking a deep look into ourselves. Perhaps we are afraid to discover that we are not what we believe ourselves to be. We all have a conservative tendency to resist change, to resist learning something new or to change our concept of ourselves and others. What is firmly established gives security and protection against anxiety.

The less we are in contact with our inner world, and the more we dread discovering our own secret 'weaknesses', the more we tend to project onto people who are different from ourselves. After forty years of working with all kinds of people, I know that we all harbour hidden parts, weaknesses, criminal tendencies, aberrations and madness. We are all tarred with the same brush as those we despise, devaluate or discriminate against. Tolerance for other people presupposes tolerance for similar, hidden parts in ourselves.

NOTES TO THE TEXT

[1] Fraiberg, S H, *The Magic Years*, Schribner, New York, 1959.

[2] Grier, W H and Cobbes, P M, *Black Rage*, Basic Books, New York, 1968.

[3] Pinderhughes, C A, 'The Black Youth of Today', paper presented in Boston 26.10.68, arranged by the Boston Psychoanalytic Society and the Western New England Psychoanalytic Society.

[4] Ibid.

[5] Brøgger, J, *Kulturforståelse. En nøkkel til vår internasjonale samtid*, Damm & Sønn, Oslo, 1993, pp.129–151.

[6] Roszak, T, *The Making of a Counter Culture. Reflections on the technocratic society and its youthful opposition*, Anchor Books, Doubleday & Co., New York, 1969.

[7] Klein, M, *Love, Guilt and Reparation*, The Melanie Klein Trustees, London, 1948, 1952, 1975.

[8] Jørstad, J, 'Narcissism and Leadership: Some differences in male and female leaders', Nord. J. Psychiatry, 1995, 49, pp.409–416.

[9] Kristeva, J, *'Etrangers à nous même'*, Librairie Arthéme Fayard, Paris, 1988.

Chapter VII
WE ARE ALL MURDERERS
The roots of aggression

I declare that we are all murderers. Not in the literal sense of the word – for we have not killed other people – but in our conscious or unconscious fantasies we are all murderers.

On what grounds do I base this assertion? First and foremost on my experiences with people while I worked as a physician, psychiatrist and psychoanalyst. Through this work I gained insight into the conscious and unconscious fantasies and motives of my patients, and into the counterforces which prevent us all from seeing important aspects of ourselves. The media gives us daily reminders of the fact that in special circumstances, far more individuals than we believe, may kill others when feeling threatened, hurt or provoked in vital areas. Collectively we can observe this phenomenon in both national and civil wars, when anyone can become a killer, or even a mass murderer.

I have not chosen this heading in order to excuse those who really do become murderers, or to reduce the seriousness and horror of taking another person's life. However, I have chosen it as a gateway to reflections about some very important issues. What are the roots of aggression? How can we understand some of the hatred and violence that may eventually lead to homicide and murder? If I am correct in my assertion that, to a certain extent, we all have murderous tendencies, what is it then that distinguishes those of us who only commit murder in fantasy from those who really act out their murderous impulses? Where are the brake mechanisms which separate fantasy from action, and what may influence, strengthen or weaken them? I will come back to this question in the next chapter.

A revealing dream

Let me first relate a dream which I had many years ago. I had celebrated the birthday of an old friend who had been living abroad and whom I had not seen for many years. The night after the birthday party I dreamed the following.

My friend and I are standing outside a building where some workers are busy carrying some welded steel drums which were found in the cellar of this house. I am very curious about the contents of these drums, and insist on having them opened. My friend is terrified about my request and warns me strongly about the dangers that may be involved. However, I carry out my intention and have the drums opened. It then becomes apparent that they contain dissected corpses. The dissected limbs are hung up on a rack, for all to see. In the background there are two sets of rails which are broken because the bridge across a ravine has collapsed; there is no longer any connection between the rails on either side of the ravine.

It was an intense dream which greatly disturbed me and which, at first, made me think of the relationship between my friend and myself. We had not seen each other for many years and had developed in completely different directions. He had always been a somewhat anxious and careful man, always reluctant to take chances or to confront other people; a truly 'kind and good-natured fellow'. When we were young, he had warned me on several occasions to curb my impulsiveness, when I had been outspoken in voicing my opinions in words neither wise nor diplomatic. At the time of our meeting, he was obviously provoked by the fact that I went to psychoanalysis, which he himself would not dream of doing. He had also chosen a very different career from mine. Altogether it seemed that our old friendship no longer functioned – the rails were broken, the bridge had collapsed.

The way I saw it, the dream revealed something about our relationship, and about our two different attitudes to that part of the mind which is hidden in 'the unconscious', and which – in the symbolic language of the dream – is represented by the steel drums emerging from the cellar. At the same time the dream revealed something about the murderous and sadistic tendencies in each of us, which, however, mobilised more anxiety and defence in him than it did in me. Being in analysis at that time perhaps made me less easily scared.

I knew already at that time that a dream has very personal aspects. This was therefore *my* dream telling something only about *me*, and it gave glimpses of the two sides in me which opposed each other. On the one hand, my primitive and murderous impulses, and on the other, my fear of facing what lay hidden in the depths and my defences against this fear. These two sides in me were split off from each other and represented by the image of the ravine and the collapsed bridge. But a third side in me wanted to confront the truth – I had nothing to hide from myself or from others. This side emerged as the winner in the dream, perhaps as a result of the analytic process?

The image with the collapsed bridge addressed itself specifically to me. The two sides in me were still separated, but working with the dream and wishing for greater wholeness and openness, gave me a ray of hope that it would be possible to rebuild the bridge. If the two sides in me could be linked by a new bridge, it would make me feel more secure and more whole, which again might make it possible to repair our friendship. The dream pointed to the future, to a possible development within myself and in relation to others.

The reader may raise understandable objections, namely that I should not draw universally valid conclusions from one single dream, which, at best, can only disclose something about me personally, but not about others. Seen isolated, this is correct. I had murderous impulses of which I had been only partly conscious.

Children's drawings and play

Before starting school, I remember that I used to make drawings of cannons, tanks and warships, as well as of soldiers fighting and killing each other. Later, Bernhard, my best friend in the fifth and sixth form, and I, would often play with tin soldiers, each side lining up its 'army' and mowing down the other with slingshot cannons and peas as bullets. One might say these are typical boy games, and probably rightly so. But we know from the play observations of children and analyses of children's drawings that games like these disclose something about the aggressive feelings and the problems with which the child works subconsciously. They are as revealing as the dreams of adults. It is also true that boys produce such drawings and play war games far more often than girls. Maybe even though this tendency may have its root in constitutional differences between boys and girls, I do not believe that this explains everything. I will return to this issue later.

I remember that when I was a schoolboy I had totally conscious murderous fantasies and daydreams about crouching behind a machine gun and wiping out hundreds of people who were crowding in on me. All this was seemingly in contrast to the nice, well behaved boy of those days, who never fought or was openly aggressive, neither at home nor outside with my friends. Bernhard and I had both been given an upbringing which made it impossible for us to fight with other boys who were tougher than us. Indeed, in our private school in Parkveien, we two were the ones who were mobbed most often by other pupils who were more aggressive and self-assertive. So it was probably not strange at all that we vented some of our rage and need for revenge on the tin soldiers when playing war games.

However, I began making martial drawings long before I started school. My murderous fantasies also found expression through other channels, especially in situations where I felt humiliated, hurt or treated unfairly, by the very people perhaps who were closest to me and whom I loved most – my mother and father. The knowledge gained from all psychotherapeutic and psychoanalytic work indicates that some of the roots of anxiety and conflicts can be found in the aggressive feelings we harbour towards those whom we love or are dependent on. It is because we are most sensitive to hurt and rejection by those dearest to us, the greatest threat being the loss of their love. Most of us solve this conflict by repression, that is to say, the aggressive part of our feelings 'disappears', and is hidden – using the symbolic language of dreams – 'in the cellar in welded steel drums'. These feelings are more deeply hidden than the pain of having been mobbed at school and experiencing humiliations later in life.

Is aggression an instinct or a result of psychic injury?

Sigmund Freud founded his metapsychological theories on two basic instincts in human beings: libido, or the sexual instinct in the broadest sense of the word, and the aggressive drive, or the death instinct as he also called it for a time. Some of his successors have raised critical objections to Freud's instinct theory. They look upon aggression primarily as a result of early environmental injuries or frustrations sustained during childhood, a viewpoint which they are able to substantiate by many examples. This has also been corroborated by my extensive psychotherapeutic and psychoanalytic work. However, this can hardly be the only explanation when one considers the great importance given to aggression, violence and destruction today and at all times, in all cultures as well in the life of the individual.

In his book, *The So-Called Evil*,[1] the Austrian physician and ethnologist Konrad Lorenz discusses the question of the roots of evil. By comparing aggressive instincts in humans and animals, and giving a number of examples, he attempts to prove that aggression is not a manifestation of 'evil', but an element necessary for maintaining the natural equilibrium and essential for the self-protection of the species. When this instinct is derailed, which can easily happen in human beings, then aggression will become destructive and dangerous. Animals defend their physical living space, their 'territories', against intruders who turn into enemies. Is it not the same with us, when nations or ethnic groups fight against each other, or when we feel like killing a burglar or a rapist in our house? They are the 'intruders' into our territory and a threat to our vital interests. Obviously, in some situations this parallel can be relevant, but in our own lives this issue is often more complicated. Do we pose the wrong question when asking: instinct or environment? It should not be either/or, but both. For that reason it is important for us to be able to understand the danger signals in developing situations that may reinforce the destructive and self-destructive potentials of aggression.

A nightmare

I would like to relate another dream which showed that murderous impulses can be totally unconscious. It concerns a nightmare which I had many years ago and which I still think of as the most important dream of my life. It became a turning point in my understanding of my own aggression and the aggression of others.

I was staying with my family in a mountain cabin and had finished reading Dostojevsky's famous novel *Crime and Punishment* late that night. This is about the poor and desperate student Rodion Raskolnikov who kills the female pawnbroker and her sister with an axe. Throughout the greater part of the novel he fights an internal and external battle with his guilty feelings and his need for punishment and atonement, while the police officer Porfyriji Petrovitsj, through repeated dialogues with Raskolnikov, and without directly accusing or arresting him, finally makes him come forward and admit his guilt.[2]

Early in the morning I nearly woke up, but not completely. I was still in the dream, and *I* was the murderer who has killed and who is now waiting for the police to come and arrest me so that I can receive my well deserved punishment. When I finally woke up from this nightmare, I was still full of anxiety and guilty feelings. The dream had a realistic quality which surprised and frightened me. I had terminated my psychoanalysis with Harald Schjelderup a few years previously. In my naivety I was convinced that the most important problem areas in my life had been worked through reasonably well, but now I was suddenly a murderer deserving punishment!

This dream caused me to embark on my second psychoanalysis, with Astri Brun, MA, a female psychoanalyst. During the course of this analysis, new dreams with similar motives kept on surfacing, and I became gradually aware of the fact that the irrational guilty feelings which I had suffered from as an adult were connected to the violent fits of rage and death wishes towards my mother which I had had when I was about two to three years old. I had been told that I had been prone to these fits at that age, and that I had been severely punished, which was the usual way of dealing with children at that time.

In spite of the fact that my mother was in the best of health at the time of the dream, I was subconsciously deeply convinced that I had killed her and deserved punishment. In this second psychoanalysis, I relived my mother's strict, reproachful face in the female analyst, and my own rage over having been corporally punished when I had been 'naughty'. In my fantasy and in my dreams, Astri Brun became the 'witch' whom I 'killed' time and time again, cutting her into small pieces, the way a child may do in its fantasy.

My mother had had a typically old-fashioned upbringing in Sweden, and my father, who worshipped her, was usually the one to carry out her orders for my corporal punishment. I can still remember how often he cited the usual clichés expounding the bourgeois views on child-rearing of the twenties and thirties: 'Your will lies in my pocket,' and 'Spare the rod and spoil the child'. These exhortations may have given him some kind of comfort, since it was without any signs of enthusiasm that he spanked my bare bottom.

On Astri Brun's analytic couch I discovered something which was not only important to me, but also for many other people, as my subsequent work would show me. A great deal of the hatred we feel, the guilt and shame, uncertainty and inferiority, stems from the earliest years of our lives, when vulnerability and emotions are far more intense than later in life, and when there is a great gulf between the adults' superiority and the child's impotence and helplessness. Before we have the necessary preconditions for understanding why adults are as they are, we are inclined to take upon ourselves the burden of guilt for their problems and mistakes. The more authoritarian and punitive the upbringing, the more hateful and murderous the impulses created in the child. During their earliest years, children do not distinguish clearly between fantasy and reality, and their thoughts may acquire a magic and omnipotent quality: whatever we think, will happen! The type of upbringing I received was conducive to creating strong and neurotic guilt feelings for all my aggressive impulses. The murderous fantasies remained well hidden in 'the cellar in welded steel drums', but emerged together with the guilt feeling in the dream which was a real nightmare.

Why is murder so fascinating?

My Raskolnikov dream shows that authors of genius, like Dostojevsky, intuitively understood, personified and staged this inner drama, so common in many of us. This inner drama also takes place in our night dreams which we stage ourselves. Sometimes, as in the above example, the literary drama kindles the inner, unconscious drama.

In his roman á clef *A Fugitive Crosses His Own Trail*, Axel Sandemose takes up the same subject: a murder committed by Espen Arnakke. It is not only Sandemose who addresses the issue of murder committed in order to vent feelings of hatred generated by injustice and suppression. Why are crime stories and crime films so immensely popular? Is it because they touch certain chords in us? Why does the tabloid press quite consciously exploit the sensational effect of murder? The more bestial the details, the larger the headlines, the better the sales. Sometimes we identify with both the murderer and the 'long arm of the law', the investigator and the policeman. We can more or less unconsciously live out both sides in us – the one that kills and the one that punishes. In this way we can give vent to our own aggressive tendencies, while at the same time satisfying our conscience. But not everybody has a well developed conscience or 'inner policeman', and some individuals have more aggression than others.

It starts in infancy

My own aggression which, in my boyhood, found an outlet in the drawings I made, in games, conscious fantasies and frightening dreams, probably had its roots much earlier on, and was due to conditions which have an impact on the lives of all children. However, the phenomena pertaining to the very first year of life have received very little attention outside purely professional circles.

Melanie Klein, a pupil of Freud, was one of the first to shed light on the earliest roots of aggression, together with a number of British psychoanalysts, among them Donald W. Winnicott. They developed the school of thought in psychoanalysis which is known as the 'object relation theory', and which has contributed to a better understanding of psychotic individuals and others with a serious mental illness. Melanie Klein gained her experience when treating small children, while Winnicott began as a paediatrician and later became a psychoanalyst. I shall attempt to present some of their thoughts which are significant for our discussion of the possible roots of aggression.[3]

Melanie Klein describes how, in the first year of life, every child's development is furthered through close emotional interaction with its mother. Through what we call 'introjection' we incorporate both good and bad experiences, at first in relation to mother's breast, later to the mother as a whole person, and through 'projection' we thrust our own bad or destructive feelings back onto the breast/mother. She becomes the receiver or 'container' of these feelings which also have an influence on her. These projected feelings will again leave their mark on the child's experience of the breast/mother which is then incorporated as an introject. In this way a mutual interaction takes place between mother and child, which then leads to the formation of what we call 'inner objects', strongly emotionally charged structures or 'images' in our psyche. Since an infant's ego and its perception is still immature at this stage, it will experience the good and the bad impressions as totally separate, and as though they originated from two totally separate 'objects': one that is only good and one that is only bad. In technical language this is called 'splitting', a phenomenon we can also observe in adults, particularly in immature persons and in persons with personality disorders. It partly reveals itself in a tendency to think only in terms of black or white. For instance, idealising someone whom one considers to be faultless and perfect, and devaluating others for whom one feels only hatred and contempt.

Based on her observations of children and adults, Melanie Klein asserts that all children, from the moment of birth, have innate destructive impulses. Impulses such as greed and primitive envy, may all lead to what we call 'aggression'. In the interaction between mother and child there will always arise frustrating situations which will call forth some of these impulses in the child, and which are then projected onto the breast/mother.

During the first three months of life, in particular, this will lead to a special form of anxiety in the child, which Klein termed persecution anxiety. The 'outer' object, the breast/mother, will be experienced in some situations as a bad and persecutory 'object', the prototype for the witch in fairytales. During this phase the child is in the 'paranoid position', according to Klein.

Later, when the child's ego has developed further, it will experience the mother more as a whole 'object'. The child's own destructive and hateful impulses will then – according to Melanie Klein – create anxiety connected to fantasies of having destroyed the 'good object', the mother. Melanie Klein termed this developmental stage 'the depressive position'.

The way in which the mother is able to meet the child and its needs, receiving and tolerating its destructive projections, is decisive for the child's further development, and how it will react in later life to its own aggression, and that of others.

Even though these theories have been much criticised, we have to admit that – on the basis of clinical experience and research – Melanie Klein may have been right in asserting that many serious mental disorders can be traced back to the first year of life, and that the tendency to paranoid and depressive reactions may be embedded there. In addition, the destructive and hateful impulses and fantasies from this early stage in life, play a far greater role in the lives of all people than most of us are aware of. To a greater or lesser extent, our close relationships to other people are influenced by our good and bad inner objects.

To express these theories very simply, we can say that the more anxiety we carry with us from the first months of our lives (the paranoid position), the more disposed we will be to see enemies in other people, and the more easily murderous feelings will be provoked in us. The more anxiety we carry with us from a later stage in infancy (the depressive position), the greater our tendency to have guilt feelings and suicidal thoughts will be when facing disappointments or stress later in life.

Death and resurrection

Winnicott has gone further by emphasising the significance of the destructive fantasies during infancy. He looks upon them as an important precondition for enabling us to distinguish between ourselves and others, and thus develop a sense of reality. At the starting point there is a fusion between mother and child, a 'symbiosis'. Later the boundaries between the 'me' and the 'not me' are still unclear, also because of the circular interaction between mother and child through projection and introjection. At the time when we begin to discover the mother as a whole person, we are in an egocentric (narcissistic) phase, where the mother and the father in our fantasies are our obedient servants, while we see ourselves as the almighty centre of the world.

In order that we may discover that the 'object' (breast/mother) is not only a part of ourselves, but also an external phenomenon from which we can receive something and which is useful, we must first destroy the 'object', says Winnicott. All of us have therefore as children, when feeling frustrated, killed our mothers in our fantasies, over and over again. If the mother can tolerate our destructive rage, without retaliating or revenging herself, we will gradually discover that she has survived outside ourselves, and that she is there for us as something which is good and can be useful. This is the beginning of our discovery that there is a whole world outside of ourselves. It is a life-and-death process, where mother has to be destroyed as a projected aspect of ourselves, in order to be resurrected as something outside ourselves. Part of the illusion of omnipotence about ourselves is then transferred onto the real person of the mother. It is therefore an important task of every mother to guide her child through these first years of repeated attacks, and yet to manage to 'survive' as a 'good' mother.[4]

Theory or reality?

It is natural to query the validity of these theories. How can anyone know what kind of feelings and fantasies an infant has? It is correct that we cannot *know* for certain. But by studying the play of children and the dreams of adults we can – to a certain extent – reconstruct early experiences, particularly those that have had highly emotional consequences. An even more important indication is the unconscious repetition of early interactional patterns, which emerge in the relationship to the therapist – what we call the transference. Psychotherapy becomes a scenario where past relationships are relived with nearly the same emotional qualities as in the past, but are now transferred onto the therapist.

The process of the mother's death and resurrection, which Winnicott attempts to describe from the infant's viewpoint, can be repeated in psychoanalyses and in-depth psychotherapies. It is when the therapist becomes the target of the patient's rage over and over again, and the therapist 'survives' without retaliating, that a decisive turning point is reached. Interpretation is not primarily one of the most important tasks of the therapist, but to be a patient and reliable mother who can tolerate the murderous rage which is often re-awakened in therapy.

During this important phase my patients have fantasised about killing, crucifying or cutting me up into small pieces. In their dreams, not all have succeeded in hiding the dissected corpses in steel drums, but have had the whole 'cellar' full of blood and corpses. The more bizarre and primitive these sadistic and murderous fantasies, the more likely it is that their roots lie in the earliest developmental stages – and then they are not accompanied by special guilt feelings.

My own two dreams revealed sadistic and murderous fantasies from the age of two to three, and guilt feelings which perhaps derived from a later stage in my childhood. I have reasons to believe that I received a great deal of love from both my parents in the first couple of years of my life. Even though there was a residue of destructive fantasies from my infancy, the problems first started in earnest when I reached the obstinate age and began saying no. By doing this, I demonstrated the beginnings of a will of my own, which greatly provoked my mother who herself had had an authoritarian and old-fashioned upbringing.

But those were, after all, only fantasies. As I gradually gained more knowledge and experience, I was able to comfort myself and others that we are all murderers in our conscious or unconscious fantasies.

Summary

Psychoanalytic experience with thousands of children and adults has taught us that we all – already in the first year of our lives – have a genetic potential for aggression, reminiscent of the aggressive instinct in animals. It is provoked by normal frustrations in relation to the early care person, usually the mother. The way in which this early interaction between mother and child develops, will determine the strength and direction taken by aggression later in life. If the mother tolerates her child's rage and murderous projections, the child will be able to overcome the paranoid and depressive tendencies in its first year of life, and be ensured a normal development. There are strong indications that aggression, already at that early stage, can constitute a dynamic force which will help us to discover 'the other' outside ourselves, thus helping us to experience ourselves as separate from others. By 'killing' the projected aspects of ourselves, we discover our real selves. This will initiate a more realistic image of ourselves and others, and thus of reality. Later in life a moderate degree of aggression may become a dynamic force in our lives, strengthening our identity and self-realisation.

NOTES TO THE TEXT

[1] Lorens, K, *Das sogenannte Bøse. Sur Naturgeschichte der Aggression.* Borotha-Scoeler Berlag, Wien, 1963.

[2] Dostojevsky, F M, *Raslkolnikof*, (*Crime and Punishment*), Nasjonalforlaget, Oslo, 1929.

[3] Klein, M, *Our adult world and its roots in infancy*, Tavistock pamphlet No. 2, Tavistock Publ., London 1960.

[4] Winnicott, D W, *Playing and Reality*, Tavistock Publ., London, 1971.

Chapter VIII
WHAT CAUSES US TO KILL OTHERS?
Circumstances which influence the boundaries between fantasy and reality

There is no simple or unequivocal answer to the question of why some people actually kill others. Neither do I have any illusions about being able to prove that there are universal causes for actions of this kind, or fantasies we may all have about them. However, there is a body of interesting knowledge available from psychoanalytic practice, as well as from research in the fields of social psychology and social anthropology. It may be expedient first of all to examine a number of individual circumstances and then the socio-cultural and collective processes which may increase the risk of violence and murder.

Anxiety and aggression

There is often a close connection between anxiety and aggression, inasmuch as anxiety can provoke aggression, and vice versa, that aggression may provoke anxiety in the person who has the aggression. The latter condition applies particularly to repressed aggression, as in my own case, and to persons who are not in contact with their own rage. The physiological reactions in the body to fear, anxiety and anger are very similar. Hormones, such as adrenaline and noradrenaline flow into the body and cause an increase in blood pressure, pulse rhythm, respiration and muscular tension. These changes in the body can be looked upon as a preparation for fight or flight. Fear or terror give warning of external danger to which humans and mammals can react in two different ways: either by fighting or by fleeing; both reactions demand a maximum of physical and mental effort. It is possible that both fear and anxiety are necessary reactions, signalling to the individual to mobilise all resources in order to survive. However, anxiety is often caused by something in us that is unknown to us and which we can neither flee from nor fight against directly. Intense anxiety can give us a feeling of being pinned down, incapable of taking any action and yet desperately entrapped by something we do not understand.

A certain amount of anxiety, however, may be a means of preparing us to fight in a positive way; as for example, when we are beset by achievement anxiety or 'stage fright', since a moderate degree of anxiety can make us do our utmost. On other occasions, our aggression may be provoked by something we cannot tolerate facing up to. Not only dogs bite out of fear. Many people have a similar aggressive readiness to 'bite' anyone who comes too close. Aggression often becomes a defence against anxiety, especially in men, who are often less in contact with their internal world than women.

Oppressive attitudes towards children

We know that authoritarian and oppressive attitudes in parents and other persons in authority sometimes reinforce anxiety and aggressive tendencies in children. Children's total dependency on adults, their natural tendency to take upon themselves the guilt and the responsibility for everything that they feel to be painful or wrong, causes as a rule strong guilt feelings in these children, and the repression of their feelings. Later in life, the adult will usually be in control of his hostility. Indeed, as it was in my case, one is often not even aware of it. The price to be paid for an upbringing of this kind may be inner conflicts and neurotic symptoms, such as anxiety, depression, phobias or obsessive symptoms. The interaction between projection and introjection will here result in the aggression being 'displaced to the upper floor', in other words, it will have an impact on the conscience which will then become strict, aggressive and punitive. The unconscious murderous impulses are then directed inwardly, and may sometimes lead to suicide. In other cases, individuals who received an authoritarian upbringing will themselves become authoritarian and take out their aggression on those who are weaker.

However, a neurotic person will only lose control and become violent or murderous under very special conditions, and only when greatly provoked.

The absence of closeness and care

We have an extensive body of knowledge about neglected children who, lacking both basic closeness, contact and caring during their first vulnerable years, had traumas in the important phase from the age of about nine months to three years (the separation and individuation phase).[1] In this phase the child gradually begins to free itself from the mother, although continuing to be totally dependent on her being easily accessible. Close contact with the father is most important during these years because it will help the child to free itself from its early mother-fixation, and to develop a stronger inner structure. Simplified, we may say, that those who were deprived of important elements of child caring during this phase, will often lack an inner structure or an inner core, and thus a mature conscience. Their psychic defence mechanisms against their unconscious, aggressive and sexual impulses will be primitive and weak, they will, therefore, have a lower level of impulse control and inhibitions, and a high level of anxiety. Since these persons unconsciously continue to place their hatred onto others through projection, they will often experience other people as evil or hostile.

Individuals with personality disorders of this type, need therefore less provocation before they transmute their hateful and murderous impulses into acts of violence[2] (Chapter XIV).

The combination of violence and child neglect

Great harm is done when parents or other care persons neglect the child's early needs for closeness, care and affirmation, and at the same time expose it to psychic and/or physical violence. We find here a set of preconditions that may easily predispose an individual to violence and even to murder. It is easy to understand that, both consciously and unconsciously, there are strong reasons for revenge. These conditions create serious personality disorders, with very primitive defence mechanisms, poor impulse control and few inhibitions. Other forms of criminality often have their root in similar backgrounds.[3,4]

It is a well known fact that violence breeds violence. The individual who has suffered maltreatment or abuse as a child, will himself become predisposed to maltreating or abusing his own children. These persons may direct their hatred against one parent or both, or against other adults who consciously or unconsciously represent parental figures. In recent years, we have repeatedly read in the press about adult children who kill their parents. It is often stated that tragic childhood conditions may lie at the root of these happenings.

As an example we can take the case of a young woman who for six years repeatedly attacked other adults, nearly killing them. Her targets were mostly women of her mother's age. She would have these sudden, violent impulses to 'take' this person. She had made many voluntary attempts at different forms of treatment and stayed at institutions, however without satisfactory results. She continued having murderous impulses and assaulting others, until one day she killed a woman in her fifties who was unknown to her. However, this young woman had never been considered insane.

Very early in her life, she had been rejected by her mother, probably because of a congenital physical handicap. For this reason she spent most of the first four years of her life in hospital and in children's homes. After returning to her parents, she was beaten and maltreated by her mother throughout her childhood and adolescence, until at the age of fourteen she escaped from home. Her father, who was weak and unable to protect his daughter, was also beaten and later thrown out of the home by his wife. Soon after the daughter left home, her rage exploded in violent acts against other adults.

Intoxication loosens inhibitions

Many assailants do not necessarily have these special backgrounds. Murder and homicide are often committed in a state of intoxication, most frequently under the influence of alcohol. Fights and scuffles in slum areas of big cities, where there is a high incidence of alcoholism, vagrancy and a certain amount of criminality, frequently end in homicide. As we have seen in several examples, it is not only in dreams that one dissects corpses. We know that the state of intoxication induced by both alcohol and drugs weakens our power of judgement, our inhibitions and impulse control. When alcohol and drugs are used excessively over a long period, the brain may be damaged, especially the parts of the brain which are vital for higher mental functioning such as ethics, willpower, consideration for others and power of judgement. Besides, scientific evidence has revealed that many chronic abusers have a personality disorder. We may therefore have a combination of three interacting factors: personality disorder, brain damage caused by chronic abuse, and the acute effect of intoxication on an already impaired individual.

Narcissistic provocations

We are also aware of the fact that seemingly normal and balanced individuals – when provoked to breaking point – may actually commit murder. The classical example is the *'crime passionnel'*, the husband who catches his wife in bed with her lover – *'in flagranti'* – and who, overwhelmed by jealousy, kills the lover and perhaps also his wife. In Latin cultures, the motive for this type of unpremeditated homicide is considered as a strongly extenuating circumstance, but not so in this country. *'Crime passionnel'* is a classical theme in operas, novels and jokes. But even today, this type of crime is still committed, particularly in connection with drunkenness. Murders are also committed as a result of pathological jealousy (jealousy paranoia), where the killer imagines that his wife has a lover. A husband's potential sexual impotence may prompt delusions of this kind. Since it would damage his self-image to become consciously aware of this fact, he lays the 'blame' on his wife which then justifies his murderous rage being directed towards her.

Other situations may also evoke strong feelings, for instance, when we catch a burglar red-handed, and especially if we have a loaded gun and have been startled or angered beforehand. Many people imagine, and even say outright, that they would kill any burglar or any other 'scoundrel'; and if the effect is strong enough, the road to action is not long. Both anxiety and fear will play a role here. In many ways, one can say that both these situations are parallel to the aggression directed by animals against intruders into their 'territory', which are then experienced as violating the vital boundaries for the individual or for the group.

So far we have focused on individuals, and seen that homicide is not always carried out by people with character disorders who were emotionally injured early in life. In real life, it is not always a question of having either a neurosis or a personality disorder. We often have to deal with complex conditions, with people who have conflicts, and also whose needs were not met in childhood. We are all tarred with the same brush and may therefore be more or less predisposed to committing violent acts, especially in emotionally charged situations, when we become anxious or are under the influence of alcohol.

Let us consider some socio-cultural factors which may contribute to the incidence of homicide.

Can television induce us to commit murder?

In recent years there has been a lively discussion about whether images of violence and killings on films and television can be an incitement to murder. The views were many and differed greatly.

We know that, generally speaking, live images can have a far greater impact on us than the words we hear or read. They reach deep layers in our minds, because our earliest thinking during childhood was image-thinking, a fact of which we are reminded every night in our dreams.

Visual influence exerted by the media has increased dramatically during the last thirty years. Within the same period, there has been an increase in the number of murders in most countries. In the United States, where there is an even higher frequency of violent acts shown on television and in films than in Norway, the approximate number of registered homicides each year is twenty-five thousand. Even in this country, the number of homicides has increased from approximately twenty in 1960 to fifty in 1990. Studies carried out in the United States reveal that twenty-two to thirty-four per cent of the individuals convicted of murder, had actually used criminal techniques which they had seen on television.[5]

Most people will agree that watching violent films is no more detrimental to adult, stable persons than reading detective novels. But not everyone has an adequate measure of stability and good enough defences against aggressive impulses. It has been demonstrated through numerous research reports that the number of unstable persons who have a personal history of childhood deprivation and personality disorders seems to have increased both in Europe and in the United States. These individuals, as well as children and adolescents who have not yet developed a stable character, may be incited to commit criminal acts by constantly watching films depicting violence and murder. Children learn by imitating the adults. When watching these films, their remonstrances against what they are seeing may be weakened, thus blurring the boundaries between fantasy and reality.

Culture and upbringing

The Spartans in ancient Greece had already discovered that they could induce boys to become aggressive warriors by subjecting them to a strict, puritan upbringing with heavy emphasis on physical toughening, physical training and the use of weapons. The individual was totally subordinated to the state.

For this reason Sparta developed into the most belligerent society in ancient Greece.[6] Similar methods were used in other cultures and other historical times by different peoples and societies in order to produce aggressive warriors. The male-dominated ideology of fascism in Italy and nazism in Germany contained similar elements. *'Gelobt sei was hart macht'* ('Praise be to that which makes us hard') was a typical ideological slogan which had consequences for child-rearing. Children were raised to become 'hard', with the aid of mythical concepts like *'Blut und Boden'*, and theories about the superiority of the Arian race. The whole population was to participate in the battle for 'The Germanic Empire', for world dominance. This enabled them to exterminate, with a clear conscience, all 'inferior' individuals and peoples, such as Jews, gypsies, slaves, psychiatric patients, homosexuals, epileptics and the mentally retarded.

The chord successfully struck by Adolf Hitler and his ideologists, as is brilliantly depicted in Sigfried Lenz's novel *The German Lesson* from 1968,[7] was the idea of the typical authoritarian and patriarchal German family structure. This Prussian, authoritarian and oppressive manner of raising children was commonly practised in many German families, and became one of several factors which helped Hitler gain power over the majority of the German people. The unconscious dynamics operating here are identification with the tyrannical father, and the accumulation of hatred and the need for revenge which is easily acted out in relation to others. The suppressed, murderous hatred against the tyrannical father vented itself in mass murders and unconscious self-hatred. This also caused the death of millions of Germans, and the destruction of the *Vaterland*.

How to become 'a good cannibal'?

Anthropological and psychoanalytic studies carried out by the couple Theodore and Ruth Lidz on the headhunter culture in the interior of Papua New Guinea, reveal the different methods by which a culture may manipulate the aggression of male children. The children live together with only their mothers and other women until the onset of puberty. At this point the boys are drastically removed from the women, who are feared, despised and regarded as dangerous for the boys. The boys are subsequently subjected to a number of brutal and painful initiation rites which include beatings and torture. This earns them admission into the ranks of the male adult members of the tribe, and they continue living in the men's house outside the village where they are in contact with and are cared for only by adult men and other boys. Here they are inseminated homosexually, particularly through oral sex (fellatio), in order to strengthen their masculine identity and turn them into great warriors. Even after they have been permitted to marry, they continue living in the men's house.[8]

An interesting aspect of this culture is that in the myths and fantasies it is the women who are considered dangerous and powerful and who have to be suppressed. The Oedipus complex (Chapter X) which plays a key role in psychoanalytic theory, is non-existent. It is not the father who causes castration anxiety, but the mother. We know from psychoanalytic experience that a culture of this kind is bound to create deep anxiety and feelings of frustration in these men after the separation from their mothers, as well as immense latent aggression due to the brutal torments they are exposed to. The strong influence of male culture in these men will also set up inner defences against the 'dangerous' and feminine aspect within themselves. They become real 'macho men'. This was expedient in former times when they were surrounded by other belligerent tribes, since it made them into very aggressive head-hunters. Their fear of women was so great that they had to abduct children from neighbouring tribes, since their own tribe's reproductive potential was understandably too small.

Mass murder in war

We react strongly to war, and particularly to civil war where mass murder is organised and legitimised. The 'others' then become the enemy to whom all conceivable negative and 'bad' qualities are attributed, while we on the other hand conceive ourselves as the 'good' ones. This gives rise to a greater tendency to think in terms of black and white: 'Those who are not with us, are against us.' Some of us still remember our attitudes in World War II when all Germans and Nazis were 'bad', while all Norwegian patriots were 'good'.

Holy War has become a current concept in today's Islam, but many other 'holy wars' were fought earlier under the sign of the cross and using the name of Jesus as an alibi, where millions of people were killed, tortured and maimed. The words *'Gott mit uns'* were inscribed on the uniform belts of German soldiers during the last World War. As we have witnessed in Bosnia or Kosovo, when religion becomes an additional factor in ethnic clashes, there are no limits to the misdeeds carried out by one side against the other. Not only does the need to assert oneself at the expense of the other create the need for scapegoats; it is also a general and collective necessity for strengthening one's own ethnic, religious or national group and thus represents the very dynamics of extreme nationalism. The mobilisation of millions of people, primarily men, to organised mass murder is made possible through interaction of the 'murderous' aspect in the individual, and the tendencies emerging in large groups.

Irrational group processes

In order to be able to understand these phenomena, we must try to examine the processes operating under the surface in large groups of people. It is possible to study irrational group processes, for example, by participating in group relation conferences of the Tavistock type, where the significance of authority and leadership is highlighted (Chapter IV).

It is most instructive, but also rather frightening, to see how healthy, well educated individuals in leading positions and from all sectors of society, succumb to irrational group processes. A certain degree of 'regression' will take place in most of them, diminishing their ability for rational thinking, while primitive fantasies and feelings will take over. Unconscious, collective and unrealistic expectations in regard to the 'leader' or the person who has been accorded a position of authority in the group will often emerge. It can also become difficult to experience oneself as an independent individual with an identity of one's own.

Tyrants, demagogues and fanatics

This has made me realise how not only tyrants and commanders of armies have succeeded in gaining power over the masses, but also how religious and political leaders play on the same chords. One horrendous example was the Reverend Jim Jones, the leader of the sect called the People's Temple in California, who compelled about nine hundred sect members to go out into the jungle in Johnston in Guyana and commit collective suicide by taking potassium cyanide. The Reverend Jones himself was too cowardly to take prussic acid and shot himself with a gun. A similar tragedy took place in 1993 in Waco, Texas, when the fanatical sect leader David Koresh set fire to the compound and perished in the flames together with the majority of the members of his parish.

In many ways this bears a certain similarity to what Hitler did to the German nation[9] – except on a far larger scale. His inflated self-esteem, hatred and misanthropy resulted in the largest mass murder in world history of citizens of other countries, Jews and the German people. We know that the combination of psychopathic and power-seeking leaders and irrational processes in great masses, can weaken the sense of personal identity and conscience in the individual, provoking murderous impulses and thereby conferring uncanny power over the masses onto the leader.

The film *The Wave* reminded us of the possibility that such things may happen even in a perfectly normal school class (p.86). Even though this was a feature film, it was realistic in its presentation of irrational group processes and the potential power they wield over individuals. Also how, in given situations, primitive and aggressive tendencies can be mobilised in most people. It therefore throws some light on the background for collective violence, mass murder and war.

Summary

In this chapter I have enumerated a number of circumstances that may disturb normal development. Early deprivation, maltreatment and violation of a child's boundaries, and injuries to its self-esteem, are factors that may predispose individuals for violence. However, even adult, relatively stable individuals may lose control over their aggressive impulses in highly emotionally charged situations, for example, when jealous, or when other vital interests are threatened. All this may evoke anxiety. Violent actions are often carried out under the influence of intoxicants.

I have also discussed the significance of a number of social-psychological factors that may influence people, such as films depicting violence, military and oppressive child-rearing, as well as the manipulation of aggression in male children in certain cultures. There are many reasons why men are usually more violent than women, among them the genetic, psycho-biological differences between the sexes, and individual psychological and socio-psychological factors (Chapter IX).

In order to comprehend the basic motives for mass violence and mass murder in war, we must attempt to recognise the irrational group processes operating in all human groups, especially in large groups. Since the individual is more or less influenced by these processes, it may lead to an undermining of common sense, to lack of conscience and impulse control, and thereby to an increase in collective fantasies, projections, anxiety and aggression in the group. Throughout the ages, tyrants, demagogues and fanatics have been able to exploit these irrational processes operating in the masses.

Human aggression therefore has a variety of roots: genetic and gender-related, conditioned by the environment, from earliest childhood till late in life. It can be aroused both internally and externally. Fantasies can be acted out when there is a coincidence of a number of circumstances, as happens in war situations. It is then that we may all become *real* murderers.

NOTES TO THE TEXT

[1] Mahler, M S, Pine, F, and Bergmann, A, *The Psychological Birth of the Human Infant*, Hutchinson, London, 1975.

[2] Kernberg, O F, *Severe Personality Disorders*, Yale University Press, 1984.

[3] Fawcett, J, *'Dynamics of Violence'*, Am. Medical Ass., 1972.

[4] Nyhus, P and Urdal, B, *Asosial og kriminell adferd hos barn og ungdom*, Universitetsforl., Oslo-Bergen-Tromsø, 1977.

[5] Kvåle, G, Fjernsyn som voldsundervisning, Aftenpostens kronikk, okt.92.

[6] Kitto, H D F, *The Greeks*, Penguin Books, Middlesex, England, 1951.

[7] Lenz, S, *Deutschstunde*, Hoffmann und Campe, Hamburg, 1968.

[8] Lidz, T and Lidz, R W, *Oedipus in the Stone Age. A psychological study of masculinisation in Papua New Guinea*, Int. Univers Press, Madison, Connecticut, 1989.

[9] Stierlin, H, *Adolf Hitler, Familienperspektiven*, Suhrkamp Verlag, Frankfurt am Main, 1975.

Chapter IX
WHY ARE MEN MORE VIOLENT THAN WOMEN?
Some ideas about the male role

In the previous chapter, I indicated that men are more violent than women, but I would like to see if it is possible to find a reason why this is so. It can hardly be accidental that the majority of violent acts are nearly always performed by men, and that three times as many men as women commit suicide. Throughout history it has always been the men who fought the bloody battles or carried out pogroms against other groups. Women and children usually were the victims of this type of mass violence. What is it that causes men to be so different from women in this area?

As a child this difference never occurred to me. Was this because my father was an unusually kind and peaceable man, or perhaps because on several occasions I experienced my mother as the one who was strict and angry? However, it was always my father's task to spank me when, according to my mother, I had done something wrong, even though he often did so only half-heartedly (Chapter VII). The roles here were quite clearly allocated. She was the judge, he was the executor. But a few times I did see my father really angry. I suppose it was in situations which frightened or startled him.

Even though I do not wish to draw too many general conclusions from this particular family constellation, does it perhaps say something about women being behind men's aggression, and men's violence being sometimes caused through anxiety? However, the question of cause is generally far more complex. Let me first say a little about the general aspects of the male role.

Rural culture and role assignment

As a boy I spent several summers on ancestral family farms in Gudbrandsdalen where I took part in haymaking and other activities. The farmers in my father's family were typical representatives of the role pattern of rural society of those days. It was very different from what I was used to at home. The farmer worked the soil, he did things which were concrete, practical and visible. He was taciturn, he never showed any signs of weakness, and rarely what he was feeling. The wife was the one who showed her feelings. She was the nurturing and caring person, even towards me, a relative on holiday. The children clung to their mother's skirt until they were old enough to accompany their father to the fields or to the cowshed. I remember seeing a 'half-wit' on one of the farms, who had been put away there. He did some repair work and carpentry. Much later I understood that he had a schizophrenic psychosis. The weak and despicable was placed (projected) onto him so that the men could make fun of him and laugh at him.

This role allocation may be a natural consequence of the hard toil of many generations with unproductive soil and under severe climatic conditions. It thus became a virtue of necessity for the man to concentrate on the external world's, practical and down to earth matters. He could not give in to weakness and helplessness without risking disastrous consequences for his family. In her own special way, the woman also had a very hard time, however the role which was natural for her to assume was that of the care person who dealt with the children, the food and 'the spiritual'. *Kinder, Küche, Kirche.*

The farmer has an advantage over forestry workers, fishermen, seamen, industrial workers and office workers. While working on the farm the farmer is visible in the landscape, the children know what he is doing and that his work represents the material basis for the family's livelihood. If, in addition, he has a certain warmth and the ability to make contact, he will be an important role model for the development of his sons' and daughters' identity and personality.

I was able to observe this traditional role pattern among my patients when, as a newly qualified physician, I began practising in a rural district. As elsewhere, there were always more women than men in my waiting room. These country women were themselves not particularly verbal, but in addition to their worn-out bodies, their aching backs and high blood pressure, they did have some contact with their own feelings. They would tell me that they were depressed, suffered from anxiety and had worries. They would also wonder – more often than the men – whether their relationship to other people, especially to their family members, could in any way be responsible for their physical ailments. The men were often more taciturn and had difficulties expressing their feelings.

Psychiatric experiences

These impression were confirmed by my work in psychiatric wards. There were approximately sixty per cent women and forty per cent men in the psychiatric ward B at the Ullevål hospital. These percentages remained unchanged from one year to another, both in the acute ward and in the outpatients department. There was an even greater imbalance in the day wards which only accepted patients who were motivated to work with themselves and with their problems. Psychiatrists and psychologists in private practice confirm these observations. The people who come to them for help with various mental illnesses are mostly women.

However, in the alcoholic care organisations, men are by far in the majority; this is also so among patients in internal medicine wards who suffer from cardiovascular diseases and duodenal ulcers. We know that the underlying emotional causes in these patients may be better concealed and therefore less accessible than in the neuroses and other nervous disorders (see Chapter XIII).

Characteristically, men in psychiatric institutions are often more prone to deny their own weaknesses, their helplessness and anxiety than women. It often seems that men simply lack the words needed to express their feelings. They are also less willing than women to come to family therapy sessions. Instead they make attempts to place the problems unilaterally onto the one family member who is hospitalised and is thus defined as the patient.

The interaction in couple relationships

During my forty years of work with people in crisis, I have observed certain constantly recurring patterns in relationships between couples. A great number of women feel that they are unable to communicate sufficiently with their partners, especially in those important areas of life where sharing is only possible in the context of a close relationship. This applies to the whole range of feelings and problems, such as worry, anxiety, insecurity, feelings of inadequacy, thoughts about the future and the development of the children, as well as everything to do with the sexual relationship. The female partner often feels rejected if she tries to approach these areas. If the man's ability to verbalise his feelings does not develop through the couple's interactions, then the woman may feel either rejected or that she is not taken seriously. Some women transfer their craving for emotional closeness and intimacy onto a child, thereby binding and burdening it. Some women react unconsciously by becoming obsessed with housework. They run around frantically every day, tidying up and cleaning for hours, as an outlet for their pent-up rage. Others get muscular pains, for example fibromyalgia (Chapter XII), or else they develop depressions and different phobia. Some women turn secretly to 'pill-swallowing' or drinking too much alcohol.

In other couples where there is a mutual lack of contact and understanding, the woman may be driven to break out of the relationship. Today there are more women leaving their partners than the other way round. Some of these women prefer to live alone rather than remaining in a frustrating relationship.

Even though, as a rule, the man quickly establishes a new relationship after a break-up, he will often be the loser. If he has not learnt his lesson from the crisis, and does not make every effort to speak more openly about his feelings and worries, then the pattern may easily be repeated in the new relationship.

How did these differences come about? Does today's pattern of role assignment still reflect the earlier agricultural society, its socio-cultural factors, which were handed down from one generation to the next, and which still have an impact on our current pattern of role assignment? What do sports idiots, yuppies, stock market speculators, technocrats and top men in business administration all have in common? They have in common a great deal of knowledge about mathematical, technical and economic matters and they all use the latest computer model. Do these people merely represent different degrees and variants of underdeveloped, immature 'zombies', typical products of post-industrial male society? Or are they the result of a mental deficiency, caused by fixations in the egocentric phase of childhood, which will persist for the rest of their lives (Chapter XIV)? But why can these tendencies be seen mostly in men?

Experience with leaders

A number of studies carried out on male leaders in the United States revealed important facts. William E Henry interviewed one hundred top leaders in trade and industry. He found that a recurring feature in the lives of most of these successful leaders was their good relationship with their fathers. Also, that they had left their childhood homes and had freed themselves emotionally from their parents, particularly from their mothers.[1] It seemed that one of the conditions for making a successful career was a good relationship with the father. The majority of these leaders were strongly achievement-oriented, active and resolute, and very self-confident. They were unilaterally oriented towards external reality, focusing exclusively on practical, concrete and straightforward issues. This, however, was at the expense of fantasy, visions and contact with their own feelings. Behind the successful facade, most of these men had anxieties about making mistakes and being a failure. Many of these leaders were uncertain, they found it difficult to relax, and they often had problems in their relationships with other people.

In his book *The Gamesman*, Michael Maccoby points to the possible consequences of making a career.[2] He interviewed two hundred and fifty male top leaders in twelve renowned concerns in the United States. A very large percentage of these leaders showed signs of anxiety, felt inhibited in relationships and lacked independence. They also had depressive and psychosomatic symptoms. For the majority of the 'game playing' type of man, their lack of contact with their own feelings and weaknesses was typical. Their career strengthened and stimulated their intellect, their technical skills and competitive abilities. The 'qualities of the heart' – such as being in contact with one's own and the feelings of others, solving emotional problems or acting according to one's moral convictions – were weakened. They had to distance themselves from their families, cut out any pity they may have felt for losers and other weak individuals. They had to react indifferently towards others, remain watchful and never display any enthusiasm. In this way they could protect themselves against all intense feelings and experiences. Maccoby discovered that many of these leaders were obsessive, they were compulsive eaters and had digestive disorders. A very great number of them were afraid of losing control. Most of them kept their feelings to themselves and had difficulties expressing what they actually meant. Many avoided contact with others.

It is perhaps a comforting thought that the USA is not Norway. However, my own experiences with leaders and organisations – in Norway and in the other Scandinavian countries – suggest that these tendencies can also be found here.[3] In his book, *Gubbestruktur* (The Structure of Old Men), Christian Ylander, a Swedish Organisation psychologist, gives a drastic description of the typical male Swedish leader. Fifteen years of experience with leaders in Sweden have given him a pessimistic outlook with regard to the future.[4] I myself have no difficulties finding examples of the type he describes, especially in the Norwegian public administration. The constant pressures in business and industry for a higher degree of efficiency and productivity, and tough competition for markets, has necessitated the selection and formation of leaders with typical 'game playing' qualities. These are the type of men who quickly rise to top positions.

Consequences for family life

In the above-cited study of male leadership, the author points to typical characteristics of the male's role in today's society, and to special qualities which can be intensified in leading positions.

But not only leaders display these tendencies. The greater the demands for specialisation and higher education, the more fathers, in particular, are taken away from their children. One only has to think of the consequences on family life of commuting, overtime, shift work, postgraduate studies, further training in evening schools, and weekend courses. Therefore, while the father is at home the quality of the contact between him and the child becomes even more important.

When working with patients, we often see the dire consequences of this development, particularly where the 'distant fathers' are concerned. Most men and women with grave nervous symptoms and mental illnesses have in their background a history of lack of contact with their father, and a bad relationship between their parents. There are, needless to say, many other conditions which play an important part here. But it is hardly a coincidence that total lack of contact or too little contact with the father, is an ever recurring element in the lives of patients who have identity problems, sexual deviations, or abuse drugs. Again and again we can observe that young boys and girls who have dropped out of school and have slid into drug abuse, and who hopelessly drift around, come from families where the father is mostly absent, rejecting, passive and distant. The same applies to many asocial males, who have become criminals or thugs, to women who become prostitutes, and to patients with serious mental illness such as schizophrenia. In contrast to earlier times, these deviations are no longer characteristic of young people from the working classes, but are encountered equally in the middle and upper classes. They often come from so-called 'good' homes.

Recent studies show that the time that fathers – and also mothers – spend with their children these days is gradually becoming less. As teenagers, these children will often come under the influence of peer groups and become very dependent on them. If the parents have failed them in early childhood by not letting them have enough closeness and contact, then it may now be too late to repair the damage. The child will only then be able to identify itself with the attitudes of its parents if it has received sufficient love, closeness and security in early childhood.[5]

It is my impression that men are often more narcissistic than women. That is to say, that they are very egocentric and excessively vulnerable, combined with having an inflated self-image and a tendency to devaluate others (Chapter XIV). This not only prevents an individual from approaching other people and from understanding them, but will also cause him to experience all criticism as humiliating. This may trigger off primitive rage and sometimes even violent behaviour. Men also tend to make human relations impersonal. In the public health sector we can find male hospital doctors who keep their patients at a great distance and also their families. This may have understandable causes, but unfortunate consequences.[6]

Differences in men and women's biological and psychosexual development

Boys and girls are born differently. This includes the differences in the structure of the brain and the great hormonal variations.[7] The latest brain research indicates that this difference between the sexes begins to develop as early as the sixth foetal week, and is controlled by genes and hormones. The male hormone, testosterone, has such a decisive effect on aggression that many scientists believe aggressiveness to be a typically male quality. They assert that competitiveness, and the striving and lust for power, must be looked upon as a consequence of the male sex hormone.[8] However, one has to add that it is the average man and the average women we are speaking of, since there are such great individual differences in women and men. Men and women have both male and female sex hormones, but in different quantities.

These dissimilarities become evident at an early stage, before social factors can have made an impact on specialised behavioural patterns. Boys show an early interest in material things, in everything which moves, cars for instance, as well as for places and areas. They are often more actively penetrating, attacking, aggressive and more curious than girls. Girls tend to have a greater interest in making contact and communicating with others, they are more maternal than boys, but also more anxious and cautious. In their play they concentrate early on dolls and clothes.

One of the most interesting results of brain research is that in the female brain there is a better balance between the right and the left cerebral hemispheres than in the male brain, which is more specialised. The corpus callosum, which contains the nerve connections between the two cerebral hemispheres, is thicker and stronger in women. It is often easier for men to understand distance and space, abstract concepts and theories. Women are more susceptible to the stimulation of their senses, such as noise, smell and touch, and to the body language of others. They are quicker to interpret social signals. Women, therefore, often have access to far more material in their interpersonal relationships than men. Is this part of what we term female intuition?[9]

However, there are also many family-related and cultural factors which have an impact on the development of boys and girls. These can either reinforce or reduce the congenital gender differences. I would like to mention some of these factors which are very little known outside psychoanalytic professional circles.[10,11,12]

In the course of their development, both boys and girls have to free themselves gradually from their early dependency on the mother, in order to be able to identify themselves with the parent of the same sex. In the years of puberty and the teens, they gradually become more independent of both parents. They develop a personal identity, a feeling of 'this is how I am, and I am different from both mother and father'. An important part of this feeling is connected to their sexual identity, the certainty of 'I am a boy' or 'I am a girl'.

There are many preconditions for this identity development, but two of them are particularly important. The girls must not only disengage themselves from their early ties to the 'almighty' mother, but they then have to identify themselves with the same person, the mother, in the adult female role. This disengagement from and identification with the same person can pose problems for some girls, especially if the mothers have bound them strongly to themselves. The consequences can be serious if there has not been a sufficiently close relationship with a good father – or father substitute – who showed his love to the little girl. In other words, every little girl needs a father as an intermediary station. A father whom she can love and idealise for a certain period of time and who will confirm that it is good to be a girl. This will help her to disengage herself from her early ties to her mother. By identifying herself with the adult mother, she will be able to develop a secure identity as a woman and a mother. However, as a rule the break with the mother is not as drastic for the girl as it is for the boy.

Boys too have to free themselves from the early ties to the mother, in order to be able to identify themselves with another person, namely the father. As mentioned before, this represents a more dramatic break and may later in life lead men to deny their own dependent, weak and feminine parts. In order to overcome the trauma which the loss of the symbiosis with mother represents, boys have to go through a process of mourning. They need to recognise the mother as a separate person and also one of the other sex. Only then can they develop a masculinity which is internalised, and integrated with elements from the mother and the feminine. In this development the father plays a decisive part. He will become a good role model if he himself has integrated his own feminine side, and is able to acknowledge it by being in close and open contact with his son. But if he denies his own weakness, the boy's denial of his own weakness will be strengthened. If the father is not physically present, or if he is distant, rejecting or aggressive towards the son, there will be greater problems.

Per Olav Tiller's classical study of the sons of merchant seamen trading in foreign seas showed that these particular circumstances basically create individuals with an insecure male identity, which they overcompensated with toughness, aggressiveness, self-assertion and competitiveness. Beneath this thin veneer these men are uncertain of their male identity.[13] A number of studies in other countries have confirmed similar findings as background for 'macho men' and male violence. Studies carried out in the black ghettos of America's great cities which have always been, and still are, marked by extreme violence are particularly well known. A typical family pattern in these ghettos is the single black mother with many children by different men. These children grow up without a stable father figure.

There is much evidence to suggest the massive denial of the lost mother symbiosis to be a gender specific factor which in men often causes lack of contact with their own weakness and that of others. Instead, a man will strive for power and control – control over everything that might reveal his weakness and his loss. This may lead to a strong urge to have control over the woman. If she slips out of his control, it may trigger primitive aggression and paranoid behaviour in the man. The man's masculine conduct will then be a compensatory reaction to being abandoned, and a defence against his unconscious anxiety and helplessness. This may explain why in certain cultures where sons grow up without fathers to identify themselves with, the male role is often propelled into extreme directions, with more violence and criminality.[14,15]

Tendencies in modern psychological literature

In the international psychological and psychoanalytical literature and in research published during the last twenty years, there are a number of converging lines which are relevant to our understanding of some aspects of the male role. In very simplified terms, some of it can be thus formulated: at the beginning of their lives, children are totally dependent on their parents for survival. They are therefore extremely sensitive to the emotions and needs of their parents. Many parents are markedly egocentric (narcissistic) and use their children to a high degree to satisfy their own needs. In the first years of the child's life, traditional gender roles often assign the role of the dominant figure in the interaction to the mother. Gradually however, the father comes strongly into the picture for both girls and boys. His attitude becomes important because he represents different aspects of life, and is able to disrupt unfortunate interactions between mother and child.

The narcissism of parents can cause children to develop a 'false self', an adaptation to the superior strength of the adult.

This is at the cost of the children's own needs and their potential for development which they unconsciously have to fight against. Children growing up with this type of background, will later on as adults continue to adapt themselves to power structures which they know so well from their own childhood.

Men can often trace back the cause of their weak male identity to having been tied to mother's apron strings – in addition to having had distant fathers. This reinforces the tendency in the male role to have contempt for the 'weak', the 'feminine' and the 'emotional'. In one of her books, Alice Miller gives three examples: Adolf Hitler, the mass murderer Jürgen Bartsch, and the case of the drug-addicted girl Christiane F., whose hatred turned upon herself.[16] Other authors, such as Helm Stierlin and Norbert Bromberg and Verna V. Small, have also taken Hitler's personality development and family background as their point of departure. They point to the parallel between his family background and the typical German family structure. Here we can find some reasons as to why Hitler had the ability both to influence a whole nation, and to play on the German people's hatred of themselves and others.[17,18]

It may not be merely coincidental that it is actually a German author who paints the most drastic picture of the consequences of family dynamics of this type. In his book *Die Muttersöhne* (Mother's Darlings), Volker Pilgrim gives a number of examples to show that throughout the ages 'great men' often had this type of family background.[19] Through exhaustive biographical studies, he has come to regard the mother's darling as the result of a family constellation, where the woman is subdued and shut in behind the four walls of the home, and remains in her classical role of *Kinder, Küche, Kirche*.

According to Pilgrim, the woman was despised, neglected and abandoned by her husband who was a soldier and warrior, or else he was at the pub. Nowadays, he is at home very little, he engages in many activities outside the home, he is disinterested in his children, and thus in his sons. In some cases he is actually brutal and maltreats both his wife and the children. However, today in Norway and the other Nordic countries, it seems that this pattern is about to change in a positive direction. In young families the fathers are often in close contact with their children right from the beginning.

The psychological consequence, says Pilgrim, is first and foremost that the woman giving birth to a son, has an ambivalent relationship to this new male individual. But she succeeds in repressing the hateful part of her ambivalence by intense intimacy and binding. Gradually this son will represent a potential for satisfying the mother's own needs, and for living out her needs for self-realisation and revenge. These mother's sons can never totally free themselves from their mothers. They are characterised by a femininity, which they repress and despise, and cannot identify with. They do not have any possibilities for identifying themselves with their fathers, and cannot therefore feel secure in their masculinity. Instead, a vacuum is created, a lack of identity, which can be filled with everything except for issues pertaining to human values. The boys will be incapable of forming close relationships with either men or women. Their unconscious hateful feelings towards both parents are partly reinforced by the strong hatred and destructive urges delegated by their mothers.

Pilgrim suggests the reason why, throughout history, men who had been mother's darlings were able to live out their destructiveness and bloodthirstiness. It is because they appealed to all the other mother's darlings, who then became willing executioners of other people, and finally willing tools in their own downfall.

Mother's darlings have three domains in which they realise their full potentialities, and which also give them the power to destroy the world: they build empires. They find an enemy, and if there is none, they invent one. They persecute those who are weak which in reality represents a projection of their own battle against their own weakness.

Hitler, Stalin and Napoleon are some of the historical figures analysed by Pilgrim in this perspective. Their constant battling led to the destruction of others as well as themselves. But Pilgrim goes even further. He demonstrates that the same tendencies are in evidence in the Catholic Church and in Lutheran Protestantism. Both schools of thought have mother's darlings at their core, to spread 'God's kingdom, 'which is not of this world'.

Throughout the whole history of Christianity this led to more mass slaughter, torture and repression than was perpetrated by any other movement. Pilgrim also takes up the subject of the witchcraft trials in the fifteenth century which coincided with the discovery and conquest of new continents. Men could not endure the here-and-now lives in their own homes. They had to go out and discover new continents and new celestial horizons.

In my opinion, Pilgrim draws an extremely biased and drastic picture of these men who were mother's darlings and the impact which they had on history. I believe that he underestimates the significance of the fact that these mother's darlings were also worshipped by their mothers and had strong ties to them. This may have contributed to the development of an inflated self-image and pathological narcissism in these sons (Chapter XIV). Pilgrim does not adequately underline the part played by their fathers – except indirectly, that they were absent. Nevertheless, some of his ideas are included here because they point to tendencies which many other authors and scientists are aware of, and which may help us to understand some aspects of men's violence.

The Dutch psychoanalyst Arno Gruen goes deeper in his analysis of modern man. In his books *Der Verret am Selbst* (The Betrayal of the Self) and *Der Wahnsinn der Normalität* (The Insanity of Normality), he debates the question of our relationship to ourselves, the issue of aggression and the relationship between man and woman.[20,21]

He too takes as his point of departure our tendency to betray our own selves and to lose contact with our real needs. Our upbringing, which teaches us to adjust ourselves to the superior strength of the adult and to deny our own feelings and needs is mostly responsible for this. This leads to a faulty development resulting in obedience, submission, conformity and dependency. Sensitivity, weakness and the understanding of others is suppressed, and we believe that success and happiness lie in adaptation and power. Later in life, we are frightened of everything that touches on the unrealised nature in us and fight against it. Our own self becomes our worst enemy, and we flee from responsibility and from everything that is vibrant with life in others, because it gives us anxiety. If we feel too strongly provoked by the freedom of others, it will produce a rage in us which is directed both against others and against ourselves. We are also eternally in search of confirmation, especially from those who suppress and deny our real needs.

Gruen shows how many men – instead of striving for freedom – strive for power. They strive to conquer things which are outside themselves in the material world as though these things could guarantee their safety. Even those who are in revolt, identify themselves with the power holders, and become unconsciously bound to them.

For many men their great enemy is their own helplessness. These men have to revenge themselves on everything personifying the weak and helpless in themselves which they unconsciously despise. For this reason they are attracted to leaders who represent the same attitudes, and who in reality hate all humanity and all men. This relieves them of the pressure of their own self-hatred. Thus the oppressor can free us from our own hidden self-contempt, precisely by being full of contempt for us. This may partly explain why Stalin and Hitler were god-like father figures for millions of people.

Gruen indicates that individuals who were manipulated in their childhood will, later in life, feel deeply dissatisfied without knowing why. In reality they are driven by a hidden rage which they attempt to channel through achievements and successful careers. However, beneath this surface there are destructive forces. We can conceal our rage and our destructivity by hiding ourselves in the group, and we can likewise adapt ourselves to the socially recognised striving for achievement, career and power. Hatred and destructivity can also be camouflaged behind lofty words, friendliness, smiles and progress. But in some individuals their rage will erupt into open violence.

In Arne Gruen's view, the fear of helplessness is particularly strong in men and can easily lead them to hate and suppress women. The woman, on the other hand, compensates by exercising her power over her helpless child. Thus the circle is closed, and the development continues from one generation to the next. Men's striving for power, superiority, control, success and conquest, conceals their ever present fear of failure, their own helplessness and weakness. In spite of great external success, many men still have doubts about their own 'masculinity'. Also, the female partner's lack of sexual orgasms becomes an accusation against the man's inadequate potency.

Summary

I do not suggest that my reflections about the gender roles and aggression are in any way supplementary, or indeed that they cover the whole field. Both areas are far too complex for that. We know that congenital, biological qualities, as well as family-related and cultural conditions, play a part in the determination of the gender roles and the degree of aggression on both women. The circumstances of childhood are here as in all other areas in life, decisive for the formation of gender roles, and the degree to which aggression will play a part in the lives of both men and women. I have attempted to throw light on some of the aspects of these early relationships.

In the balance between mother and father, and between them and the child, there are strong emotional forces which will influence the development of each individual's personal and sexual identity. In the case of the girl, the problem area is her early dependence on the mother. The father's presence is crucial as it enables the girl at this stage to free herself and later to identify herself with the mother in the adult woman's role. In the case of the boy, the breaking-off with the mother is more drastic and potentially traumatic, and may become the Achilles' heel of many men! They have to deny their own weakness, helplessness and femininity to a far higher degree than girls. Instead they develop compensatory fantasies about omnipotence and a compulsory striving for career success, power and control. The father's attitudes and values will here be of importance.

Many men need to have control over women. If this control is threatened, it may activate paranoid aggression and violence.

These reflections may confirm the hypothesis mentioned in the introduction, that anxiety may partly be the cause of men's aggression and predisposition for violence. Behind this anxiety lies a denial of the overwhelming power of women and their significance at the beginning of our lives – a denial of the wound inflicted by the loss of the mother-symbiosis.

Narcissism, which many psychoanalysts consider to be the core problem in the relationship between parents and children, can be one of the reasons for men's inclination to violence. Male narcissism can easily be reinforced by the narcissism in a parent, as for example, when the mother favours a son and binds him to herself, and/or when the father is distant, rejecting or aggressive towards the son (Chapter XIV). A weak male identity is compensated for by grandiose ideas and by a vulnerability which can lead to aggression and violence. Under these influences, the man will also distance himself from his female partner and his children, and from his own real self (see examples in Chapter XI).

There is no easy solution to these problems. We have to accept that men and women are biologically and psychologically different. This has consequences for our aggression. However, these differences can be reduced or reinforced in the early interaction with parents, and by cultural influences. As mentioned earlier, the change in gender roles and the fact that the women's lib movement succeeded in boosting the self-confidence of women in many countries, was conducive to breaking the vicious circle. In the last thirty to forty years, there have been dramatic changes in Scandinavia as regards the role of the father. In young families the father now has close contact with his children more often than before, and takes over some of the caring work in the family. This, I believe, will have considerable consequences.

I hope that men will gradually learn to accept their own weaknesses and limitations. This will make it easier for them to renounce their ideas of omnipotence, and to be less motivated to act out their primitive and destructive rage. Being in contact with their own helplessness, weakness and sensitivity gives a different kind of strength than having external power. It provides a feeling of wholeness and of inner security which is a precondition for a relationship of greater equality and a higher potential between men and women. It will make men better fathers and better role models for their children.

NOTES TO THE TEXT

[1] Henry, W E, The business executive, the psychodynamic of a social role. *I: The irrasjonale executive, psycho-analytic studies of management*, Eds.: Manfred F R & Kets de Vries, Int. Univer. Press, New York, 1984.

[2] Maccoby, M, *The Gamesman*, Simon & Schuster, New York, 1976.

[3] Jørstad, J, 'Contemporary Leaders: Power and Powerlessness', Leadership & Organisation Development J. 1991, MCB University Press, Vol. XII, No. 15, pp.21–31.

[4] Ylander, Chr, *Gubbstruktur*, En bok om männens ledarskap, Stockholm, 1981.

[5] Bowlby, J, *Maternal Care and Mental Health and Deprivation of Maternal Care*, Schocken Books, New York, 1966.

[6] Jørstad, J, Utbrenthet – et økende problem I helsearbeid, Nordisk Medisin, 1988, 103, pp.102–105.

[7] Moir, A and Jessel, D, *Brain Sex*, Michael Jospeh Ltd, London, 1989.

[8] Ibid.

[9] Ibid.

[10] Blos, P, *On Adolescence. A Psychoanalytic Interpretation*, The Free Press of Glencoe, New York, 1962.

[11] Erikson, E H, *Childhood and Society*, Northon & Co., New York, 1950.

[12] ———*Identity and The Life Circle*, Int. Univers. Press, New York, 1959.

[13] Tiller, P O, 'Father absence and personality development of children in sailor families', *Nord. Psychol. Monogr.* Series 9, 1958.

[14] Tiller, P O, Når far er borte, Tidskr. F. samf. Forskn. 1, 13–27, 1960.

[15] Mitscherlich, A, *Society Without the Father*, Tavistock, London, 1969.

[16] Gyllenhak, U, *'Var är pappa?'* Natur o. Kultur, Stockholm, 1993.

[16] Miller, A, *An Anfang war Erziehung*, Suhrkamp, Frankfurt, 1983.

[17] Stierlin, H, *Adolf Hitler, Familienperspektiven*, Suhrkamp Verlag, Frankfurt am Main, 1975.

[18] Bromberg, N and Small, V V, *Hitler's Psychopathology*, Int. Univer. Press, New York, 1983.

[19] Pilgrim, V E, *Die Muttersöhne*, Klaassens Verlag, Düsseldorf, 1986.

[20] Gruen, A, *Der Verrat am Selbst*, Deutscher Taschenbuch Verlag, München, 1986.

[21] ———Der Wahnsinn der Normalität, Küsel Verlag, 1988.

Chapter X
SEXUAL CHILD ABUSE – FANTASY OR REALITY?
How reliable is our childhood memory?

The background for my topic is the ongoing debate about sexual abuse and incest, as well as all the cases that are 'disclosed' in the media these days. These cases are based either on stories told by children, who are often under the influence of grown-ups who suspect that the child has been exposed to sexual abuse. Or they are based on the fact that adult individuals undergoing different forms of psychotherapy begin to remember that they have been exposed to abuse. Other influences sometimes cause such memories to emerge, or they may rise to the surface apparently spontaneously after having been consigned to total oblivion for many years.

In addition to individual cases referred to in the media, which are shocking in themselves, we see examples of cases comprising many individuals, and even whole communities may have been more or less involved.

Naturally the question asked by the public is, can this really be possible? Are there actually so many people with deviant sexuality and paedophile tendencies? Do the stories told by children during interrogation refer to what actually happened, or are they fantasies? We know that the suspects in these cases are put under terrible strain, whatever the final outcome.

Freud's dilemma

As an introduction to this problematic and diffuse area between fantasy and reality, I would like to say a few words about Sigmund Freud and the views held by psychoanalysis about this dilemma.

In his book *Studies on Hysteria* from 1895 which Freud published together with Josef Breuer, he asserted that all his patients with hysterical symptoms said that they had been sexually abused in their childhood; the adult perpetrator was always a close relative, usually the father. In the treatise he claimed that these traumatic experiences were the root cause of the symptoms and neuroses of his female patients. 'The hysteric suffers mostly from reminiscences', i.e. repressed memories of sexual abuse, and only by making these memories conscious and reacting against the accompanying strong affects through 'the cathartic method', the repressions could be lifted and the symptoms dissolved.[1] We can quite understand that these assertions met with strong reactions in the Vienna of those days.

Freud himself however, began to have doubts about the truth of his own observations. In a famous letter dated 21 September 1897 to his friend Wilhelm Fliess, he relinquishes his earlier standpoint.[2] He now considers a great deal of what his patients are telling him to be their own fantasies which have been anxiety- and guilt-ridden and have therefore been repressed from their consciousness. He recorded the reasons for this change of heart in his letter to Fliess: it was because he had difficulties achieving the desired results with his patients, because many of them broke off their treatment prematurely, and especially because he considered it unthinkable that so many fathers, including his own, could be perverts. In fact, one of Freud's own sisters also had hysterical symptoms, and with most patients it was their fathers who were involved in the stories they told. In recognition of the fact that symptoms always were the result of several traumas, the number of perverse fathers had to be far greater than the number of patients with hysterical symptoms. Freud wrote that he had now discovered that the unconscious fantasies which are accompanied by strong affects, can be completely disconnected from reality, in other words, it is totally impossible to separate truth from fiction.

This realisation represented a decisive breakthrough for Freud. The discovery of the *reality of fantasies* led to the discovery of infantile sexuality and the Oedipus complex, two of the cornerstones in his psychoanalytic theories.[3] The work he carried out with his pupils was now focused on the investigation of *the intra-*

psychic phenomena: the unconscious fantasies, the drives (the libidinous and the aggressive drive, Eros and Thanatos), dreams, and from 1921 the structural theory of the three intra-psychic component: the id, ego and superego, and the conflicts between them.[4]

Criticism of Freud

I cannot here go into details about the developments which took place in psychoanalysis while Freud was alive, and those taking place after his death in 1939. His theory of drives was one of the great controversial issues, that is to say, his emphasis on libido and aggression as the fundamental drive forces in the individual. Greatly simplified, we may say, that through their work with patients in psychoanalysis, many psychoanalysts have come to the conclusion that the real interaction between the child and the adults is of far greater importance than the innate drives. The British school of thought which we call *the theory of object relations*, has become of great importance (Melanie Klein, Fairbairn, Guntrip, Winnicott), and later also the school of thought in the United States called self-psychology (Kohut).[5,6,7]

From this perspective the basic motivation of the child is seen as an intense need for an object, that is to say, for attachment to another human being through physical and mental closeness, dependence and mutual emotional interaction – an object relation. Those who are more consistent, consider this to be the sole fundamental need, while others give greater weight to this theory, rather than to the theory of innate drives without, however, discounting its significance.

The Swiss psychoanalyst Alice Miller, and the American Jeffrey Moussaieff Masson, who was neither a doctor nor a psychologist but a professor in Sanskrit, have been Freud's most aggressive critics in the last twenty years. Due to many special circumstances, Masson did not only undergo a personal analysis, but he also started training to become a psychoanalyst and was finally recognised as one. He had a brilliant career and was put in charge of the Freud archives which also contained a great number of Freud's hitherto unknown and unpublished letters and manuscripts. The reason for mentioning these two analysts in particular is that they have both written a number of books addressed to the general public which have been translated into many languages – Miller's books was also translated into Norwegian. These books have consequently made an impact on the present debate on child abuse. [8,9,10,11,12,13]

In my opinion, there are many important viewpoints in Alice Miller's books, but not in Masson's. But they do have one point in common which is important for the present topic: they both accuse Freud of having abandoned the truth when, in 1897, he no longer accepted that the stories told by his patients had been real occurrences, but came to regard them mostly as expressions of their fantasies. These two authors now accuse psychoanalysis of giving far too much importance to 'the intra-psychic' aspect, while neglecting the real relationship between parents and children. With this they imply that Freud and psychoanalysis is laying the blame on the 'innocent' child, while exonerating parents and other adults from abuse of power and other forms of child abuse. The result of this is that today's hostile and repressive attitudes towards children are maintained in the whole of the western world, in all education, pedagogy and the established power structures, including psychoanalysis.

The background for the criticism and one misunderstanding

I cannot here give a detailed account of the professional discussion, and all the counter-arguments which have been voiced against this criticism. It seems that Alice Miller's growing bias may have been caused by negative experiences, both in her own training analysis and when confronted by the orthodoxy in some sections of psychoanalysis in Germany and Switzerland. When reading Masson's last book *Final Analysis* in which he tells about his own training analysis in a self-revealing manner, I can understand some of the personal tragedy underlying his spiteful attacks on Freud and on psychoanalysis.[14]

However, I wish to clarify one important misunderstanding that has followed in the wake of this criticism. Freud himself never denied the significance of real traumatic events in the life of an individual. He only pointed out that the way in which the child experiences and works through the real events in his own fantasy, will be crucial for whether the outcome will be traumatic. In other words, the decisive factor will be the interaction between fantasy and reality. Nor does Freud look upon the child as merely a passive receiver of what adults do to him, but also as an active partner on an unconscious and emotional level – reacting to events in accordance with his own drives and needs.[15]

However, there is reason to believe that some of Freud's most orthodox successors, in their writings at least, have concerned themselves mostly with the intra-psychic domain and have perhaps laid too little stress on the real traumas of childhood. This, I believe, concerns mostly those who have worked with patients with classical neuroses.[16] It is interesting to note in this connection that when working with children and with seriously disturbed patients, as for example, schizophrenic patients, it is difficult to avoid seeing the significance of the early relationship between parents and children, and thus also the limitations of the drive theory.[17] It is precisely this type of work which has led many psychiatric therapists to gain a deeper understanding of the 'interpersonal relations'[18] and the importance of the early 'object relations'.

Our reactions to sexual child abuse

As mentioned at the beginning, we have had an explosive increase in media focus on sexual child abuse during the last ten years, which has actualised Freud's dilemma: what is fantasy and what is reality?

The moral indignation and general condemnation aroused by such actions can be understood on several levels: it can be on a conscious and rational level, where it is completely natural for all of us to react against brutal child abuse by adults, be it sexual or violent, or both at the same time. It can also be on an unconscious and irrational level where we disassociate ourselves from, and project onto others, the fantasies, impulses and tendencies which are partly our own. The more anxiety and taboos are linked to such fantasies and impulses, the more dramatic and vociferous the need becomes in us to punish the 'guilty'. Both this tendency to become fascinated, the sensational effect and the mass hysteria, disclose the widespread presence of these anxiety-filled taboo areas in our unconscious.

Children's feelings and fantasies

What was it that Freud discovered which led to his dramatic turnabout operation? His discovery was that all children have sexual feelings and fantasies about their closest care persons, mothers and fathers. However, one should note that these feelings and fantasies are on the child's developmental level, and are very different from adult sexuality. A common trait, however, is that these fantasies have something to do with the body, with being close and with pleasure. In psychoanalysis, sexuality – Eros – is a far wider concept than is usually understood. In its primary form, it emerges in the obvious pleasure and delight often shown by the infant when breast feeding, which has its parallel in the physical and mental pleasure experienced by the mother when suckling her baby. Many mothers say that they feel something resembling an orgasm when suckling. The mouth, the skin and the female breast are erotically loaded – they become what Freud termed erogenous zones. It is relevant here to point out the sexual significance of the mouth, skin contact and female breasts for most of us throughout our lives.

Later, the child's sexual pattern will change. During the so-called oedipal phase between the ages of three and five, it is well known that the little boy is in love with his mother, and the girl with her father. On their childish level, the children have fantasies about marrying mother and father respectively, and they look upon the other parent as a rival. However, it is not so well known that both sexes will experience the opposite in another stage of the oedipal phase: the boy will then love his father and the girl her mother, while the other parent will become a rival.

Today we know that these feelings in children are completely normal, and one does not have to be a psychoanalyst to recognise the first constellation.

Childhood oblivion

If the relationship between the mother and the father is good and their relationship to the child is adequate, then these fantasies and feelings will not cause any serious problems later in life, that is to say, except for one: We forget practically everything we have felt and experienced during these first four to five years of our lives. This in spite of, or precisely as a consequence of, the fact that these years of our lives are characterised more than any other by strong and passionate feelings. I would like to emphasise that in the different developmental phases, these feelings are always more or less ambivalent, containing both love and hate, and gradually also anxiety and guilt in relation to both mother and father.

According to psychoanalytic experience – and this is also included in the theories, most of us emerge from the oedipal period without too many wounds to our soul, and with a fresh gain: we have developed a more mature conscience which helps us to keep our formerly passionate and ambivalent feelings and fantasies towards out parents unconscious (primary gain). Instead of feeling anxious about being rejected or punished by our parents, we have developed the type of anxiety which we call pangs of conscience, or guilt feelings.

This childhood oblivion is perhaps the strongest and most important reason why we do not remember much from the first four to five years of our childhood, which I unreservedly consider the most important years of our lives. This is a paradox and a chief problem in all the work with psychic illness, whether it concerns the dissemination of knowledge, psychotherapy/psychoanalysis or research: for how can we possibly know anything that is unconscious? The characteristic feature of the unconscious is precisely that it *is* unconscious and therefore cannot easily be evoked into consciousness. Freud did, however, create the concept of the preconscious, a kind of grey zone between the conscious and the unconscious and the contents of which are somewhat more easily accessible. But it would take too long to elaborate on this.

The unconscious reveals itself

It is precisely in connection with the unconscious that we recognise the genius of Freud. Years of painstaking observation of himself and his patients led him to discover how the unconscious reveals itself. Let me mention some of the most important areas:

1. The imagery of dreams which he himself called the 'royal road to the unconscious'.

2. Parapraxes, such as slips of the tongue and lapses of memory.

3. The method of free association which is an important part of psychoanalytic technique. Seemingly incoherent thoughts can often reveal unconscious connections.

4. Symptoms and personality traits often have hidden psychodynamic connections. As a rule they represent compromise solutions and unconscious survival strategies for the individual.

5. Repetition compulsion, that is to say, the tendency we all have to a certain degree, to a constant repetition of the same reactions and behavioural patterns in spite of the fact that they often are neither expedient nor beneficial to us or others. It is an unpleasant reminder that in spite of our pretence, we are not the master in our own house.

6. The phenomenon of transference, which became a decisive concept of the psychoanalytic method, may be looked upon as a special outcome of repetitive compulsion. A great number of psychoanalysts consider this to represent the crucial difference between psychoanalysis and other methods. Freud noticed that patients in psychoanalysis regularly expressed feelings or showed reactions and behaviour that obviously had nothing to do with him as a person. They reacted to him as though he were another person. He discovered that patients in treatment unconsciously transferred fantasies, feelings and reactions from important persons in their childhood to him. In their fantasies he himself became these important persons.

In the analytic room, the drama of the past with regard to the near care persons of childhood is re-experienced. With almost the same feelings and fantasies as at that time, though detached from their original context. In the course of the psychoanalytic treatment, the intensity of these feelings and fantasies is usually heightened, while at the same time the resistance to speak about them increases. At the height of the analytic process most of the neurosis will manifest itself first and foremost in the relationship to the analyst (transference neurosis).

By recognising this transference, the analyst will gradually be able to understand and reconstruct the most important emotional relationships in the patient's childhood which the patient himself or herself has forgotten (repressed). In due time, and when the available material is sufficiently convincing and clear to the analyst, he can help through interpretations to make the repressed material conscious. However, not infrequently, the analysand will himself have experiences enabling him to see through his own repression. Working with dreams, in particular, is often helpful for bringing self-revealing material to consciousness.

A great deal can be said about the phenomenon of transference which not only manifests itself during psychoanalysis or psychotherapy, but is also a general human phenomenon. It more or less colours all our close relationships, our attitude towards authority and superiors, out sympathies and dislikes, our falling in love and choice of partner, and especially our prejudices. I could also say much about counter-transference, the fantasies, feelings and reactions experienced by us, the analysts and psychotherapists, which are often triggered by the patients' transferences. Simplified one might say that we 'catch' the fantasies and feelings directed towards us by a patient and this calls forth similar feelings in ourselves. One of the reasons why we analysts have to undergo a personal analysis is that we must learn to be able to control our counter-transference. This ability is necessary to be able to utilise these feelings for an understanding of what goes on beneath the surface between the patient and the analyst. Our feelings can also tell us something about the patient's childhood, and about the feelings the patient then called forth in the persons who were important to him as a child.

Other factors which influence childhood memory

There are other factors which are of great importance when talking about childhood memory. One of them is that children during their first years of life do not distinguish clearly between fantasy and reality; they endow fantasies with a realistic quality. This can easily be observed in the play of small children, and it is for this very reason that play is used as the most important tool in child therapy. The intervention by an adult in the play can have an influence on the child.

Another factor is that children in the first years of life have not yet developed language or logical thinking, and therefore lack a precondition for what we usually mean by memory, in other words, they are unable to express themselves in words. At the beginning of life we are almost only body and feelings, although there is a well developed sensitivity for everything concerning our relationship to our important care persons, usually first the mother, somewhat later the father. Consequently early strong, emotional impressions are only remembered physically. Here we touch upon some of the reasons for the development of what we call psychosomatic disturbances, i.e. illness where early and highly emotional conflicts find their outlet in bodily symptoms and organs.

At first all children have a primitive defence mechanism which we term 'splitting', a way of keeping two impressions, feelings or areas quite separate from each other. This is a forerunner for repression which presupposes a somewhat higher degree of maturity. When splitting, the child may experience 'the good mother' or 'the good father' as persons who are only kind and totally different from 'the bad mother or the bad father' who only hurt it. This splitting may also lead to a split between head and body – 'this does not happen to me, it only happens to my body'. This type of alienated relationship to the body is typical for many prostitutes and for patients suffering from anorexia. Splitting as a defence is also common among people with personality disturbances and may explain their symptoms and tendencies.

Splitting may contribute to the tendency in all children from the age of two to three years to blame themselves for everything which they experienced as painful or wrong in the family. Whenever the mother or the father is angry, if they offend the child, beat or maltreat it in other ways, if they are drunk, disappear, or whenever the atmosphere in the home is tense and insecure, then the child at a certain age will easily believe itself to be the cause. Several other factors may contribute to this tendency, the natural self-centredness of children on the one hand, and on the other the fact that mother and father are our first gods who appear almighty, omniscient and perfect to us, regardless of their real nature. Indeed, when we are children it is of vital importance for us to maintain this image of mother and father during our first years, since we are totally in their power and dependent on them. They are the basis for our security and confidence in the world and in ourselves.

Therefore, if a mother or a father injures the child by rejecting it, by failing to take care of it, by psychic or physical violence, or by sexual abuse, it is after all easier for a small child to place the evil within itself rather than having to realise that it is the mother and/or the father who are evil. If the child did believe this, it would not be able to 'survive'. We can here find an important source of irrational guilt feelings, and the reason why many people idealise their parents and 'the green valley' of their childhood. Also, why the deep hurt inflicted by parents is often effectively split off from consciousness – and forgotten.

I would also like to remind you that a child's first thinking takes the form of images. Freud termed this primary process thinking and we are reminded of these images every night in our dreams. These nightly hallucinatory 'films' often contain important experiences from the first years of our lives, before, at around the age of five, childhood oblivion brought down the 'iron curtain'.

It is only through a lengthy psychoanalytic or psychotherapeutic process that the wounds inflicted in childhood come to light and are thus made conscious. First perhaps as physical sensations, later perhaps as dreams, or an unconscious staging and re-experiencing within the transference to the analyst, accompanied by strong emotions.

Examples

I have had several patients, both young and elderly, whose symptoms were physical sensations that something was growing in the mouth, becoming bigger and bigger, and forcing its way in an unpleasant and painful manner. These sensations were partly accompanied by nausea and vomiting, and the patients did not connect them with anything of a sexual nature. Only later during the treatment did images emerge of a man who put his penis into their mouth when they were still very small.

The passionate nature of the transference which develops in psychoanalysis or psychotherapy can be traced back to the oedipal period, but is at the same time coloured by the fact that the patient is no longer a child, but an adult. Therefore the childish passions and longings for closeness and to own and control mother or father, often acquire a more discernible layer of adult, genital sexuality which conceals the childish quality of the feelings and fantasies.

I once had a seriously disturbed female patient in long term psychoanalysis, who for a long period had intense fantasies and wishes that I should put my hand between her legs; she felt that it was only then that she would come alive and become well again. Some of this would be repeated in her dreams. She dreamt that I put my hand between her legs and in these dreams as well as in her daytime fantasies she felt strongly sexually aroused. Gradually, in her dreams and fantasies, I was replaced by her father. Memories of him began to surface, of situations when she was two to four years old and he had pawed her.

Because of her mother's absence and illness, her father had been the only care person in the home during that time. This father had been exceptionally interested in his daughter's body during her adolescence. He himself had grown up in an eccentric and pietistic family, and had at one time been hospitalised, probably because he was psychotic. Also the mother of this patient had been seriously disturbed and egocentric, and had also been greatly preoccupied with her daughter's body.

What is real and what is fantasy?

How can we know that this has actually happened to her? Maybe it has only happened in her fantasies? Indeed, it does not prove anything that she was gradually beginning to remember such episodes. However, paradoxically, this is perhaps not so important, since it is precisely in the interaction between reality and fantasy, between the outer and the inner world that the traumatic quality comes into being.

At times there is also reason to believe that the trauma comes into existence first later on, *'nachträglich'*, when it is activated later in life by new mortifications of a similar nature. It is only then that the early experiences are understood on an adult level, as offences committed by a person on whom the child had been totally dependent, whom it had trusted and loved with a child's passion.

I would again like to remind you that a child is unbelievably sensitive to the feelings of the adult care person, irrespective of external actions. The feelings and fantasies of adults can be perceived by a child, irrespective of the content of their words and actions. In particular, it seems that eye-contact is of importance, but also mother's and father's facial expressions, their movements, postures and voice quality. The eyes, the face and the voice are the first things perceived by the child and it absorbs emotional undercurrents long before it understands the content of the adult's conscious or unconscious communication. A child responds automatically with similar feelings as the ones it is met with, but on a child's level. To express this even more explicitly one can say that a small child is totally defenceless against the feelings, impulses and desires which it encounters in an adult.

Sexual feelings between parents and children

I would like to call your attention again to Freud's discovery that the child's sexuality begins at its mother's breast, and continues through the anal phase to the oedipal phase. Today we know that it is normal for parents and children to have sexual feelings and fantasies about each other. Also, that every child, boy or girl, between the ages of three and five, passes through phases in which it loves its mother and feels its father to be a rival, and the other way round – loves its father and feels its mother to be a rival. However, the child's fantasies about its parent and the parents' fantasies about their child, are on two totally different levels. This may give rise to feelings of frustration, anxiety and guilt in the child which are later concealed behind the curtain of childhood oblivion. If the relationship between the parents is fairly satisfactory, and this is reflected in their relationship to the child, then the chances are good that the child has not been injured or overtaxed in its interaction with its mother and father throughout the different developmental phases. However, problems – also those from the oedipal period – lie hidden and may unconsciously be activated when for example, news about sensational sexual abuse hits the headlines in the media. Or when neighbours or work colleagues are suspected of having been involved in this type of abuse, or when serious conflicts have arisen between two spouses.

If the parents have had serious problems, for instance, with regard to an exceptionally unsatisfactory or problematic sex life, then it may have consequences for the child. The intimacy between the parents and the child may then be coloured by the sexual problems and the desires of the adults. If, for example, in his fantasy a father looks upon his child as a potential sexual object, though without translating it into action then the child will be confronted with a confusing situation which it cannot possibly interpret, and which will force it to submit to the father's fantasy.

A glance can be eloquent

A number of years ago, a woman in her twenties came to see me because she was suffering from anxiety, felt remote and had some physical symptoms. During the last few years she had withdrawn from other people, but had managed to keep up a certain standard in her work as a secretary.

Her behaviour during the sessions changed gradually, she became increasingly tense and tearful, said that she dreaded coming to the sessions, she was afraid of becoming dependent on me, and believed that sooner or later I would reject her. Soon she came up with fantasies about other people being able to implant their feelings into her body. This included me too. It made her feel defenceless and exposed to my glance, and she noticed that the front of her body became taut. She felt like turning the chair around so that she would not be seen by me from the front. She felt totally defenceless, as though my eyes were controlling her. Closeness to me and to other people represented a menace to her, and for that reason she had to withdraw and, above all, keep her own feelings under control.

In one session she told me a dream:

> I am a small child and am sitting in the back of our car. Father is sitting in front at the wheel. When we reach a spot near to your house, I have to get out of the car and pee. While I am peeing, father stands in front of the car and looks right into my crotch. I look up at father with an uncertain glance, I have tears in my eyes, am confused, feel humiliated and terribly ashamed. I cannot understand why I look like that, and why I just accept it (that he looks at me like that). When I go back into the car, I am an adult person sitting there, and there is something or other that does not make sense.

When I asked her what came to her mind in connection with this dream she realised that her dream revealed a sexual tension between her father and herself in which she felt hopelessly caught up.

She produced more material concerning her relationship with her father. She had been very close to him as a small child, but as she reached puberty, her father withdrew from her. She could not understand this at the time and felt rejected. The dream now made her wonder whether she had been exposed to abuse. But there were no real indications, nor did any emerge later in the therapy.

It had been the father's glance in the dream that had brought her to the verge of tears, and made her feel confused and ashamed. A glance can symbolise receiving special attention, and it can also exercise a strong influence on another person. I pointed out that this resembled the way she had earlier described her relationship to other people, and reminded her of her anxiety during the sessions about me and my glance. In other words, I interpreted her transference from her father to me. The whole dream took place near my house. We now saw the dream in connection with her anxiety and behaviour during the sessions, and with her relationship to her father as a child. We began to understand that his feelings had probably been more than usually sexually laden as he stood looking at her. But she also loved her father. Much later she understood that the marriage of her parents had been full of conflicts and lacking in intimacy, although this had never been spoken about. She remembered that the atmosphere in her home had been tense with anxiety, uncertainty and sadness. Her parents were subsequently divorced.

This dream contains a number of elements which are outside the scope of our subject. Later in the therapy, she became aware that her anxiety was even more connected to her mother than to her father. She felt that her mother had always looked at her in a special way, which had always made her feel very uncomfortable. She described her mother as a very insecure and weak woman, who could not bear being criticised, and who responded to criticism with glacial rejection. At some point the patient actually perceived her mother as an evil persecutor, from whom she fought desperately to break away. This became a contributory factor to her fear of intimacy and dependency, and her withdrawal from other people.

A possible interpretation here could be that behind the patient's oedipal problems and sexual feelings towards her father, there were earlier ambivalent feelings towards her mother, which were unconsciously experienced as even more dangerous than the oedipal threat. It is not unusual for the mother to be the first to abuse her child in order to satisfy her own needs, often far too intensely, or far too long. These feelings and needs should by rights have been satisfied within the relationship to her husband.

But usually they cannot be detected from the outside, and are not 'sexual' in the adult sense of the word (Chapter XIV).

Summary

If I am to answer the question put forward in the title of this chapter, whether our childhood memory is reliable, then my answer will be both yes and no. If our unconscious childhood memory is included here which also embraces the body's memory and the imagery of dreams, then my answer will be yes. Psychoanalytic experience indicates that everything we have experienced from the very first moment of our lives until the present is stored with countless details, feelings and affects. In theory, this can all be mobilised. In practice, on the other hand, large segments of this memory remain inaccessible to adult cognitive recollection, for the following reasons:

1. Our earliest feelings and experiences are wordless, they are only remembered bodily.

2. The lack of boundaries in childhood between fantasy and reality, where fantasies can take on a semblance of reality. If a child is still at an age where the boundaries between fantasy and reality are fluid, it may, for instance, easily be able to confirm abuse, when confronted with dolls, official interrogation, etc.

3. Our childhood oblivion generally bars the way to most of our recollections from the first four to five years of our lives. This is why we often cannot remember our dreams, and fail to understand the imagery and symbolic language of our dreams and childhood, which hold the keys to our earliest and seemingly forgotten experiences.

4. Our tendency to split off and later effectively repress the painful or traumatic events of our childhood, and especially our ambivalent feelings towards mother and father. This is also connected to a characteristic tendency in childhood to believe ourselves to be the cause of all that is painful, frightening or incomprehensible.

Our unconscious fantasies, passions and incestuous feelings, accompanied by anxiety, shame and guilt, dating from the first five years of our lives, can be unconsciously provoked in different situations. For example, if we are exposed to similar situations or injuries later in life. Or when the media focuses on sexual abuse and incest and during a psychotherapeutic process.

Since these feelings are ambivalent and taboo, they are easily projected onto others, and may result in both an obsession with this subject and the denouncement of the possible 'sinners'. In a family where, for example, the mother transfers her unconscious guilt-feelings onto her husband, the father may then be suspected of child abuse. But this may also go the other way, when the mother 'fails to see' that the child is actually being abused by her husband. Sometimes these individual intra-psychic phenomena will not only lead to consequences within a family, but will extend to larger groups, and thus lay the foundation for 'mass hysteria' in a whole community, causing everyone to suspect everyone else.

Therapists may be led astray by their own unsolved sexual conflicts and by the most extreme views of authors like Alice Miller and Jeffrey Masson, to believe that physical sexual abuse is enormously widespread, and the cause of most mental illnesses. I know of several instances where such therapists have 'seduced' their patients, on false premises, to believe this to be true, with tragic consequences for these patients and for their families. In one particular case, the therapist's own lesbian orientation and her hatred of men had clearly contributed to her 'seduction' of the patient – a typical example of counter-transference which had not been understood, but acted out with grave consequences.

By far the most difficult issue to understand and to explain to others is that the vulnerable child, when interacting with its close adult care persons and their sexuality, is confronted with something that is incomprehensible, confusing and shameful. This becomes particularly traumatic when the adult uses the child as his sexual object in concrete acts; this is something we all strongly condemn and which must not be minimised or explained away.

Far more common and even more concealed is the narcissistic abuse of children, in cases where the conflicts and unsatisfied sexual and other needs of fathers and mothers are used as a means of emotional exploitation and binding of the child, without necessarily resulting in concrete sexual acts. A glance can be sufficient, if it transmits strong drives and desires.

If we widen our scope to include this as a type of child abuse, then I do not hesitate to assert that this forms part of the background in the lives of very many individuals with mental illness. The parents, however, have usually been the victims of similar injuries and abuse when they were children. Here we can often gain insights into tragic currents running from one generation to the next, the 'original sin'. This is by way of explanation – not an excuse.

In this chapter it has been my intention to try and illustrate the difficulties and the complexities we encounter when balancing between fantasy and reality. Also, how difficult it is to give simple answers to the questions raised in the introduction. Even though my conclusions only refer to some theoretical fragments and to my own experiences, I hope they will show how cautiously we must tread in this area, and how easy it is to make a false step.

NOTES TO THE TEXT

[1] Freud, S and Breuer, J, (1893–95), *Studies on Hysteria*, S.E. Vol. II, The Hogarth Press, London, 1955.

[2] Masson, J M, *The Complete Letters of Sigmund Freud to Wilhelm Fleiss*, The Belknap Press of Harward University Press, Mass. and London, 1985.

[3] Freud, S, (1905), *Three Essays on the Theory of Sexuality*, S.E. Vol. VII, The Hogarth Press, London, 1953.

[4] Freud, S, (1923), *The Ego and the Id*, S.E., vol. XIX, The Hogarth Press, London, 1961.

[5] Guntrip, H, *Schizoid Phenomena, Object-Relations and the Self*, The Hogarth Press, London, 1974.

[6] Winnicott, D H, *Playing and Reality*, Tavistock Publ., London, 1971.

[7] Kohut, H, *The Restoration of the Self*, Int. Univers. Press., New York, 1977.

[8] Miller, A, *Du sollst nicht merken*, Suhrkamp, Frankfurt, 1981.

[9] ——*Am Anfang war Erziehung*, Suhrkamp, Frankfurt, 1983.

[10] ——*Der gemiedene Schlüssel*, Suhrkamp, Frankfurt, 1988.

[11] ——*Das verbannte Wissen*, Suhrkamp, Frankfurt, 1988.

[12] ——*Abbruch der Schweigemauer*, Hoffman & Campe, Hamburg, 1990

[13] Masson, J M, *Freud: The Assault on Truth. Freud's Suppression of the Seduction Theory*, Father & Father, London, 1984.

[14] ——*Final Analysis. The making and unmaking of a psychoanalyst*, Harper Collins, London, 1990.

[15] Freud, S and Breuer, J, *Studies on Hysteria*, Penguin Books, USA, (Footnote p.201, added 1924), 1974, 1978, 1980.

[16] Fenichel, O, *The Psychoanalytic Theory of Neurosis*, W.W. Norton & Co. Inc., New York, 1945.

[17] Lidz, T and Fleck, S, *Schizophrenia and the Family*, Int. Univers. Press, New York, 1985.

[18] Sullivan, H S, *The Interpersonal Theory of Psychiatry*, W W Norton & Co. Inc., New York, 1953.

Chapter XI
HOMOSEXUALITY – DO WE KNOW ANYTHING ABOUT ITS CAUSES?
The balance between male and female

Following my reflections in Chapter IX on a number of aspects of the male role, it seems only natural to proceed a step further and to take a look at the sensitive and difficult subject of homosexuality – the strong sexual attraction felt by a number of people towards members of their own sex. If we only take into account the individuals who are manifestly homosexually oriented, then this group represents one to five per cent of the population.[1] A great number of people are attracted to both men and women in varying degrees – they are bisexual. According to Kinsey, ten to twenty per cent of all men have at one time had a homosexual experience without this having led to permanent homosexual practice.[2] Do we know what causes homosexuality?

Freud maintains that our congenital bisexuality, in the interaction with the significant persons in our childhood, becomes a decisive factor for our sexual orientation later on in life. Then he thought of all sexual deviances as a defence against pre-oedipal anxieties and affects.[3] Other psychoanalysts differ slightly in their views regarding the possible significance of childhood circumstances. However, the majority attach more importance to the early environment rather than to congenital factors. The early mother–child relationship has been particularly emphasised,[4,5,6] and some analysts even consider the role of the father as equally important.[7] They all look upon homosexuality as a result of unconscious conflicts and anxiety, and therefore not as a normal variant of our sexual orientation.

The French psychoanalysts Janine Chasseguet Smirgel and Joyce McDougall, who are recognised as some of the most deeply penetrating researchers in this field, agree that neo-sexualities, including homosexuality, are due to a narcissistic injury in the sexual arena, related to loss of sexual identity. The triumph and grandiosity that may be present under sexual enactment are the means of achieving recovery precisely where the original wound was located, that is the sexual pride. These researchers also see a common dynamic in the denial of difference and complementarity of the sexes, and the difference between the generations.[8,9,10]

The attack on separation, differentiation and specificity leads them to construct a substitute reality where anything can become anything else, as a defence against accepting one's relative place in life. But the consequence is a breakdown of perception, knowledge and awareness, and that many are trapped in a vicious circle with increasing enactments. Many psychoanalysts link these neo-sexualities to addictions and compulsive behaviour which have the function of avoiding painful affects and fundamental psychic realities.

In the United States, a number of scientists claim that the explanation for many of the variants in human behaviour can be found in our hereditary qualities, in our genes.[11] These include not only mental disorders, such as serious depression, schizophrenia, personality disorders and free-floating anxiety, but also homosexuality. According to the most recent studies carried out by the Salk Institute for biological studies in San Diego in the United States, homosexuality is, in all likelihood, caused neither by family nor childhood conditions, but by a potent hereditary factor.[12] These studies are based on two hypotheses: partly on the possibility of hormonal influence on the brain already at the foetal stage, partly on the study of the genetic impact by looking at the number of homosexuals in families in which there are homosexuals, and also by studying the genes directly. However, the findings are not unequivocal, and strong criticism has been launched against these claims by biologists.[13]

This new trend may come as a relief to a number of people. However, there have been mixed reactions among the homosexuals in the United States. Their uncertainty is connected to the question of whether these 'findings' could strengthen or undermine the battle waged by the gay community for being accepted as equals of heterosexuals. It is also connected to the question of whether these findings should be seen as expressing nature's diversity within the sexual domain. Family members and relatives of gay individuals will certainly react positively to these 'findings'. If our sexual orientation is predestined from the moment of birth, there should be no reason for self-scrutiny or feelings of guilt!

In most human behavioural patterns there is a combination between hereditary factors and environment, nature and nurture. The hereditary factors will usually indicate tendencies, possibilities and limitations, while the early environment in particular will be crucial to the direction taken by the development. Our sexual orientation depends on a large number of complex factors, which I have attempted to illustrate in Chapter IX. Some forms of homosexuality are more genetically conditioned than others. Psychoanalytic work and research has offered significant insights into family and environmental conditions which play an essential part in forming the background for homosexual development. Some of this will be further elaborated on in this chapter.

In order to illustrate the great importance of the relationship between the mother and the father for the sexual identity of a boy, let me give you a few case histories.

An excessively dominating mother

Ole was admitted to a psychiatric ward at the age of twenty-nine. After a certain period of planning, he had attempted to hang himself in a pine tree in the hills surrounding Oslo. However, when the rope broke, he regretted his decision and sought help. It had been a serious attempt; he still had rope marks on his neck and was deeply depressed and in despair.

The cause of his depression soon became clear. Ole was an only child. All his life he had been totally dominated by his mother whom he described as a hard, cold and wilful woman obsessed with the idea of cleanliness and tidiness. She herself had been the third child of fifteen siblings, her large family living close to where Ole grew up. His father was a weak and reticent man.

He was totally unable to stand up to his wife who openly demonstrated her contempt for him by ignoring him and pushing him around. The atmosphere in the home was described as ice-cold. Feelings and spontaneity were taboo. Ole's parents had to get married when his mother became pregnant with Ole. Openly, she bitterly complained that this marriage had been forced upon her. The mother had always spoiled Ole by giving him all that he asked for. She was also excessively solicitous and ambitious on his behalf. She wanted him to become 'something big', like the son on the neighbouring farm who had become a professor. His father had soon been kicked out of the marital bed. Ole took his place in the bed and kept it until he was seventeen or eighteen years old.

Ole had always felt dependent on his mother and critical of his father with whom he did not have much contact. As a boy – and later in life – Ole was always good, weak and shy.

He blushed easily when meeting strangers. He was never allowed to go to parties with friends. Ole was good at school. After grammar school he was sent to Oslo to study law. This had been his mother's decision. He would have preferred to become an engineer or to work in an office. He had even been offered a place in a college in the United States, but his mother vetoed this project. He himself had no say in the matter. While he was a student he was reserved and kept himself to himself, he made no friends, could never assert his own opinions or show his feelings. When he gradually began to lose his ability to concentrate and was unable to complete any of the examinations, he lied to his family saying that he had passed them. He became increasingly depressed and finally attempted suicide.

I shall say no more about the situation at that particular time, except to mention that after three months of psychotherapy in the psychiatric ward, he came out of his depression, and was discharged. He discontinued his studies and launched out with something quite different.

More than thirty years later he came to me because of his sexual problems. Professionally and financially he had managed well, but socially he lived a very isolated life. He had never established close friendships with either men or women. The previous year, at the age of sixty, Ole had for the first time in his life ventured to approach a woman sexually, only to realise that he was impotent. This resulted in the woman leaving him, and once more he felt himself to be a failure. In spite of the fact that Ole was a talented man who had a great deal of insight into the connection between his present problems, the circumstances of childhood, and his relationship with his mother and father, he did not have the courage to undergo psychotherapy. He understood that his impotence was a symptom of deep-seated problems connected to his entire personality and sexual identity, and that it could hardly be solved in isolation. Did his courage fail him now once again, or was it a realistic resignation?

The reader may ask why I mention this example in a chapter about homosexuality. Surely Ole was not homosexual? True enough – he had never felt sexually attracted towards men or had had any homosexual experiences. However, as a man he did have a weak personal and sexual identity which probably caused him to be impotent. This can be an important factor in the development of homosexuality.

Ole had little contact with his father, and had been deeply dependent on and tied to his extremely domineering mother. This was a dependency which proved to be ambivalent since it contained both love and hate, anxiety and a sense of guilt. This mother fixation had made him extremely afraid of coming close to other women.

Let us look at another example, a man with a similar background, but whose reactions were diametrically opposite.

The masculinity of Don Juan

Reidar was an attractive man of fifty-six years who looked masculine and had a fit, well trained body, but somewhat evasive eyes. He was a lawyer with his own firm, and he had specialised in one particular field where it would not be necessary for him to appear in court. Financially he was very well off, he lived in a large mansion, owned several country houses, cabin cruisers and luxury cars. He was unmarried and had no children. He briefly sought professional help in a critical situation and offered the following information: He had a brother, seven years senior to him, who had a good position and a family, as well as a successful social life. Their father had been a taciturn and reticent man who had died when Reidar was three years old. Their mother, who had neither remarried nor entered into a new relationship with a man, was described as an obese, insecure and dependent woman. When she became a widow, Reidar became her great comfort in life. He was her 'golden boy' whom she spoiled and fussed over long after he had become a teenager – indeed, she even continued after he became an adult.

While Reidar was a student and later, when he practised as a lawyer, his mother constantly visited him. She prepared his food, washed his clothes and fixed practical things in the house. Reidar had always been a lone wolf. He had never made close male friends. He avoided social gatherings and meetings. When he did have to attend a meeting, he always left long before it was over. He admired and envied his older brother as well as an older colleague of his.

He had always been drawn towards women. He was a typical Don Juan who constantly needed to conquer new women but who quickly discarded them, especially if they began to show signs of deeper feelings for him. He spoke about several episodes where he had greatly enjoyed subjecting the woman to humiliation and ridicule after having had sex with her. He clearly had sadistic impulses which emerged in sexual relationships, and he was terrified of becoming emotionally attached to anyone.

Why then do I tell this story about a man who was also not manifestly homosexual? Because this is another variant of a man with a weak sexual identity. Strong indications suggest that an unresolved dependency on his mother, as well as the absence of a father figure have had an impact on his relationship to women. He invariably needed to convince himself that he was a man, while at the same time he acted out the sadistic, aggressive part of his ambivalence towards women, through his 'use and discard' attitude. Common to both Ole and Reidar is the fact that neither of them had had a normal, close relationship to their father. In his fantasies, Reidar longed for an older man, his brother and the colleague. Both Reidar's and Ole's mothers were domineering women, binding their sons to themselves, although Ole's mother was more extreme in her total 'engulfment' of her son.

A gifted artist

Anders was a thirty year old man who was voluntarily hospitalised in a psychiatric ward on account of his depression, his alcohol abuse and conflicts with an older live-in partner with whom he had had a homosexual relationship. There had been strong ambivalent feelings in both parties and now, after many rows, they had finally broken up. This had brought about a depression in Anders and also episodes during which he behaved threateningly and violently towards his former friend.

Anders was an intelligent, charming and talented painter. From the very beginning in the sessions he was extremely candid about himself and his life, and his depression disappeared quickly during his stay in the ward. He told me that he had lost his father through an accident when he was only four years old. He could therefore not remember him. His mother succeeded in supporting both herself and her two children, Anders and an older sister. She was, however, particularly attached to her son whom she dominated, overprotected and spoiled during his childhood and adolescence. This was not only the subjective experience of Anders, but it was also confirmed in sessions with the family.

From the time of his puberty onwards, Anders had had a number of homosexual relationships, but never any sexual relationship with a woman. I was therefore surprised when I met him a few years later and he told me that he was married and had two children. He was therefore bisexual. He continued having extra-marital male partners. Many years later I heard that he had become an alcoholic and had developed psychopathic behaviour. It ended tragically. At first there was a divorce. And later, after several stays at institutions for alcoholics, he committed suicide.

Common to these three men is that they all grew up with a domineering and binding mother, and that they lacked a good relationship with their fathers. However, all three developed differently and only one of them was bisexual and also attracted to members of his own sex.

During all the years of my work in psychiatric hospitals I noted that the homosexual men who were hospitalised because of the critical situations they were in, all had certain similarities in their family backgrounds, as mentioned above. However, many boys grow up with similar family backgrounds without becoming either socially lone wolves, Don Juans or homosexuals. What knowledge do we have at present about possibly more specific causes of homosexuality?

The play of unconscious forces

In order to approach this question it is not enough to consider the family constellation which is evident and which, at least in part, can be registered by the family members themselves. It is only through psychoanalytic work on a long-term basis that we may recognise the hidden and unconscious mechanisms which are instrumental in forming us, and not least our sexual identity (Chapter IX).

One of the most comprehensive studies of homosexual men was carried out by Irving Bieber and his collaborators.[14,15] This study comprises one hundred and six homosexual men and one hundred heterosexual men who were treated by seventy-seven different accredited psychoanalysts over a period of ten years. The material consisted of a thirty-page long questionnaire with four hundred and fifty questions addressed to the analysts of these patients. All the answers were computerised and analysed. The one hundred heterosexual men functioned as a control group.

In brief, this study clearly showed the significance of the parents' role for the homosexual son. None of these parents had a normal relationship with their homosexual son, and all the parents themselves had grave emotional disturbances. The classical triangle was in fact a domineering, binding and seductive mother, and a distant, aggressive or rejecting father. Half of the mothers were domineering women who tried to diminish their husbands. As a rule, the son was the mother's darling. Most mothers were openly seductive, the intimacy with the mother being sexually provoking and partly over-stimulating for the boy. The background was an unsatisfactory marriage between the parents which led the mother to satisfy her own needs through the son. This again satisfied the son's unconscious incestuous fantasies, reinforcing his jealousy and fear of the father. The mother thus alienated the son from the father which resulted in the father being aggressive towards both the mother and the son.

On the other hand, the mother became over-sensitive to her son's sexual behaviour towards herself, repressing all the suggested sexual elements and indicated virile masculinity in the boy. This may be understood as an expression of her own unconscious fear and guilt about misusing her son to satisfy her own incestuous wishes. She therefore sent diametrically opposed signals to the boy, by both stimulating and at the same time rejecting his sexuality.

The study showed that the father's importance for the boy's psychosexual development is at least as great as the mother's. In this material not many men were totally fatherless, but most of the fathers proved to be distant, aggressive or rejecting towards their sons. All the fathers had considerable mental problems, and they were unusually aggressive towards other men whom they experienced as rivals. At the same time they felt rejected by their spouses. Many of the fathers satisfied their own emotional needs in their relationship to a daughter in the same way as their wives did to a son.

None of these homosexual men had felt that they were accepted by their fathers, and not one of them had had a good relationship to a father or a father substitute during adolescence. Each son lacked a father figure as a good model in his development towards a masculine identity. The son's conscious feelings towards his father were dominated by hate and fear. Unconsciously, the fear of being attacked by the father was coupled with the longing for his love. Typically characteristic for these sons was that in their pre-puberty they had been anxious and dependent, as well as feeling inadequate and self-contempt.

The authors of this study came to the following conclusion: a supportive and warm father rules out the possibility of a homosexual son. Such a father becomes a protective element against a mother's possible attempt to seduce or to bind the son too strongly to herself. A good relationship to an older brother, for example, can compensate for a poor relationship to the father.

Bieber and his collaborators held the opinion that in addition to the family dynamics, there is a distinct element of unconscious longing for union and reconciliation in homosexual attraction and practice. This longing can be symbolically expressed in fellatio, for example, an attempt to have a share in the father's power through oral sex (Chapter VIII, 'How to become 'a good cannibal'?').

A lesbian woman

Marianne was a single, thirty-six year old woman who went into psychotherapy because of an anxiety neurosis. It started with an acute attack of free-floating anxiety when her father fell ill and had to undergo an operation. It soon came to light that she had had sexual relationships with other women from her puberty onwards. However, she could not accept this because of her moral outlook on life. She also hid these activities from her family.

In many ways her family background was a mirror image of the typical family background for homosexual men, as is described above. Marianne had strong emotional ties to her father and was dependent upon him, but there was also an ambivalent and incestuous undercurrent which emerged during the psychotherapy. She experienced her father as an insecure, weak and over-sensitive man, who felt a great deal of anxiety and guilt in relation to her. She described her mother as an immature, hysterical, unpredictable woman who was given to extreme fits of rage. It seemed that her mother had never accepted her own role as a woman, a wife or a mother. Marianne had never had a close relationship to her mother, neither physically nor emotionally, and she had always believed herself to be rejected or attacked. The family sessions confirmed these impressions and showed that there were great difficulties and conflicts in her parents' marriage.

Marianne had been dependent upon her father all her life, and it was with him that she had identified herself. And yet their relationship had never had an open-hearted quality. They never spoke about personal matters or feelings. There was always a great deal between them that was unsaid and frightening. These unknown and frightening elements coloured all Marianne's relationship to men. The subject of men and sexuality became a taboo in her life, while at the same time she did not know what it meant to be a woman. To all appearances she herself developed strong, independent and masculine ways which covered up her uncertain identity, her low self-esteem and loneliness. This had important consequences for her relationship to other people.

During her prolonged psychotherapy Marianne came to realise how much her relationship to her father had limited her all her life, and had blocked her relationship to all other men. Her mother's personality and the lack of contact with her had prevented her from a normal identification with the female role. Moreover, she was caught up in the conflicts between her mother and her father. Her anxiety conveyed a number of things, the deepest of which was a lack of security and an awareness that she was not anchored in her own personal and sexual identity. The illness of her father threatened the only fixed point in her life. It was at that point that her anxiety was fully activated.

In the course of the psychotherapy, in her transference, her strong, regressive longings for a good and close father and mother which she had never had, came to light. In her previous lesbian relationships these longings seemed to have been the underlying driving force. However, these relationships were also marked by ambivalent feelings, by symbiotic longings as well as fear of dissolution and loss of control, by aggression and a sense of guilt. For Marianne, all close relationships were dangerous. I have seen a similar pattern in other lesbian women. It is not difficult to understand that this type of family constellation makes it difficult for a daughter to develop a secure identity as a woman and have normal relationships with men. This background may serve as a partial explanation for the lesbian orientation in women. But the causes of such a development in women may be different and more complex than a mirror image of the psychosexual development in homosexual men.[16]

Critical reflections and reactions

A great deal of criticism has been levelled against the conclusions drawn by Bieber and his collaborators. It was pointed out that all the homosexual men in the study were patients under treatment, and that they therefore were not representative of ordinary homosexual men. Their symptoms and problems made them dissatisfied with their life situation and they therefore sought help. Thus the study says nothing about homosexual men who are *not* patients. The same objection can also be raised to my example of Marianne.

It is correct that most homosexual men and women do not wish to be treated for their homosexual orientation, and in the main, they do not have more mental disturbances than heterosexual individuals. If they are hospitalised in psychiatric wards, it is in order to get help for their mental problems and crises – but not for their sexual orientation. A number of homosexual men seek contact with psychiatrists on account of severe depressions after the breakdown of a relationship with a partner, as was the case with Anders in our example. But this is a common cause of depression and crises in heterosexuals too.

However, Bieber's viewpoints are corroborated by a number of additional studies. Among these is a study comprising fifty homosexual men in the United States who were brought in by the military police for homosexual activities, and another study comprising forty-six men who were dismissed from military service for the same reason.[17] A more comprehensive study by Evans comprises seventy-three homosexual and heterosexual men who were *not* psychiatric patients.[18] The findings in all these studies as regards parent/child relationships and family pathology were similar to those presented in Bieber's study.

A study group which compiled all the available knowledge about male homosexuality, published its results in the International Journal of Psychiatry in 1973.[19] The results reached by Bieber and others are confirmed by eleven prominent psychiatrists and scientists in this report. They conclude with, among other things, that homosexuality is attributable to family circumstances. One key factor is an unconscious fear of the opposite sex. Follow-up studies of homosexual men who had been in psychoanalytically oriented psychotherapy indicate that between one third and one half of the male homosexuals who had sought treatment, had become heterosexual after the treatment.

Needless to say, these studies do not imply that the only explanation for the sexual orientation of homosexuals is the special triangular situation in their family backgrounds. We must assume that there are many different contributory causes of this deviant sexual development, that genetic dispositions play a role, apart from the family constellation at early and later stages in the development of the individual.

These results called forth violent reactions in the homosexual community in the seventies. They felt themselves branded as 'sick', and believed that the connection that had been established between family problems and homosexuality reinforced the already existing discriminating tendencies in society against them. Whether it is true that they are more branded for that reason is a moot question. On the other hand, many homosexuals have also felt the hypothesis that homosexuality may have genetic roots to be a controversial issue.

Once upon a time we were all homosexual

In the course of a psychoanalysis or a psychoanalytic therapy it is normal for patients to develop strong, passionate feelings for the therapist, irrespective of sex. It is well known that a female patient can 'fall in love' with her male therapist, and the same situation may occur with a male patient in treatment with a female therapist. We know that an important reason for this reaction is the strong and loving feelings which all children between three and five harbour for the parent of the opposite sex. Underneath the adult's 'love', there are a child's passionate feelings at the oedipal phase for its father or mother (Chapter X). These 'incestuous' feelings are more or less weighed down with anxiety and feelings of guilt, all according to the adult's attitude to the child and to sexuality. However, these feelings are always repressed after the oedipal phase. In psychoanalysis or psychotherapy the patient will re-experience some of these powerful emotions in his or her 'transference' to the therapist, the link to childhood being initially unconscious.

What is far less known is that as children we harbour just as intense and passionate feelings towards the parent of the same sex.[20] This constitutes an important stage in our psychosexual development and can emerge in psychoanalysis or in similar forms of treatment as a transference of 'homosexual' and infantile fantasies to a therapist of the same sex. In particular, men are often so deeply alarmed by these feelings in themselves that a strong resistance is set up against having to recognise them.

Their 'incestuous' and 'homosexual' feelings may provoke men in several ways. Most men have built up a strong unconscious defence against the homosexual reminiscences from their childhood, and in many instances their self-image may be threatened by the infantile quality of these feelings. Let me illustrate this with two examples.

Lars was a thirty-seven year old academic. He had been in psychoanalysis for two years when he became very silent in the sessions. I respected his silence by not asking questions or not pressing him, but I conveyed to him that I understood he had important things on his mind. After several weeks of near silence in the sessions, he suddenly told me one day that he had fantasies about being a small boy who was allowed to sit on my lap and be caressed. Lars was a tall and strong man who felt ashamed to admit this, but it led to a turning point in his psychoanalysis. He was now able to recall that as a boy he had sorely missed being emotionally and physically close to his father whom he felt to be distant.

Einar was a married man aged about forty-seven, with two children and a good position. Already in the first session of his psychoanalysis he told me of a dream: a house was burning and the fire brigade turned out. He was a fireman struggling to put on his protective kit and helmet in order to avoid being injured. A fireman wearing many medals on his chest walked towards him and a homosexual man came running out of the burning house.

His spontaneous comment was that the dream told him that he was afraid he might have hidden homosexual tendencies which might come out in the psychoanalysis. In the dream he struggled to prevent such 'fire damage', hoping that the fireman with the medals, whom he believed to be me, would help him to put out the fire. Later in the analysis he had several dreams and fantasies about being physically close to me. Einar's mother had been unable to give him closeness. As a small child his father had let him lie in the crook of his arm but in other ways he had rejected him and been a bad model for him.

Neither Lars nor Einar had a binding and seductive mother. Nor did either of them become homosexual. In childhood both men's need for an intimate and good relationship to their father had not been met. This is of equal importance as when a mother for different reasons is unable to meet her child's needs, or when she uses her child far too much in order to satisfy her own needs. Here again we can see the importance of the father's role.

Women who are in treatment with a female therapist are usually not so afraid of their lesbian fantasies about the therapist. In general, women have a more relaxed attitude to physical contact with other women. Also, they are not so quickly frowned upon if they exchange caresses or live together. One of the reasons for this may be that daughters do not usually break off so definitely with their mothers as is the case with most sons (Chapter IX).

However, breaking off her relations with a mother, or the lack of closeness to her, can become disastrous for a daughter, as in the case of Marianne. Her father's strong emotional ties to his daughter increased her problems and probably contributed to a lesbian development in her.

Summary

In the present chapter I have attempted to show that in many cases homosexuality is not merely genetically determined. Psychoanalytic empirical knowledge and research clearly demonstrate that family relationships can play an important part in the development of homosexuality. The balance between mother and father, between the feminine and the masculine, becomes a crucial precondition for our development into manhood or womanhood. Very simplistically we can state that too much mother and too little father may create problems for a boy's psychosexual development towards a male identity. Correspondingly, too much father and too little mother may create problems for a girl's development towards her identity as a woman. In addition to 'too little' and 'too much', there are many other circumstances and unconscious factors which contribute to the problems concerning identity, and which may lead to a homosexual development. There are particularly strong indications that narcissistic problems in both parents play a role (Chapter XIV).

We have all had 'homosexual' fantasies and feelings at certain stages in our childhood, but they were on a child's level and very different from adult sexuality. However, most of us develop in the direction of heterosexuality.

There are many indications that a good relationship with a father or father substitute can prevent a homosexual development in a son, and that a good relationship to a mother will correspondingly prevent a daughter from becoming a lesbian. A 'good relationship' implies that both the mother and the father are normally in good emotional and physical contact with their child, without binding it too strongly to themselves or without misusing it to satisfy their own emotional or sexual needs. Moreover, it is possible that unconscious remnants of childhood 'homosexual infatuations' in the parents create anxiety which may lie at the root of homophobic tendencies which are more prevalent in men than in women. However, the relationship between the parents is also of utmost importance for the child. Here again we have a fine balancing act.

During the last twenty years the gay community in many countries has fought out a battle aimed at removing homosexuality from the list of psychiatric diagnoses. In Norway as in other countries homosexuals are accorded the same rights as all citizens. The frankness with which the subject of homosexuality and other human behaviour is treated has helped to reduce prejudices and discrimination. There must be no doubt about the question of human dignity. However, does this result in making homosexual orientation a normal variant?

Even though we make an all-out effort to eliminate prejudices and discrimination against homosexuals, and recognise that we are all tarred with the same brush in this area too, we still do not have to go to the other extreme and declare all forms of sexual behaviour as 'normal'. If we look at the natural order of things, and the need of the human race to propagate and preserve itself, then homosexuality cannot be considered adequate for this purpose. We know that if family life is to include children, then both boys and girls need a man (father figure) and a woman (mother figure) for reasonably normal development. Therefore there must be no taboo on investigating the conditions which may help us to a better understanding of phenomena like homosexuality which has such profound consequences.

I believe that it is important to impart the knowledge we have today, even though we realise that there is still a great deal we do not know. What we do know may result in important preventive work with families and with the relationship between parents and children.

NOTES TO THE TEXT

[1] Kinsey, A C, Pomeroy, W B and Martin, C E, *Sexual Behaviour in the Human Male*, Saunders, Philadelphia, 1948.

[2] Ibid.

[3] Freud, S, (1905), *Three Essays on the Theory of Sexuality*, S.E. Vol. VII, The Hogarth Press, London, 1953.

[4] Bergler, E, *One Thousand Homosexuals*, Paterson, Pageant Books, New York, 1959.

[5] Marmor, J E, *Sexual Inversion*, Basic Books, New York, 1965.

[6] Socarides, C W, *The Overt Homosexuals*, Grune & Stratton, New York, 1972.

[7] Limentani, A, Neglected fathers in the aetiology of sexual deviations, Int. J. Psychoanal., Vol. LXXII, No. 4, 1991, pp.573–584.

[8] Chasseguet-Smirgel, J, *Creativity and Perversion*, Free Association Books, London, 1984.

[9] McDougall, J, *Plea for a Measure of Abnormality*, Free Association Books, London, 1978.

[10] ——*The Many Faces of Eros*, Free Association Books, London, 1995.

[11] Le Vey, S and Hamer, D H, 'Evidence for a Biological Influence in Male Homosexuality', Scientific American, May 1994, pp.20–25.

[12] Ibid.

[13] Byne, W, 'The Biological Evidence Challenged', Scientific American, May 1994, pp.26–31.

[14] Bieber, I et al., *Homosexuality. A Psychoanalytic study of Male Homosexuals*, Basic Books, New York, 1962.

[15] Jørstad, J, 'Homoseksualitet hos menn', Fokus på Familien, Vol. V, No. 1, 1977.

[16] Dorey, R, 'The Male Homosexual Organization, a Structural Approach, Psychoanalysis in Europe', Bull. 44, 1995, pp.9–29.

[17] Snortum, J R et al., 'Family Dynamics and Homosexuality', *Psychological Reports*, 24, pp.763–770, 1969.

[18] Evans, R B, 'Childhood parental relationships of homosexual men', J. of Consult. & Cl. Psychology, 33, pp.129–135, 1969.

[19] Socarides, C W et al., 'Homosexuality in the Male, A Report of a Psychiatric Study Group', Int. J. of Psychiatry, Vol. I, No. 4, 1973.

[20] Freud, S, (1905), op. cit.

Chapter XII
BODY AND SOUL, MUSCLES AND FEELINGS
A hypothesis about fibromyalgia

Muscles are not merely muscles. They are also closely connected to our nervous system and are part of our defence against our feelings. In particular the feelings which we do not accept in ourselves, or those which threaten our relationship with the people on whom we are dependent.

In my book *Sånn er livet, sånn er du og jeg* (This is the Way We are, You and I),[1] I describe some of the background for the interaction between muscles and feelings. I would like to mention some of the aspects of this topic here.

It starts in childhood when we are taught to control our spontaneous impulses and feelings. Instead of hitting or kicking, we often lock the muscles in our arms and legs. Instead of screaming and raging, or being overwhelmed by anxiety and despair, we learn to block the breathing muscles in our diaphragm, chest, neck and shoulders.

To begin with we are driven by the awareness of our dependence on our parents and our fear of losing their love. Gradually however our conscience becomes an 'internal' authority, and, in the majority of cases, will take over the parental function of restraining our aggressive impulses.[2,3]

These impulses tend to trigger the movements for attack, defence or flight, especially the bending muscles, the flexors. Anxiety, fear or guilt have a tendency to tauten the muscle groups which have opposite functions, the stretch muscles, especially the extensors. In this way the movement becomes blocked and both groups of muscles remain in a static contraction. The result is stiff, tight muscles in one or several parts of the body. Experience has taught us that these taut muscles play a part in the repression of emotional conflicts. Therefore our muscles become part of our psychological defence against non-acceptable impulses, feelings and thoughts. This is particularly true in regard to people on whom we are dependent. Conflicts caused by conflicting emotions can therefore become frozen in our muscular tensions, without our knowing what causes this.

A painful arm

Let me illustrate this with an example from my own experience. When I was a young doctor training to become a psychiatrist, I started having symptoms in certain muscles in my right arm. These symptoms are well known; they consist of an increasing pain in the outer or radial muscle group of the lower arm, and a soreness located especially in this muscle's attachment to the lower socket of the upper arm bone, the lateral epicondyl. This tension can exist in the entire forearm. In medical terms this is called epicondylitis. In everyday language we call it 'tennis elbow' or 'writer's cramp', because it can develop in keen tennis players or in people who do too much paperwork involving sustained tension in the muscles of the right arm.

In my case, the latter activity must have been the reason for my symptoms. In the ward where I worked we had to write all the medical case records by hand. It was an acute psychiatric ward with a large turnover in patients. This was before the days of the Dictaphone, when also it was quite unthinkable that junior doctors would be permitted the use of typewriters. When I was on night duty in this ward there were always many patients. All the case records had to be written up during the night and lie ready on the chief physician's desk in the morning. Heaven help those poor souls who had not done their job properly! The boss was an authoritarian who quickly lost his temper and never hesitated to complain in these or other situations. Even though I had had two years of psychiatric experience in another hospital, I was still at the bottom of the medical hierarchy, with many duties and hardly any rights.

After several months, I had all the symptoms typical of writer's cramp. It became increasingly difficult for me to get the paperwork done on my night duties and also at other times. I contacted a physiotherapist who recommended a special form of physiotherapy which at that time was called the 'Bülow–Hansen method'. This method had been worked out by the physiotherapist Bülow–Hansen together with the chief physician Trygve Braatøy at the Ullevål hospital. Today it goes under the name of psychomotoric physiotherapy.[4,5,6,7]

I started physiotherapy with Tove who was very competent and had a great deal of experience in using this method. For nearly two years I had weekly one-hour sessions. To my great surprise, she not only treated my painful arm, but my whole body, from top to toe. I lay on the couch in my bathing trunks, sometimes on my belly and sometimes on my back, while she treated my muscles with a special type of manipulation. At first very gently, with deep massaging movements. My first reaction was a feeling of well-being but also a vague feeling of pain when she 'pinched' or massaged certain areas.

In the course of this treatment, I had a number of surprising reactions, both physical and mental. When Tove began to massage my neck, I had an apparent physical reaction: I had goosebumps all over my body. Later, when my muscles began to loosen up in my neck, shoulders and back, there were clear signs of anxiety in the form of 'sighing dyspnoea', a feeling of not getting sufficient air, which results in some deep breathing in (inhalation) followed by short blowing out of air (exhalation) with a sigh. During certain periods, I also felt a strong and inexplicable aggression, a rage which I strongly needed to take out on my family at home. At other times my body reacted with diarrhoea, obviously a reaction to the loosening up of some groups of muscles. My bodily posture began to change. Of special importance to me was that along this road I became aware of the connection between muscles and feelings/effects.

Tove explained to me that the main consequence of having so many tense muscles was that they inhibited or blocked my breathing. It therefore became the aim of the therapy to liberate my breathing. I began to realise that the muscles had a hidden function as the controller of feelings. Much of this control was linked to breathing. By inhibiting or blocking my breathing, I prevented feelings and effects from becoming conscious and thus the possibility of expressing them to other people.[8]

Even though this method has its origin in general physiotherapy which is traditionally somatically oriented, it also 'touches' very much upon deep and repressed parts of the psyche. In this way, psychomotoric physiotherapy contributes to a process of making the unconscious conscious.

Tove was a sensitive and confident therapist. She was able to accept my reactions without ever overstepping the boundaries of her profession. She never attempted to act as a psychotherapist which later I greatly appreciated. However, after being with her for almost two years, I was more than ready to start in psychoanalysis with Professor Harald Schjelderup. It now became possible for me to integrate some of the connections which I had literally experienced on my body during physiotherapy with Tove.

Psychoanalysis made me understand that there were several reasons for my writer's cramp. The writing up of the medical case records had certainly been a provoking factor for the pains in my arm. But just as significant was the emotional reason for my tense right arm, namely my attitude towards the authoritarian boss on whom I was dependent and, against whom at the same time I strongly protested. The bending muscles (flexors) in my right arm and the stretching muscles (extensors) were in constant tension. My right clenched fist was both ready to strike and to hold back – it was immobilised. We know that persistent static contraction is one of the causes of muscular pains.

This was only one aspect of my symptom. Certain personal traits also contributed to the conflict. They were partly connected with similar situations with significant figures in my childhood. And with my fear of authorities and of aggression (Chapter VII).

The importance of Wilhelm Reich

One of Freud's pupils, the psychiatrist Wilhelm Reich, in his book *Character Analysis*, published in 1932, describes how our emotional conflicts manifest themselves in facial expressions, and in bodily postures, in our manner of breathing and our movements.[9] He also uses the phrase 'muscular armour' to express generally tense and hard muscles. This may, in some people, become an unconscious defence against external and internal dangers, and impede their '*élan vitale*', their joy of life and creativity. Reich asserts that psychoanalysis can only be effective if the physical and character-based aspects of our emotional life are incorporated in the treatment. He developed theories and techniques which have been partly integrated in modern psychoanalytic therapy. Other therapists have elaborated on the physical aspect and developed special therapeutic methods such as 'vegetotherapy', 'bio-energetics' and different physiotherapeutic methods.[10]

Wilhelm Reich holds a special significance for Norway as he lived here for several years before the Second World War. Both Nic Waal, the child psychiatrist, and the psychiatrist and psychoanalyst Trygve Braatøy, chief physician at the psychiatric department at Oslo City hospital Ullevål, from 1946–53, based their work on some of Reich's theories and experiences.

In his book '*De Nervøse Sinn*' (The Nervous Minds) and in two further articles Trygve Braatøy reflects on the possible connection between the physical and psychic pains patients were suffering from.[11,12,13] In 1947, after meeting the physiotherapist Aadel Bülow-Hansen, they started working together and this resulted in the unique method, used only in Norway, of psychomotoric examination and treatment. This has led to exciting research on the connections between muscles and feelings/effects.[14,15]

The 'mystery' of fibromyalgia

Fibromyalgia seems be the modern common national complaint which lead increasingly to prolonged sick leaves and permanent disability, especially in women. For this reason it is given special attention by the media. This coincides with a period in which politicians are doing their best to reduce the growing expenses in the health and social services. In 1992 there were one hundred and sixty thousand patients in Norway with this diagnosis. Of these ten thousand were given invalidity benefit. However, the rules for invalidity benefit are becoming more stringent. One now needs to have a defined 'illness' in order to be entitled to this benefit. But is fibromyalgia an illness? Doctors disagree on this. In spite of a consensus conference which was held in Copenhagen in 1992, and a public health conference held in Oslo in 1993, there is still a great deal of disagreement and confusion among doctors.[16]

What is mainly agreed upon are the symptoms: the condition often starts with prolonged local pains in muscles, muscular attachments or joints, but this spreads sooner or later to a large part of the body's muscles. In women, these pains are mostly localised in the shoulders, in men, in the back. There is reduced muscular strength and increased tiredness and irritability. Most of the time, the pains alter in intensity and locality, but physical activity always makes them worse. Many patients have general symptoms, such as headaches, stiffness in their bodies, sleep disturbances, laboured breathing, cold hands and feet, and difficulties with concentration and memory; seventy to eighty per cent have mental symptoms, such as anxiety, depression and a tendency towards social isolation, which doctors, however, regard as being secondary consequences of the pain. Ninety per cent of the patients are women, predominantly between the ages of twenty-five to fifty-five, but the symptoms may also occur in other age groups.[17]

Characteristically, most patients have had numerous and expensive examinations, on account of their local pains and their general condition. But no 'objective' sign of illness has been found, neither with X-ray nor laboratory testing. In two articles published in 1993, the rheumatologist Kåre Leif Spongsveen wrote that there is no effective method of treatment. He also asserts categorically that 'fibromyalgia is *not* a psychiatric/psychogenic illness, it is *not* an imagined illness or hypochondria, it is *not* a women's disease, it *cannot* be healed with training, physiotherapy, psychotherapy, surgery, incantations or word magic'. On the other hand he maintains, that it is probably 'a stress induced illness'. Further on in his articles he indicates that lack of oxygen in the muscles can be an active mechanism.[18,19] The thrombosis specialist, Professor Helge Stormorken, ascertains in another article published in 1993: 'Fibromyalgia is *not* a women's disease, and does *not* have psychogenic origins'.

These and other contributions to the debate are probably attempts at defending the national insurance rights of these patients, but they do not offer a deeper understanding of the reason why precisely these people develop fibromyalgia, or why it has become such a widespread illness in our country in the last fifteen to twenty years.

A country doctor's story

During a train journey, a country doctor who worked in one of the valleys in Eastern Norway and I were talking about fibromyalgia. I asked him about his experiences with these patients. He said that he had seen many of them in his part of the country, where the typical pattern, based on the still existing traditional gender roles in the villages, was that the husband worked outdoors and the wife inside the house. The novel aspect was that in addition to taking care of the house, the food and the children, the wife also often had a full time job outside the house. In most cases, this certainly has not resulted in the farmer becoming more helpful about the house. He still takes a nap after dinner, reads the newspaper, watches television, and does not lend his wife a helping hand. In this doctor's experience, this represented the typical family background for women with fibromyalgia. Also it was his impression that these women were perfectionists and conscientious above the average.

I believe that he had observed some important points, which I would like to elaborate on with two case histories.

An active and energetic woman

Signe is a forty-five year old married woman who tells me that she has felt anxiety and muscular pains for twelve years. Her initial anxiety came out of the blue, with acute panic, palpitations of the heart, dizziness and a fear of closing her eyes, as she was convinced that if she did so, she would then not wake up again. Since then she had been using anxiety-reducing drugs with good results.

Soon after the first symptoms of anxiety she began to feel muscular pains. The first signs were diffuse pains in her back and her neck, but gradually the pains also spread to her legs and arms. During one period they were particularly strong at the muscular attachments in her left shoulder. She was given a cortisone injection used for the treatment of stiff, painful shoulders, the so-called 'frozen shoulders'. This had a fairly good effect. But otherwise her condition gradually deteriorated; her whole body became so stiff that she ended up having to use crutches. Her knees and feet swelled and became stiff. She had intense pains and stiffness in her hips and pelvis. She felt constantly tired and worn out, as tired when she got up as she was when going to bed. Signe had now been on sick leave from her job as a secretary for more than two years. The second year she received rehabilitation benefit. The diagnosis was fibromyalgia.

Regarding other illnesses, she had suffered from migraine from the age of eleven to thirty-two, but this vanished with the onset of her states of anxiety and her muscular pains. Now however the migraine had returned. She was referred to psycho-motoric physiotherapy, but the therapist considered her too ill for this type of treatment which makes great demands on the patient. Psychiatric help was then recommended to her.

During her first session with me, she told me about her complaints and symptoms which are described above. Then spontaneously she said: 'All my life I have been hyperactive, and I find it terrible that I can't do anything now! It really distresses me as I have always needed to get things done straight away, I just can't relax until they are done! I enjoyed having three children and a full-time job outside the home, but now I realise that for a long time I have taken far too much upon myself. When my mother fell ill, being an only child, I had to continue to keep at it.'

Signe told me that she could remember little about the first ten years of her life. What she did remember were mostly painful episodes about her father when he was drunk, but these she had tried to push away from herself and could not bear to recall them. She remembers that he became vulgar, that he often fell asleep naked on the floor, and that he constantly drove while drunk. Her mother was extremely house-proud, everything had to be spick and span and all the food had to be cooked from scratch. 'I just had to continue along the same lines.' Signe describes her mother as being extremely industrious, strict but fair. She was very particular about how the children were dressed, also that they should be well behaved. 'I have taken over a lot of my mother's attitudes. I used to be house-proud myself, but now I no longer have the strength!'

There was no openness or intimacy in the home, and there were many taboo areas which one never talked about. When she first started menstruating at the age of eleven, she had no idea what it was all about. She was shocked, afraid and began screaming. It was her father who came and who consoled her with the words: 'Mother says it isn't dangerous.' He had great respect for his wife. As long as she was alive, she kept him in order to a certain degree. But when she died, he broke down completely and his alcoholism became even worse. The father married again soon, continued to drink, and received disablement benefit. Signe continued to feel responsible for him. Even though she was aware of the irrationality of it, she still phoned him several times a week.

Signe was fourteen years old when her mother died of cancer. But already two years earlier, she had been obliged to take over all the housework. At the time she was still at grammar school. 'That cost me a lot.' She has never been able to mourn her mother's death, she did not have the courage to examine her feelings. She married at the age of twenty and now has three grown-up children. She describes her marriage as good and her husband as kind. 'If it hadn't been for him, I wouldn't have survived.' In her own opinion she has been an extremely conscientious person, who always placed great demands on herself, and always felt compelled to do a great amount of work at home, in spite of working full-time as a secretary. In recent years, when she was no longer able to cope, she had feelings of guilt. It was as though, by being in full activity, she was atoning for something, but she did not know what. Like her mother, she had an inclination towards perfectionism, particularly as long as the children were small. She could not stand rows, and never grew angry herself. Instead she withdrew, 'preferring to knead a bread dough'. She did not always say what she meant, or give herself away. She believes that she was always too good-natured and compliant, and that she had spoilt her children.

A typical pattern

I use this case history because it contains a number of factors which I have observed in many patients with fibromyalgia. It may give us a deeper understanding of the psychological background for the symptoms suffered by some of these greatly afflict persons.

The most obvious fact which the country doctor from the valley had noticed, was that these afflictions usually strike women who work very hard, both in and outside their homes. This would justify the term 'stress-related illness', a collective diagnosis used by many doctors in somatic medicine. If we look unilaterally at the physical stress factor, then the treatment suggested by the doctor, or his 'good' advice, will be to reduce the workload. The patient may also be referred to physiotherapy, in order to 'soften up the tense muscles'. None of this will have any effect, and as a rule, the patient will also be unable to reduce her workload. Something is 'driving' these patients, as in the case of Signe who always felt that she had to atone for something.

Let us take a closer look at these people who feel compelled to work so much. They are usually extremely conscientious perfectionists who make great demands on themselves. They 'have to' work so much, otherwise they are beset by guilt feelings, like Signe. They take too much upon themselves and are unable to set their firm limits against the demands and expectations of others. They are often too good-natured and compliant, they cannot tolerate quarrelling and cannot become angry themselves. The reasons for these character traits can be both numerous and vary a great deal. In the case of Signe, it was a pattern which she had inherited from her mother with whom it was natural for a daughter to identify. Also the fact that, already at the age of twelve, she had to take on her mother's tasks and duties in the home. In addition, she had to nurse her mother while still at grammar school. This must have been too overtaxing for a twelve year old!

In Signe's case, her father's alcoholism also contributed to her fear of rows and loss of control, in other words, of becoming angry. She knows that it had been necessary for her from an early age to repress many of her feelings. At first, there were no memories about her first ten years, gradually, however, many painful memories emerged in connection with her father's misuse and her mother's strictness. We know that Signe's free-floating anxiety had made its appearance twelve years earlier. Shortly afterwards, she developed her muscular symptoms, at the same time as her anxiety was brought partly under control by anxiety-reducing drugs.

This interaction between the muscular symptoms and anxiety is well known to all those who work with anxiety patients in physiotherapy or psychotherapy. For many years Signe had laboured to keep her feelings in check, and for this reason had been unable to surrender to her grief about her mother's death. Later in therapy it emerged that she had put a particularly heavy lid on her aggressive feelings. Already as a child she had to develop neurotic character traits such as goodness and compliance, an inner compulsion to put far too much effort into her work, and muscular tensions. All of this was necessary as a defence against her feelings of anger, grief and despair.

However, her muscular defence was gradually alerted – and the symptoms made their appearance. It was not until she was totally crippled that she was able to let go of this painfully vicious circle in which she was trapped by her own inner demands and the demands of others.

Between the devil and the deep blue sea

Ada was a fifty-seven year old refined and well dressed woman who came to the session together with her husband. He had taken the initiative for this meeting. The reason was that for several years there had been episodes when Ada had taken Valium tablets or alcohol and then gone to bed. This had made him very angry. He felt that these episodes were a threat to their marriage and to their whole existence. 'After an episode like this, my whole world collapses.' He was afraid that others would notice something. He described his wife as being more extrovert than himself, and needing more contact with other people. His own social needs were met mostly through his job. Ada was the perfect hostess when they had guests, and she had good contact with their own four children.

When I turned to her, she told me that she had worked very hard all her life. She owned her own bookstore which did well. At times she had worked night and day for long periods. She kept their house in perfect condition and had been responsible for four children who were now grown-up. In addition, she had been a member of many societies and had held a number of honorary posts. All the years of their marriage they had lived in the same house as her mother. The mother, a very active lady, constantly interfered in their lives, and Ada felt she always had to keep her mother informed about everything. 'Mother has accompanied us on all our holidays since becoming a widow fifteen years ago. I have never managed to refuse her or to become angry.'

Ada told me that for many years she had had fibromyalgia, with stiffness and pains from the moment she woke up in the mornings. These pains were in her muscles and muscular attachments, and moved around to different parts of her body. Seven years ago, her strong pains forced her to give up her work. She had been examined many times and had tried many treatments, but to no avail.

In a later session Ada told me that she was an only child, also that they were a close-knit family on both her mother's and her father's side. Everyone admired her mother, seeing her as a strong, wise and talented woman. The daughter however experienced her as a strict and demanding woman who was mostly interested in her work. Her mother never expressed her feelings, except when she was angry, and she would often explode into a rage. Throughout the years she had been in control of Ada. But now it seemed as if Ada herself had incorporated this controlling function in the form of a strict and punishing conscience. Ada said that it had not been possible for her to free herself of her dependency on her mother.

Speaking about the reason for her episodic misuse, Ada said that neither her husband nor her mother could tolerate her being angry or weak. This is why she always felt that she had to pull herself together and hide her true feelings. Neither was there any frankness in her marriage as there also she had to keep up appearances. She had suddenly realised that she had married a man whose character traits resembled those of her mother.

When she 'cracked' and started on drugs and alcohol, it was after a long period of accumulated defeats in her relationship to both her mother and her husband, and disappointment with herself. At that point everything had seemed totally insurmountable to her, and she had gradually begun to feel a deeply repressed aggression towards both her mother and her husband.

She was truly between the devil and the deep blue sea. Not only in relation to her mother and her husband, but also between the demands and expectations of others, and her own demands on herself. Also between aggressive impulses and the strict judge inside her, her conscience.

What do they have in common?

We can observe a certain similarity of pattern in these two women, Signe and Ada. They both have a tendency to take upon themselves far too much work, which may be a consequence of the expectations of people around them. They both have an even stronger inner drive to live up to their own expectations, indicating a strict conscience. They are both conscientious and perfectionists. They both have problems with their aggression towards persons on whom they are dependent. This is reflected in their compliance and inability to become angry and set limits for themselves and others. In the defence against the aggressive impulses the muscles also play a part, combined with the character-based qualities which I have mentioned.

Both Signe and Ada have symptoms often observed in neurotic people which represent a balancing act between impulse and unconscious defence, partly character-based and partly muscular. Signe's free-floating anxiety is a neurotic symptom, as well as her migraine resembling headaches which I consider to be psychosomatic symptoms. Ada's misuse is a neurotic symptom and an unconscious flight from problems with which she can no longer cope. But this may be the beginning of grave and chronic misuse. Apart from having an effect on anxiety, Valium (benzodiazepam) also has a muscle-relaxing effect. Having said this, I do not suggest that all patients with fibromyalgia have a neurotic character structure, but my hypothesis is that many of them do. If this hypothesis is correct, the best treatment would be psychotherapy or psychoanalysis. It could bring about a change in the deeper layers of the character neurosis, with the conflicts about aggression and dependency. But how many people can avail themselves of this form of help? The possibilities are very limited because almost everywhere there are still too few psychotherapists.

I have also seen patients with similar muscular symptoms which represent a more serious psychopathology, and where there was a great risk of psychotic breakdown. The muscles can become part of the defence against the psychosis, and it can become overtaxed and painful. In addition, these patients often have several other symptoms, such as withdrawal from other people, social isolation, suspicion or paranoid tendencies. In my experience also there is typically open and more conscious aggression, and not infrequently, these patients harbour murderous impulses towards members of their own family. This strong aggression tends to emerge when someone comes too close. This may be one of the reasons why these patients withdraw into themselves.

A medical problem

Many of my colleagues in somatic medicine feel helpless with patients who have been given the diagnosis fibromyalgia. They can often recognise the overpowering physical stress which many of these patients have in their daily lives, but laboratory tests and X-ray examinations yield very few concrete results. The entire picture of this illness seems diffuse and unclear. It does not fit into the usual categories of illness. Some of these colleagues are also aware of the character traits common to these patients, as, for example, that they are unable to set limits, that they demand too much of themselves, and that they overreach themselves. But very few of them are aware of the deeper-lying problems concerning aggression and muscular defence.

When we feel helpless, we often try to solve the patient's problems and our own by referring them to specialists. These will discuss the problem on the basis of their own speciality, but do not always include other perspectives. In the meantime, many patients will be referred to physiotherapy which at best can only give brief relief.

We have not advanced particularly far in our understanding of the interaction between body and soul, which we can also observe in our muscles. This is partly due to the fact that there is far too little interdisciplinary collaboration, and that each speciality has a limited field of vision and we therefore only see what we have been taught to see. Medical education and research still advocate a dualistic view of human beings. The subconscious driving forces are seldom taken seriously.

Many patients fall therefore between two schools. One of the reasons is that many patients with this type of psychosomatic illness do not themselves accept the idea that there may be emotional and interpersonal reasons for their pains, their tense muscles and other physical symptoms. If a doctor points to these possible connections, then the patient may interpret it as an accusation, and feel rejected. Perhaps the doctor's attitude does contain a certain rejection because many doctors, for personal reasons or the pressure of time, wish to define these patients away from their sphere of interest and disclaim any responsibility. Some doctors may even feel provoked because in dealing with these patients they are confronted with unrecognised and problematic aspects in themselves.

The Fibromyalgia Association, the organisation for these patients, is intent on emphasising that these patients do not have more psychic problems than other people. Why is it so important to emphasise this?

In patients with fibromyalgia, I believe, we see another example of our human balancing act between dependency and independency, aggressive feelings and defence, attempts at setting limits for the demands and expectations of others, a stern and demanding conscience, and a lack of limits. These are the problems which especially women in our culture often struggle with. It is therefore not so remarkable that women are over-represented in this category of patients with these symptoms.

Furthermore, patients with fibromyalgia are victims of a divided medical science which lacks a comprehensive view of human beings. However, in medical training, there already have been some changes towards a wider scope in interdisciplinary teaching. We can only hope that a greater understanding of the importance of the subconscious forces will help future physicians to acknowledge that body and soul are two sides of the same coin: the human being.

NOTES TO THE TEXT

[1] Jørstad, J, *Sånn er livet, sånn er du og jeg,* Aschehoug, Oslo, 1986, 1987, 1989, pp.197–213.

[2] Fraiberg, S H, *The Magic Years*, Schribner, New York, 1959.

[3] Erikson, E H, *Childhood and Society*, Northon & Co., New York, 1950.

[4] Johnsen, L, *Integrert respirasjonsterapi*, Oslo University Publ. Co., 1975.

[5] Bülow-Hansen, Aa, 'Problemer ved behandling av muskel-spenninger', J. Norwegian Dentist Ass. 77, 1, Oslo, 1967, pp.6–13.

[6] Houge, N H, 'Psykomotorisk fysioterapi og psykomotorisk behandling', J. Norwegian Medical Ass., 15, Oslo, 1979, pp.287–288.

[7] Sundsvold, M Ø, 'Muskelspenning og psykpatologi', Fysioterapeuten, 39, Oslo, 1972, pp.33–51.

[8] Sundsvold, M Ø, Vaglum, P., and Østberg, B., 'Respirasjon og psykopatologi', Fysioterapeuten, 47, Oslo, 1980, pp.103–107.

[9] Reich, W, *Character Analysis*, Orgon Institute Press, New York, 1949.

[10] Faleide, A, Grønseth, R and Urdal, B, *Det levande muskelpanseret*, Oslo University Publ. Co., Oslo-Bergen-Tromsø, 1975.

[11] Braatøy, T, *De nervøse sinn, Medicinsk psykologi og psykoterapi*, Cappelen, Oslo, 1947.

[12] ——'Psychology vs. anatomy in the treatment of arm neuroses with psychotherapy', J. Nerv. Disease, 1952, 115, pp.215–245.

[13] ——*Fundamentals of psychoanalytic technique*, Wiley, New York, 1954.

[14] Sundsvold, M Ø, Vaglum, P and Østberg, B, Movements, Lumbar and Temporomandibular Pain and Psychopathology, Psychother. Psychosom. 35, pp.1–8, 1981.

[15] Sundsvold, M Ø, Friis, S and Vaglum, P, Psychiatric disorders and differences in muscular patterns. *Psychosomatic Medicine, Past and Future*, Ed. Christodoutori, Plenem Publ. Co., 1987.

[16] Norges Forskningsråd, Fibromylagi, Nasjonal konferanse, Oslo, 27–28 September 1993, Report, Oslo, 1994.

[17] Strømman, T, Fibromyalgi. Med smerter som fellesnevner. Legemidler og samfunn, Oslo, 5 July 1993.

[18] Spongsveen, K L, Aftenposten, Oslo, 5 July 1993.

[19] ——Fibromyalgo, komplisert bleastnings-syndrom som rammer stadig flere, Image, Hafslund Nycomed, 4, Oslo, 1993.

Chapter XIII
THE BODY TELLS US SOMETHING THAT REASON DOES NOT UNDERSTAND
Some psychsomatic fragments

Words without feelings

I have said earlier, in Chapter IX, that some people do not have contact with their feelings. They have difficulties finding words for their own feelings – indeed, they may not even know what is meant by feelings.

We can take as an example the business manager who had an acute attack of backache, which gradually became chronic and therefore crippled him for a long period. After seeing various specialists, and many unsuccessful attempts at treatment, he came to consult me as a psychiatrist. During our first talk, he told me among other things, that when he was four years old he had been placed in a children's home for six months while his mother was having another baby. Later, he had to travel alone by bus to this children's home every day for several months, because both his parents had to work at the shop which they owned. As he was telling me this, I noticed a somewhat sad expression in his eyes and therefore asked him: 'Can you remember what you were feeling when you stood there waiting for the bus?' He looked rather surprised as he replied: 'What do you actually mean by feeling? I don't really think I know what you mean. Do you mean like the pains in my back? Of course I feel them.'[1]

A common feature in our culture – though more typical for men than for women – is a lack of contact with our own feelings, and an inability to put them into words. In Chapter XII which deals with the topic of musculature and feelings I have described the syndrome which has been termed fibromyalgia and which primarily affects women. Patients suffering from fibromyalgia are precisely those who very often find it difficult to come into contact with their own feelings. But it is not only in the interaction between musculature and feelings that the inability to express oneself in words manifests itself. I will come back to this later.

This phenomenon has been given many names, one of them being *alexithymia*, which is Greek and means lack of words.[2] French researchers call it *pensées operatoire*, which in English can be translated as 'operational thinking'. It is a way of thinking which is concrete and technical, concretistic thinking, and which implies superficial, unfeeling and insensitive contact with other people. This has consequences *inwards* in relation to 'the inner world', and *outwards* in relation to others.[3]

Alexithymic personalities speak very little about personal experiences, they use the word 'one' more often than 'I' and their fantasy life lacks richness. They have a marked tendency to conformity, that is to say, they adapt themselves so strictly to current forms of accepted behaviour that they may be considered over-adapted. They seem perfectly 'normal' to other people. The French psychoanalyst Joyce McDougall therefore calls them normopaths.[4,5] She maintains that behind this facade, deeply hidden from themselves and others, there is deep anxiety. In fact, it is the unconscious defence against this anxiety that ensures that feelings are 'eliminated'. These individuals also use denial as a defence mechanism far more than is usual, by denying things which are perfectly obvious to others.

Detaching oneself from pain

Haakon was a forty-six year old man who started psychoanalysis because he felt anxious in social situations, and because he often became angry with his subordinates at his job without having a rational reason. In the sessions he sometimes reacted with physical symptoms, such as pains in his chest, a need to urinate, as well as feelings of numbness and pain around his mouth. His wife and adult children reproached him for always thinking of himself and Haakon himself admitted that he was self-centred and had difficulties entering into the feelings of others. He lacked empathy. He had to be constantly active, doing something, creating something. A great deal of progress and success had been the result, but in spite of this his self-confidence remained low.

In the analysis, which lasted for several years, he kept up an even flow of words during the sessions which revealed much intellectual understanding, but he remained totally unaffected. If I said something important, it often 'got lost', he remembered nothing afterwards – a typical example of unconscious resistance.

In one session Haakon told me about a meeting with colleagues where he had presented something that concerned him very much but found that the others were totally uninterested and scarcely listened to him. He said that it had made him a little sad but then he had dismissed it. Afterwards when he told me about another situation where something similar had happened, I commented that he must have felt both hurt and rejected in these two situations. As soon as I had said these words, Haakon fell into a deep sleep. When, after a couple of minutes, I woke him up and repeated what I had said, he immediately fell asleep again, and this time he snored. This repeated itself for a third time, and each time he had forgotten what I had said. Falling asleep was obviously an effective escape and a defence against the feelings which my words had evoked in him.

In the following session he reported that he had been totally worn out after the previous session. When I reminded him about my words about injury and rejection, he said: 'At home I was always overlooked, I was never taken seriously. They never noticed how unhappy I was.' He now spoke about how often he had felt afraid, lonely and helpless during his childhood, and how all signs of weakness or tears on his part had been belittled or ridiculed by the grown-ups. The rage he had felt then was now reactivated in situations when workers in his factory were not sufficiently quick or helpful. His rage was also directed at those who did not 'see' him (as when he was small) and did not help him (against his feeling of being helpless). Haakon now began to realise that underneath his exaggerated need for constant activity and achievement there might be a wish to escape from something or other. He now understood that it had been necessary for him at an early stage in his life, as a small child, to encapsule the unbearable pain he felt and protect himself from feeling anything at all, except for rage. Words and feelings had been separated from each other (Chapter XV).

I include this story because it firmly suggests a possible background for alexithymia and lack of empathy.

What is psychosomatic?

The reason why psychiatrists and psychoanalysts in many countries have been studying alexithymia is because they believe they have discovered a connection between alexithymia and the occurrence of more serious illnesses such as gastric ulcer (*ulcus duodeni*), high blood pressure and cardiovascular diseases, asthma, colitis (*colitis ulcerosa*), chronic arthritis (*rheumatoid arthritis*), increased metabolism (*thyreotoxicosis*) and some chronic skin diseases (*psoriasis* and *neurodermitis*). In the opinion of a number of psychiatrists, psychological factors may often be contributory causes for these diseases, and it is therefore correct to call this group psychosomatic illnesses.[6]

This concept has gradually been extended, and is now being used more often from an overall perspective: in every illness there is an interaction between body and soul since our body is susceptible to influences both from psychological factors and social conditions which may lead to illness. On the other hand, physical illness, strain and injuries may have psychic consequences and symptoms. We can all react psychosomatically in certain situations when we are under strain, as for example, when I got writer's cramp (Chapter XII). However, we are differently predisposed to psychosomatic reactions and those afflicted with marked alexithymia, the normopaths, seem to have a greater tendency to becoming chronically and seriously ill.

The findings of recent research suggest that alexithymia is a complex concept and may derive from disturbances in the relationship to early, close care persons. In some cases it may be a symptom of personality disorder. However, alexithymia does not necessarily have to be a character trait of the personality. It may also reflect a regression of the ego-functions and may therefore be a temporary state.[7,8] In this case alexithymia may act as a psychic defence mechanism, (cf my 'insensibility' on returning from imprisonment in Germany Chapter II)

The body's immune system plays a central role

It is a common experience that a cold or influenza may develop into a lengthy, or serious infection, for example pneumonia, if we are physically or mentally run down, exhausted or depressed. Today we have a fair amount of knowledge about the central role played by the body's immune system in fighting microbes and viruses, and even cancer cells. Many micro-organisms which are usually found in our mucous membranes without causing illness, may 'launch an attack' and invade the body if the immune system is weakened or out of balance. We know that stress and other forms of psychic strain may influence the immune system.

We know as well that atypical cell divisions, which regularly take place in our body, produce cancer cells. Normally the body's own immune cells (cytotoxic T-killer cells and NK cells (natural killer cells)) which are part of our immune system, destroy these cancer cells before they have time to multiply. A weakening of, or an imbalance in this defence system may therefore be looked upon as a contributory factor to the uncontrolled division of cancer cells in one or the other organ. Let me tell a story which made a strong impression on me and which may serve as an illustration.

A tough policeman

When I was a young doctor I was visited by a thirty year old policeman, Eivind. He was unhappy in his job. He had stomach pains and was chronically bad-tempered. Eivind was a lonely man, without close friends, men or women, and the only family he had was his father. In the course of a few sporadic talks he told me about his tragic background. He had lost his mother at the age of five and had no memories of her. Eivind described his father as a cold, aggressive, authoritarian who had devaluated and ridiculed him throughout his adolescence, and had dealt out corporal punishment. Eivind became a tough and self-assertive man, an eager bodybuilder and sportsman. He had a marked tendency to deny his own weaknesses, anxiety and feelings of loneliness. His self-esteem was poor.

When speaking about his childhood, much bitterness and a violent hatred towards his father welled up in him – a hatred which was directed partly against himself, and turned into self-contempt. During the period in which we had our talks, he fell in love with a beautiful girl who was also interested in him. He tried for the first time in his life to approach a woman sexually but discovered that he was impotent. The girlfriend left him after a time. This was a shock for him, and led to a deep depression. He felt that he was a failure as a man, and that life no longer had any meaning. Everything seemed hopeless.

Seven months later he developed a particularly malignant tumour in his back (sarcoma) and died in the course of a few months.

My meetings with Eivind, and hearing about his tragic background and fate made me reflect upon the possibility of a link between the early loss of his mother, the loss of his girlfriend and the cancerous tumour. Had he perhaps already been predisposed on account of his bitterness, his hatred towards his father, his self-hate, his low self-esteem and his dissatisfaction with his life situation before meeting the girlfriend?

I do not have a clear answer to the question of what caused Eivind's illness and death. However, in subsequent years, I have come across several people whose fate was as tragic as Eivind's and this makes me wonder today whether there might have been a connection after all.

Complex causality

With this I do not imply that all forms of cancer are caused by psychic traumas such as loss, introverted hatred and an alexithymic personality structure. The causal relations are too complicated and complex for that. However, a number of studies have come to my knowledge pointing to likely connections between personality factors and emotional strain; the body's own defence system is weakened which may, together with other factors, contribute to the development of cancer.[9,10,11]

Other factors we know about are physical and external causes such as ultraviolet radiation, excessive consumption of alcohol over a longer period, excessive smoking, and to a certain extent, excessive eating, particularly of food containing carcinogenic additives. There may be many reasons why people lack notions of the danger involved or the ability to exercise moderation in these areas. However, those who develop lung cancer, stomach cancer or cancer in other organs have in common that they have, for a long time, denied to themselves and others that excessive smoking, drinking or eating may have unfortunate consequences. They are often 'deaf' to the language of their bodies, and they deny the danger signals when these symptoms are beginning to appear. Therefore many are first examined and treated when the symptoms are already apparent and have become troublesome. By then it may be too late.

Neurotic symptoms and alexithymia

Symptoms such as anxiety, depression, obsessive thoughts and acts, and some physical symptoms which we call conversion symptoms, reflect neurotic conflicts which are repressed, i.e. the person is unconscious of them. The most usual defence mechanisms used by a neurotic person are repression, reaction formation, rationalisation and intellectualisation and, to a certain extent, denial, projection and splitting (dividing the world in two: into a good and a bad part, see p.83). Neurotic persons are in contact with their feelings to a certain degree. They can feel their anxiety and depression, and they give expression to their desperation and helplessness. They can therefore more easily acknowledge their need for help; sometimes indeed the very symptom will constitute an appeal to their surroundings for support and help. They are more often able to admit that they believe their symptoms may have a connection with their relationship to other people, both past and present. They also generally have a rich fantasy life, and a dream life, and are as a rule able to have profound relationships with others.

In many ways neurotics are therefore the opposite of alexithymic individuals who lack contact with their own feelings and therefore have more superficial contact with others, while their fantasy-life, thinking and language appears to be inadequate. However, making such a strong distinction does not tally with reality since most of us may have both tendencies. We may all regress in certain stressful situations, i.e. function on an earlier developmental level and thus make use of more primitive defence mechanisms, as well as reacting psychosomatically. Neurotic individuals too may be alexithymic, especially those with conversion symptoms (hysteria) and panic anxiety. Alexithymic individuals do not necessarily need to develop psychosomatic illnesses.[12]

Some fundamental questions

The problem areas of alexithymia and psychosomatics raise several fundamental questions to which many have attempted to find an answer over the years. For example: what is the connection between body and soul, physiology and psychology? What is primary and what is secondary? In what way do psychological factors act on the body?

A pioneer in the psychosomatic field, the psychoanalyst Franz Alexander, assumed that psychological stimuli have a directly triggering effect on the nervous system and the hormone system, thus giving rise to physiological and later even to organic changes. Scientists with a biological orientation who have had an impact on traditional medical education and research, have often maintained that physiological changes are primary, and that possible psychological reactions are secondary.

An example would be the internists who assert that patients with anorexia (an eating disorder) suffer primarily from a hormonal disorder affecting the metabolism, and that the mental reactions of these patients are a natural consequence of the physiological disorder. They firmly reject the concept of emotional conflicts in these young patients, or their relationship to their parents, having any significance with regard to the cause of this affliction. They can often produce good results from their treatments, which is not surprising since they give an explanation which relieves both patients and their families of a great deal of doubt, insecurity and guilt feelings. They may also save some lives by breaking the vicious circle these patients are caught in. Then they have done a good job. But it still does not prove that their explanation of the causal connections is correct.[13]

A third hypothesis has been formulated among others by the neuro-psychiatrist Herbert Weiner in the United States. He says that the physiological and psychological mechanisms may possibly be parallel and simultaneous. This leads to the holistic perspective which is most widespread today, that there is an interaction between our external and internal world where both biological, psychological and social factors can lead to physical symptoms.[14]

But there are many other important questions we can ask. What is it that predisposes some people to psychosomatic reactions? What is it that causes certain organ systems to react with illness in one individual and not in another? Why are some persons struck down by illness at a certain moment in their lives? A great deal of research has been carried out in order to find answers to some of these questions, and even though many questions still remain unanswered, we do have a certain amount of knowledge. I shall attempt to present some of it.

Social and economic conditions

We know that low social status, poverty and unemployment increases the prevalence of all types of illness, such as high blood pressure, cardiovascular disease, premature birth and child mortality, physical and psychic deficiency diseases, tuberculosis, cervical cancer in women, mental illness, alcoholism and drug abuse.[15]

Tests have shown that blood pressure and serum cholesterol levels increase when persons lose their jobs and that these levels return to normal when they are back at work again. Investigations of groups which are socially or culturally mobile, i.e. persons who move often, commute or emigrate, have proved that these have a high prevalence of cardiovascular diseases, lung cancer and sarcoid tumours.[16]

The connection between a diet rich in fat and serum cholesterol, and a higher risk of cardiovascular diseases, was established long ago, especially in combination with obesity and lack of exercise. Even though this theory is still valid, there are some new findings pointing to even more important factors. An extensive investigation of Japanese immigrants in the United States is particularly well known. The immigrants who kept to an American diet, rich in fats but who lived according to Japanese traditions, had a far lower prevalence to cardiovascular diseases than those who had the same diet but had adopted the American way of life. Similar findings have created the concept of lifestyle diseases.[17]

Loss and separation, changes and contentment

We know that loss and separation play an important role in psychic illness (Chapter I). Today many researchers are of the opinion that real loss, or the threat of loss, may be a releasing factor for many physical illnesses, for example, cancer, tuberculosis, diabetes, leukaemia and heart failure. But there are great differences in the degree of vulnerability to loss. The psychological significance accorded to loss by the individual is reflected in physiological changes in the body. The decisive factor will be how deeply the loss is experienced and to what extent the individual has the will or ability to cope with it.

Loss and social mobility have in common the fact that they represent a change from traditional attitudes, as was shown by the investigation of Japanese immigrants in the United States. Too much change, or too little change, as for instance in the case of understimulation, leads to the same changes in the cathecolamine metabolism.

One hypothesis is that both high and low social and economic status, life in cities, industrialisation, loss of employment, emigration, geographical mobility, divorce, loss of a partner and other sudden changes in life, weaken the individual's resistance.[18] These general factors increase the receptivity to illness, while the specific nature of the illness is due to other causes. Many attempts have been made to find out why some persons fall ill while others do not, even though they have been exposed to similar personal and social pressures. A special line of investigation has focused on finding specific personality qualities which might dispose one for certain diseases, as, for example, cardiac infarction. However, no definite results have been reached.

On the other hand, a number of investigations suggest that those who fall ill, have been subjected to great demands from their surroundings, are dissatisfied with their jobs and their life situations, and unhappy in their marriages and other close relationships.[19]

Why did I fall ill just then?

I was sixty-six years old and had decided to retire from my position as chief psychiatrist of the psychiatric department at the Ullevål Hospital as soon as I reached the age of sixty-seven. My last years in this senior position had been strenuous in several ways, also on account of economic and political conditions at the hospital and in the municipality of Oslo. There was a great deal of turbulence and insecurity in Oslo as well as in the rest of the country regarding the position of psychiatry. The plans that many of us had worked with for years were not realised, the budget was reduced and appointments were retracted. A great deal of what we had planned and built up professionally and administratively during the Seventies and Eighties was about to be destroyed. Professional viewpoints were ignored more often than previously, both on the local and municipal level. The key priorities of the politicians and the administration were economy and retrenchment. At the same time, the pressure brought to bear upon our acute ward increased owing to a rising number of very ill patients being hospitalised and needing immediate help, but who often had to be discharged far too soon because there were not enough beds available. Even though in many ways it was a very good and effective department, with the staff doing an excellent job, I, as the leader, found the situation – to put it mildly – frustrating. I looked forward to my retirement a year from then.

At that time the hospital's management and my colleagues urged me to accept the position of head of the clinic, which implied acting as chief of psychiatry for the whole of Ullevål's psychiatric sector which embraces half of Oslo's population. On the one hand, I felt this to be a vote of confidence, while on the other hand, I was under considerable pressure. If I accepted the position I would have to postpone my retirement. I was aware of the fact that if I accepted a position of this kind during this turbulent period, it would entail having to confront some very unpleasant conflicts. Even though I clearly declined the offer, attempts were made to persuade me. I began to sleep badly.

Without any warning, I had an acute cardiac infarction and was hospitalised at the Bærum Hospital where I was treated well and effectively. I had not been prepared for something like this to happen. Now it became easy for me to make a decision regarding the job – I adhered to my original plan and would not be persuaded otherwise.

Afterwards I gave a great deal of thought as to why the infarction had struck me at that very moment. It was 'a shot across the bow', a warning from my body which I took heed of. This was, however, only a subjective experience and not a scientific proof of a causal connection. I realise that my age also played a role in my decision. Had I been younger I would probably have regarded the offer as a positive challenge and would have mobilised my resources in order to manage the task. But I was sixty-six years old and was looking forward to a different life in which I would fully be able to use my resources, both professionally and privately. I have since been very happy about the choice I made.

Every age and life phase has its tasks and challenges. A disparity between the life phase and stress may result in illness.

Biological rhythms and stress

We know that in addition to life phases the body also has biological rhythms which affect its susceptibility to disease. The diurnal rhythm fluctuating between daylight and the darkness of night influences the length of day. We have gained experience from, for example, jet lag and shift work. The lunar phases and the changing seasons also have an effect on us. We have hormonal rhythms such as women's monthly cycles triggered off by ovulation. This again is controlled by the hypophysis, the superior endocrine organ. These biological rhythms create oscillations in the body's cells, organs and biochemical processes, and in certain phases our resistance to illness is lower than in others.[20]

Animal experiments have shown that there is increased activity in the part of the brain called the reticular substance when the production of immune bodies increases. Experimentally provoked stress situations may influence the immune system. It has also been demonstrated in animal experiments that stress can affect the growth of tumours.[21]

There is not yet sufficient knowledge available about how the brain regulates and affects our immune system. Much research is being carried out in order to find an answer, but what we do know today is that there is a complex interaction between the nervous system, the endocrine system with the hormones, and enzymatic processes in the cellular systems.

The early relationship between mother and child

Psychological and psychoanalytical research has for many years pointed to the vital importance of the early relationship between mother and child, and to the fact that many psychic illnesses may have some of their roots in this early relationship (Chapters I and XIV). Psychosomatic research has now enlarged our understanding of why separation between mother and child may also have far-reaching consequences for our body, and moreover that this separation may often lie at the root of our vulnerability to losses later in life.

We know that the mother regulates the infant's behaviour, physiology, biochemistry and development of the brain. On separation, this regulating effect by the mother is interrupted, with serious consequences for the child's behaviour, physiology and development. Experiments with apes and other animals have shown that:

1. The young animal's balance apparatus (*vestibularis*) is stimulated when the mother carries the offspring and

plays with it. It reduces the rocking movements in young apes. When separated, they rock in order to stimulate themselves, they suck things more intensely, slap themselves and develop other stereotypical behaviour.

2. The milk from the mother regulates the offspring's sleep rhythm, the heart rhythm and respiratory rhythms. On separation the sleep rhythm is disturbed and the heart and respiratory rhythm is depressed.

3. Skin contact with the mother influences the level of the enzyme ornithinedecarboxylasis (OCD) in the brain and the heart. OCD is essential for the maturing of the brain, and influences the growth hormone. Skin contact also affects the young ape's ability to make sounds and it stimulates normal motory activity, thus counteracting the tendency to hyperactivity and self-stimulation which are typical consequences of separation. A number of other experiments have demonstrated that early separation or social isolation also effect changes in other important enzymes (for example, thyrosine hydroxylasis and phenylethanolamine-N-methyltransferasis).

4. The nest-warmth given by the mother decides the offspring's body temperature. This again regulates the cathecolamine level in the brain. If the body temperature sinks below three degrees, the young become less active and begin to stimulate themselves. If the temperature in the nest rises to a higher level than normal, it causes a reaction in the mother who will then leave the nest. We see an example here of how the circular interaction between mother and offspring influences the behaviour and physiology of both parties.[22,23]

The important aspect of these animal experiments is that they demonstrate how early experiences in a child's life may change its bodily functions. Through these experiments we have also gained more knowledge about how conditioning, separation and isolation may affect the endocrine apparatus, the autonomous nervous system and behaviour, and how these systems are modified through feedback mechanisms. However, we still know too little about what happens on the cellular and molecular level, and what it is that causes one organ system to be more vulnerable than another.

Summary

We have long known from psychoanalytic and other psychological experience and research that there is an interaction between body and soul, and that bodily symptoms and illness may partly be caused by psychosocial factors. We have also been aware for a long time that the foundation of this interaction is laid in the early relationship between mother and child, where there is no sharp boundary between the mother's body and feelings and the child's body and feelings, and before the child has developed an ego, a mature sensory apparatus and the ability for cognitive thinking.

Perhaps some of the causes for the phenomenon called alexithymia, the inability to express feelings in words, may be found in this early phase of our lives. This inability has been connected to individuals with a marked proneness to serious physical diseases, the so-called psychosomatic diseases. Current medicine is gradually beginning to regard the concept of psychosomatic as indicating mechanisms that apply to most diseases. It expresses a holistic perspective which concerns itself – not only with 'disease' – but with the entire individual as a bio-psycho-social unity. All the part-perspectives in this unity have a reciprocal effect on each other.

Biological research has become increasingly preoccupied with psychosomatic connections, while scientific methods and experiments with animals have expanded our understanding of some important mechanisms in the interaction between body and soul. Animal experiments have disclosed that a number of psychological and social influences cause physiological and bodily changes which are very similar to clinical diseases in humans. There is therefore strong evidence that social influences can change bodily functions via the nervous system.

Regarding the early mother–child relationship, there is also sufficient evidence to show that a mother initially functions as an external psychobiological regulator for her child's physiology and behaviour. She is therefore of the utmost importance for the child's development and maturation. The mother's importance for the child's psychobiological functions will gradually diminish, as the child's behaviour and its bodily functions become self-regulating and the inner autonomous mechanisms take over.

If this does not come about, the individual may later in life still be dependent on another person as external regulator. Can this be one of the causes why some people's psychological development and maturation has come to a halt and is characterised by what we call dependency? Is there perhaps also reason to believe that the loss of important persons may become a releasing factor for both psychic and physical illness?

However, protracted attachment and dependency on the mother may also have unfortunate consequences. The role of the father is also of decisive importance for the human child since he represents different aspects of the world of reality from the mother, and may help to loosen the bond between mother and child and their dependency on each other which has become too strong, or has lasted for too long (Chapters IX and XI).

Even though we have learnt a great deal from animal experiments, it is just as important to look at the qualities that distinguish us humans from animals. The development of the cerebrum in humans is a presupposition for our acquisition of language and thus the possibility of imparting knowledge and experience to new generations – the basis for all culture. Our higher degree of consciousness enables us to work through and postpone the gratification of our needs and drives, and to make choices. But choice implies both possibilities and risks.

Animals have better developed instincts which, to a large extent, direct their behaviour, while the fate of the human child is to be, for a long time, totally dependent on its nearest care persons and the psychosocial influence they represent. Here lies the foundation for our human and cultural potential, as well as for the risk of going astray and facing destruction. Again a balance between Scylla and Charybdis. The German professor of internal medicine, Arthur Jores, formulated this dilemma thus: 'the harmony that animals have been given as a gift, we humans have been given as a task'.[24,25]

NOTES TO THE TEXT

[1] Jørstad, J, *Sånn er livet, sånn er du og jeg,* Aschehoug, Oslo, 1986, 1987, 1989, pp.197–213.

[2] Sifneos, P, The prevalence of 'alexithymia' characteristics in psychosomatic patients, Psychoter. Psychosom. 22. pp.255–262, 1973.

[3] Taylor, G J, 'Alexithymia: Concept, measurements, and implications for treatment', Am. J. Psychiatry 141, pp.725–732, 1984.

[4] McDougall, J, 'Alexithymia, psychosomatosis and psychosis', Int. J. Psychoanal. Psychother., 83, 9, pp.379–388, 1982.

[5] ——*Theaters of the body,* W W Norton & Co., New York, 1989.

[6] Alexander, F, *Psychosomatic Medicine,* G Allen & Unwin, London, 1952.

[7] Nemiah, J C, 'Denial revisited. Reflections on psychological specificity in psychosomatic disorders', Psychother. Psychosom. 38, pp.39–45, 1982.

[8] Weinryb, R M, *Alexithymia – old wine in new bottles? I: Consutrction of a rating instrument for psychodynamic assessment (KAPP),* Karolineka Instituttet, Stockholm, 1992.

[9] Greer, S, 'Cancer and the Mind', Brit. J. Psychiatr, 143, pp.535–543, 1983.

[10] Stierlin, H and Grossarth Maticek, R, *Krebsrisiken-Überlebenschansen. Wie Körper, Seele und Soziale Umwelt Zusammenwirken,* Carl-Auer-Systeme Verlag, Heidelberg, 1998.

[11] Jacobs, T J and Charles, E, 'Life Events and the Occurrence of Cancer in Children', Psychosomatic Medicine, Vol. XLII, No. 1, pp.11–24, 1982.

[12] Weinryb, R M op.cit.

[13] Bassøe, H H and Eskeland, I, 'A prospective study of 133 patients with anorexia nervosa', Acta psychiatr. Scand., 65, 1982 pp.127–133.

[14] Weiner, H, 'The Prospects for Psychosomatic Medicine', Psychosomatic Medicine, 44, 6, 1982, pp.491–517.

[15] ——'Psychobiological factors in bodily disease', I: *Handbook of Health Care Clinical Psychology,* Eds. Millon, Green & Meager, Plenum Publ., New York, 1982.

[16] Syme, S L and Berkman, L F, 'Social class, susceptibility and sickness', Am. J. Epidemiol. 104, 1976, pp.1–8.

[17] Marmor, M G and Syme, S L, Acculturation and Coronary Heart Disease in Japanese-Americans, Am. J. Epidemiol., pp.104, 225–247, 1976.

[18] Syme, S L and Berkman, L F, op. cit.

[19] Weiner, H, op. cit.

[20] Weiner, H, op. cit.

[21] Weiner, H, op. cit.

[22] Weiner, H, op. cit.

[23] Hofer, M A, 'On the relationship between attachment and separation processes in infancy', I. *Emotion, Theory, Research and Experience*, Vol. II, Eds. Plutchick, Academic Press, New York, 1983.

[24] Jores, A, *Der Mensch und seiner Krankeit, Grundlagen einer antropologischen Medzin*, Ernst Klett, Stuttgart, 1956.

[25] ——Die Medizin in der Krise unserer Seit, Huber, Bern & Stuttgart, 1961.

Chapter XIV
THE INVISIBLE TRAUMAS
Loss, narcissistic injuries and generational narcissism

What do we have in common and what is individual?

One of the lessons I learned as a psychiatrist is that it is not easy to point to general causes for human suffering. Each individual differs from all other individuals. A confirmation of these differences can be found in every life history and case history. Moreover, there is always a complex interaction between external and internal conditions which together may bring about a crisis, a breakdown or mental illness.

However, I have lately been wondering about the similarities I have observed in many individuals who came to see me because they were in crisis and suffering from a mental illness. The fact that many of our underlying motives and drives are unconscious, poses problems when investigating the reasons for our specific reactions, I have attempted to illustrate this in several chapters of this book.

How then are we to make a general statement at all – one that will apply to the majority of people?

In spite of these objections, a number of studies have suggested certain general tendencies and consistent patterns observed in groups of people. These results have been incorporated in several sciences such as psychology, psychiatry, social anthropology and sociology. It has been possible to put individuals into different categories by using various points of departure and different methods. Sigmund Freud was the first to include the unconscious and irrational parts of the human mind, in an attempt to comprehend and explain the reasons for – not only psychic suffering – but also many aspects of human behaviour. Psychoanalysis put stronger emphasis on the individual perspective than on diagnostic categories and hence became a hermeneutic science, that is to say, it developed an empathic and interpretative attitude and method to human behaviour, similar to the attitude of historians and archaeologists towards historical finds.

This had far-reaching consequences for psychiatry which mostly relied on natural science, biological thought and method, and centred on descriptive, phenomenological diagnostics. Today, a psychoanalytically oriented, psychodynamic perspective, represents another new dimension in our psychiatric work. This perspective enabled me, and many others with me, to gain a far deeper understanding of what goes on in the minds of individuals. This has enhanced my daily work and made it far more meaningful.

What is psychic trauma?

Psychic trauma can be a sudden happening or protracted strain which injures us mentally. This is corroborated by the experience of many therapists who have found that crises and psychic symptoms often make their debut following external stress situations.[1] However, we are fully aware of the fact that different people react differently to the same trauma, so that the individual who is reacting becomes just as important as the trauma itself. Indeed, in many cases the trauma is basically the releasing factor, and in order to understand the individual's reactions to a traumatic experience, one has to focus on his or her *vulnerability*. Consequently, one of the prerequisites for understanding the backgrounds for crises, breakdowns and mental illness is an understanding of the interaction between the individual and the trauma he or she has been exposed to.

The psychodynamic perspective is particularly concerned with this interaction. It is founded on basic psychoanalytic concepts such as the power of the unconscious, the fundamental significance of childhood and the meaning of symptoms. When working psychoanalytically, or doing psychoanalytically oriented (psycho-dynamic) psychotherapy, we discover that a person's reaction to a trauma nearly always has a prior history containing additional traumas which have been active over a period of time.

Our life histories demonstrate that our vulnerability to present traumas nearly always has its roots in early childhood traumas of which we are not conscious. These early injuries are for the most part never due to isolated occurrences in childhood, but to a defective or conflict-laden relationship to close care persons, to a mother and father, under whose influence we had been for years, often spanning over several developmental phases. When old wounds are re-opened by later occurrences, our reactions may be very strong and may even cause psychiatric symptoms. The fact that the reasons for our vulnerability are often unconscious, represents one of the challenges confronting us in psychodynamic psychotherapy. There will always be unconscious defence mechanisms resisting painful experiences and preventing feelings from becoming conscious. These counter-forces can explain why many people have a need to idealise their parents and their childhood. Some behavioural patterns and attitudes are unconsciously transferred from generation to generation, quite apart from our genetic inheritance which also may contribute to our vulnerability.

The effect of summation is revealed by the fact that there are nearly always a number of reasons why an individual becomes mentally ill, one exception, however, being reactions to great catastrophes and accidents. In most cases the previous life history often contains several coinciding or consecutive stress situations. The same applies to conditions in childhood which may have been defective or traumatic. Sometimes the environment sees only the releasing factor of the reaction which may merely be the tip of the iceberg under which a great deal is concealed: experiences of loss, assault and inflicted harm, rejection, negligence and defeat, all of which had been harmful for years to the individual's self-esteem.

Sometimes this development will lead to symptoms which first make their appearance when 'our cup is full' and we have come to the end of our tether. This may sometimes occur seemingly without a releasing traumatic experience.

Two important questions arise:

1. Which traumas have the greatest influence on us and become most important as releasing factors of psychic illness?
2. When suffering traumas, what makes some of us more predisposed to psychic illness than others?

If we attempt to answer these questions, the importance of the link between them will soon become apparent.

Separation and loss

Psychiatric and psychotherapeutic experience and research suggest that we are most vulnerable to loss and separation, or the threat of it, from someone or something that is of special importance to us.[2,3] This vulnerability may be an important reason why we become anxious and depressed, and even psychosomatically ill, as I have mentioned in Chapter XIII. But this does not only apply to individuals who become patients. In an extensive study which graded the changes considered most traumatic for the majority of people, loss of the partner came out on top, next came divorce, separation, a prison sentence and the death of a close family member. Losing one's job or having to retire were graded as numbers eight and ten.[4]

Our general vulnerability to loss and separation has its roots in our total dependence on our mothers at the very beginning of our lives. This is vital for our survival, and we may all have experienced situations in our childhood when we were separated from our mother. However, it depends greatly on how often we were left alone, for how long, and the manner in which this happened.

Another core issue is the question whether the early mother–child relationship in the first year of our lives gave us a basic trust and confidence in ourselves and the world. We are most vulnerable to separation and loss in the phase termed separation–individuation phase, between the age of nine months and three years. In this phase we take the first steps towards freeing ourselves emotionally from our mother, but we are still totally dependent on having easy access to her.[5]

It is during these important years that transitional objects,[6] like the comfort cloth and the teddy bear become valuable symbolic substitutes for mother. It is also during these years that the foundation for separation anxiety is laid, which is at the core of the anxiety we may experience as adults – the actual fear of being abandoned by our mother. For a small child who is totally dependent on its mother, abandonment means catastrophe. In many cases, separation anxiety is a result of the ignorance of former generations of parents who still believed that picking up babies when they cried would spoil them. We know better now: a small child cannot be spoiled. The best help for an anxious or unhappy child is to be taken up and comforted, to let the child feel the mother's or father's warm body, hear their soothing voices, to be given milk when it is hungry and a dry nappy when it is wet.

A few decades ago it was usual for mother and child to be separated if one of them had to be hospitalised. Fortunately this is one of the areas where increased knowledge and better information have lead to a totally different practice.

Separation anxiety is one of the reasons why many of us cannot be alone, and why we all in different ways try to safeguard ourselves against loss. Some people's strategy is an attempt to control others, to bind or manipulate them, or to gain power over them. Others develop an opposite strategy – they safeguard themselves by rejecting close contact with others for fear of becoming dependent on them, and then having to experience the loss of those on whom they have become dependent. Most of us try to find a middle course between these two extremes, and are clever at finding compensations for our need for security, and for safeguarding ourselves against loss. Some people become deeply involved in politics, religion or club activities. Others may collect money or expensive items by way of compensation. But, this is of course, not the only motive for taking up interests like these.

The fear of losing a mother's or father's love may resemble separation anxiety, but its origins are to be found in a later period of childhood. The child's dependence on a father's or mother's love and on their approval, may easily be exploited by parents who cannot tolerate their child's natural need for self-expression, its need to test the limits of how far it can go, and its need to protest. This intolerant attitude may bring forth 'good' and submissive children whose self-confidence and need for independence has been impaired for life. Loss may consequently become traumatic, even if it is not linked to the loss of a person. For example, if we lose something else that is important to us, such as a part of our body, for example, an arm or a leg. Or, in the case of a woman, a breast which has to be removed because of a tumour. A change in our body image or our looks may also be experienced as a traumatic loss. The same applies to losing a job, becoming unemployed, having to leave one's house – or 'losing face'. Being publicly humiliated, and being the loser when competing for a job, or in sport.

The common denominator for all such losses is lower self-esteem. The more vital the object of our loss for our self-esteem, the greater the trauma of the loss. Many of us are very dependent on relationships with people, and loss of them – or impending loss of them may therefore affect us deeply and possibly trigger off a psychic illness. In particular, anxiety, depressive reactions, and suicidal attempts in people with borderline disorders.

Injuries

Injury to one's self-esteem may also be part of the background to psychic illness. We can often observe a combination of loss and injury when, for example, we lose our prestige or our job. Some people feel that illness or growing old is a mortification, while others feel hurt by any form of criticism or disagreement. Here we can again observe great differences in the degree of our vulnerability and in the areas in which we are most vulnerable. It is therefore important to understand what lies behind extreme vulnerability.

The past twenty years have provided a greater body of knowledge about the defects and traumas which have grave consequences for children during the separation–individuation phase, inasmuch as they may lead to the development of a personality disorder.[7,8,9] The most common disorder is called borderline personality disorder. Individuals with this type of personality disorder often have characteristically unstable, shifting personal relationships. Low self-esteem and a weak identity, primitive defence mechanisms (the tendency to place their own feelings into others by means of projection, and to split the world into black and white, thus experiencing other people and themselves as either only bad, or only good). They often have difficulties controlling their own aggression. Some end up abusing alcohol or other drugs, or leading promiscuous or criminal lives.

A common trait in many of these cases is extreme vulnerability which we can better understand when long-term psychotherapies provide us with a knowledge of the defects, injuries, abuses and serious traumas these individuals had been exposed to during their childhood. As a rule, they never had the opportunity to develop confidence in either themselves or in others.

Research which was done on families of patients where there was a history of grave mental illness, particularly schizophrenic psychoses, point in the same direction.[10,11,12,13,14] Here too we often find that in these families both parents are mentally extremely disturbed and egocentric. The family dynamics in these families may include extreme forms of either binding or rejection, disturbed communication and the transgression of boundaries as in the case of incest. This, however, cannot fully explain the incidence of schizophrenic psychosis in some individuals, but it may point to a significantly traumatic background for those growing up in families as described above.

In her books, the Swiss psychoanalyst Alice Miller raises the point that pathological narcissism does not only characterise those who become psychiatric patients, but that it can also be observed in many parents in today's society.[15] Children of these parents will as a result adapt themselves to the demands and the self-centredness of the adults at the expense of their own selves. They will develop 'a false self', an adult well-adjusted and socially well-functioning shell which conceals a neglected, underdeveloped, lonely and unhappy child. But this will only be revealed during long-term psychotherapy or psychoanalysis (Chapter IX).

The myth of Narcissus

A story in Greek mythology has two protagonists: Narcissus and Echo. Narcissus was a very handsome young man, so spoiled by his mother that he believed himself to be one of the gods. He was admired by all, but he was arrogant and had a cold heart. The nymph Echo had the unpleasant habit of incessant chatter, which so irritated the goddess Hera that she decided that from then onwards Echo would only be able to repeat the last words said by others. One day in the woods, as Echo caught a glimpse of Narcissus between the trees, she fell deeply in love with him, but was unable to utter a word. Only when he shouted: 'Is anyone there?' was she at last able to answer 'there'. She ran to him and threw herself into his arms. Narcissus rejected her coldly and Echo, deeply disappointed, ran away and hid herself in the woods. There she remains, a lonely voice answering our calls.

Later, Narcissus came to a spring with a smooth clear surface and bent down to drink the water. When he saw his own reflection in the water, he fell so much in love with it that he wanted to kiss him whom he saw down there. However, each time he tried, the image of the loved one disappeared. After three vain attempts, he grew so furious that he shouted, 'You are rejecting me! I cannot live without you!' He then pierced his heart with his knife. As he was collapsing, he called out, 'Farewell – my beloved!' And from far off Echo answered, 'My beloved!'[16]

Echo and Narcissus personify two aspects of the same problem, namely, a reaction to lack of self-esteem and the ability to love oneself in a healthy and natural manner. Narcissus's ideas of grandiosity prevent him from loving anyone but himself. He believed himself to be one of the gods; that is his hubris, his arrogance. For that reason he rejects heterosexual love but is trapped in his own reflection and self-hate and must therefore die. Echo's endless chatter demonstrates her defence against her inner emptiness and lack of identity; she needs to be loved by others to gain confirmation of her own worth. When she does not receive love, she loses her identity and becomes a mere echo of others.

This myth therefore tells us that there may be two factors leading to the loss of the self being spoiled by one's mother and being exposed to the wrath of the goddess (mother). Perhaps there are also certain implications in the myth that mothers and fathers treat their sons and daughters differently, and this may result in differences in the narcissism of men and women.[17]

Normal narcissism

Freud made use of this myth in his metapsychological theories about normal and pathological phenomena, a subject which I do not intend to enlarge upon here. What we call normal narcissism is partly connected to a stage in our childhood, and partly to a very important element in the self-esteem and self-confidence we all need to possess. We may say that we are all dependent on being mirrored by one or several people who will confirm the image we have of ourselves, that we are special and of value, and worthy of love. This is particularly important during the second year of our lives, when we consider ourselves to be the very centre of the universe, and have fantasies about being powerful and strong; this is the time when we conquer the world. Mother and father are our first gods, as well as being our obedient servants, who are there to satisfy all our needs. Kohut gives the term 'self-object' to a mirroring person, whom we do not experience as an independent individual, but more or less as part of ourselves.[18]

This normal narcissism can be explained psychologically as a defence against being so small, so helpless and dependent. It is therefore important that parents do not deprive us of this illusion too early. On the contrary, they should support us during this period. This comes naturally to most parents. Most of us have therefore been able to mirror ourselves in the admiring love of mother and father – they were our first self-objects.

As children, we were also self-objects for mother and father, we mirrored them as part of themselves and confirmed their good parenting. As time went by, most of us gradually started to discover reality and were slowly able to renounce our egocentric picture of the world, and our inflated self-esteem, our grandiose self.

Most parents with normal self-esteem will gradually be able to let go of their child as a mirror and confirmation of their own worth. But it is most important that during the first years of their child's life, parents are present and accessible. That they respect the child and its feelings and that they make the child the centre of their own activities.

Normal narcissism can be expressed as simply that: we have to love ourselves in order to be able to love others. In other words, that we possess a fair amount of self-esteem, self-confidence and an ability for self-expression, that our feelings are confirmed and that we feel both understood and are able to understand others. Also, that we can give, take and tolerate both praise and criticism; and last but not least, that we feel worthy of being loved without believing ourselves to be so much better or of more value than others.

Narcissistic vulnerability and grandiosity

There may be many reasons for complications in a child's development. As in the myth, mother or father may spoil us, in the sense that we may remain mother's or father's self-object far beyond the normal narcissistic phase. Or perhaps we may receive too little 'mirroring' and confirmation during the period when this is of the utmost importance to us. We may be deprived of our illusions too early or too brutally, if the mirroring suddenly and unpredictably turns into rejection or punishment. These and other conditions may coincide with the result that the child's development becomes fixated at this stage.

At this point I would like to recall the concept of optimal frustration, which is an important factor in the child's gradual process of separation and individuation. It explains why too much or too little may be equally harmful. Too many frustrations caused, for example, by an authoritarian upbringing, will weaken the child's self-esteem. The grandiose self will be repressed but may emerge in the adult at a later stage as latent self-destructive behaviour. Too few frustrations with over-protective parents who spoil the child, will prevent its necessary experience of reality testing, and the grandiose self will continue its existence.

The third and most harmful form of frustration is the one caused by parents not being present; when parents are unable to make the child feel sufficiently secure by their closeness. Under these conditions the child's self-esteem is damaged, reality is not tested, and the child's feelings become 'voiceless' because it receives neither response nor confirmation. I believe that we may find here one of the causes of the phenomenon called alexithymia, lacking words for expressing feelings, which – when the symptoms are pronounced – is considered as a predisposition to psychosomatic disturbances (Chapter XIII).

The results of these narcissistic traumas may differ greatly, depending on the degree and the manner in which these injuries are compensated for. Some people are able to hide their wounds from themselves and others behind the facade of an apparently well-adjusted personality, but are more or less blocked in their contact with their own feelings. These are people who – according to Winnicott – have developed 'a false self', and whom Joyce McDougall calls 'normopaths'.[1920]

Others do not succeed in compensating their narcissistic vulnerability, and will therefore more or less avoid all situations that may lead to provocations or confrontations, criticism or conflict. They retreat into loneliness and social isolation and may find compensation in daydreams and fantasies of grandiosity. Others may develop pathological narcissism, which is characterised by the individual's grandiose self.

According to our present knowledge, pathological narcissism can be seen as a result of serious defects and traumas in early childhood, and as an unconscious defence against the unbearable pain that lies hidden in the depths. Any attack and any form of criticism may then be experienced as a threat against the individual's self-esteem, as an insult or as rejection, and may provoke violent rage. Indeed, mere doubting or questioning about the opinions held by such an individual will cause offence. 'He who is not with me is against me!' In fact, a good deal of pathological narcissism can often be observed in authoritarian individuals. This applies even more to psychopaths who, in addition to pathological narcissism, also have asocial or antisocial character traits.[21]

I wish to emphasise five qualities that are characteristic of pathological narcissism:

1. Pronounced egocentricity.
2. Pronounced projective tendency. Little or no ability to acknowledge weaknesses or faults in oneself. The others are always to blame.
3. Pronounced vulnerability. Small frustrations may provoke fits of rage.
4. Lack of empathy. Little or no ability for a deep understanding of others.
5. Fantasies of grandiosity, conscious or unconscious. They may influence attitudes and behaviour in the form of grandiosity, arrogance and dominance.

In our psychoanalytic and psychotherapeutic work we very often come across narcissistic injuries stemming from childhood. There is often a core of narcissistic vulnerability in psychopathology, with a possible background in the pathological narcissism of one or both parents. In other words: lack of mirroring and confirmation during childhood, and narcissistic abuse of children by their parents, causes deep vulnerability, and is particularly injurious to the self-esteem. This does not only apply to individuals with psychic illness or an obviously narcissistic personality, but also to many others who seemingly are normal and well-adjusted. Indeed, perhaps we are all tarred with the same brush.

Some examples

David is a forty-six year old man who sought therapy on account of depression and anxiety, trembling, and difficulties with his breathing and speech. He complains of lacking self-confidence, of constantly having a bad conscience, having anxiety about achieving and feeling defeated. It is as though brakes are put on any pleasure or joy that he may feel. He withdraws socially, but is able to 'put on an act' of being social whenever it is necessary. In recent years he has resorted to alcohol, a few drinks daily; it helps for a while. David is a talented and well educated man, married and with children. He functions fairly well in his work.

Speaking about his background, he says that his father was very religious, depressive, he was introverted, self-centred and a hypochondriac. He never acted naturally, but was pompous and stilted in his manner. He spoke about how often David had disappointed or hurt him, and that David ought to be grateful. His mother prattled all day long, she 'killed us with her prattle', she 'thought aloud', was self-centred, and eager to keep up appearances. She had lost her own mother when she was eight years old. David had never been in personal or close contact with either of his parents, he could never talk to them about anything. 'Mother closed the door, father only spoke in biblical terms'.

Mary is a thirty year old woman with panic anxiety. She is suffering from muscular tensions, dizziness, nausea, palpitations of the heart and sleeping difficulties. Mary lives a socially secluded life, 'only a quarter of a life' as she says. She is a lesbian, has never had a close relationship with a man, and in the only lesbian relationship she ever had, there was a great deal of conflict which made her feel very guilty. Her anxiety started when her father fell acutely ill. Mary is the eldest of two sisters, and her parents never concealed how disappointed they had been at her birth because she was not a boy. Her upbringing had been authoritarian and rigorously Christian – 'spiritual torture' in her own words. Opposition was unthinkable and one never spoke about feelings or personal matters. Her father, who held a position of authority in society, was remote, impersonal and socially insecure, yet strongly attached to this daughter, with incestuous undertones. Her mother was extremely immature, egocentric and hysterical, she had violent fits of rage which terrified the girls throughout their childhood. Mary always felt rejected by her mother, she cannot remember ever having come into physical or emotional contact with her. From an early age, she had been strongly attached to her father, and felt responsible for the life and well-being of both parents, as though she were their parent. All her life she has felt the necessity of keeping her own weaknesses and feelings under control, of acting rationally and in an adult fashion, or else they would all be struck by a catastrophe. She gradually developed a typical character neurosis, or a false self. Outwardly, she gave the impression of being strong, sober, rational and independent, but underneath there was grandiosity, as a defence against her low self-esteem, inner loneliness and helplessness.

Ingerid was a thirty year old unmarried woman with a borderline personality disorder. She had great problems with close relationships and sex, she had periods of depression and suffered from social anxiety. When she was sixteen, she developed anorexia nervosa which improved when she sought short-term psychotherapy after some years. In her twenties there was a period of alcohol abuse, but she succeeded in overcoming it and doing well in her academic studies. Her father came from an eccentric, pious rural community and when Ingerid was a small child he became psychotic and was hospitalised for a while. Her mother was manifestly egocentric and had depressive periods, she had not established boundaries between herself and this daughter who was an only child. In Ingerid's childhood the mother had strong haemorrhages which necessitated a lengthy stay in hospital. Ingerid was then left with her father as the only available care person. Her parents' marriage was unhappy and full of conflict. When she was a small child, Ingerid had an incestuous relationship with her father who pawed her genitals. When she became adolescent, her parents showed a keen interest in her body. Her father enjoyed making food for her and during the period of her excessive alcohol intake, he also bought her beer.

Even though the histories of these three patients are sketchily drawn, it is not difficult to find a common element in all three of them. This one can also be observed in the case of very many other patients: all these three patients had two parents with narcissistic problems. None of these parents had been sufficiently present, none of them had mirrored and confirmed the child during its separation–individuation phase or later. They had therefore not been able to give the child physical or psychic nearness, except a closeness compromised by incest. In the one case, the parents had not been able to accept the sex of the child, in the other two cases, the parents had been aggressive towards the child and had used it excessively to satisfy their own needs.

It gradually emerged that these parents had themselves experienced serious losses and/or injuries in childhood.

Summary

My experiences and those of my colleagues can be interpreted as follows: Apart from loss, the parents' narcissism is the most common and serious cause for the traumatisation of children. From a three-generational perspective, we can often see that both parents had experienced losses, injuries or other traumas when they themselves had been children, which had undermined their security, their self-esteem and identity development. They were therefore not able to give to their child an adequate mirroring presence, confirmation and respect. Instead, they used the child to satisfy their own narcissistic needs, exploited its dependence and guilt feelings, by using overprotection as a cover, or by spoiling the child, or giving it a so-called 'Christian upbringing', or by not setting limits in their mutual relationship. In this way, the parents took centre stage, at the expense of the child's own self and its own life. A great deal of this takes place in the unconscious of both parties and can be totally concealed from the outside world.

Narcissistic problems start early in a child's life and continue for years through many developmental phases. They cause all types and degrees of psychopathology: neuroses, personality disorders or psychoses, which are characterised by both defects and conflicts.

Physical violence and incestuous abuse of children can be seen as a partial problem and as a result of underlying narcissistic problems in parents. The same applies to separation traumas, even though we must take into account that these were partly a result of the ignorance of previous generations, and were not dictated by insensitivity to the dependence, and vulnerability of children and their need for closeness.

There is always an interaction between traumas and the individual's reaction. Since a child cannot in the beginning differentiate between fantasy and reality, the child's fantasies may contribute to, and reinforce the consequences of external traumas. This does not minimise the significance of external traumas, but it may help to enhance an understanding of the consequences of traumas. This is overlooked by those who accuse Freud of having discarded his original seduction theory (Chapter X).

If psychiatrists only focus their attention on the present life situation of a patient, they may come to neglect the early roots of this patient's problems, as well as the generational issues involved. If social-psychiatric studies of the significance of social conditions for the incidence of psychic illness are the only concerns in therapy, then important issues will also be overlooked.

In some patients, the narcissistic core can be reached and worked through in the course of long-term psychoanalysis or psychodynamic psychotherapy. In the transference to the therapist, loss and injuries can be re-experienced and worked through, and the therapist's countertransference may be an effective tool for understanding the patient's suffering and pain which reaches back into childhood.

One of the results of our having 'forgotten' most of our childhood is, that we are apt to continue 'forgetting' and disregarding our knowledge about how dependent, sensitive and vulnerable we had been as children, in those days, when all our reactions had been physical and emotional. A child's feelings must indeed be taken seriously and met with respect, so that a firm basis for genuine self-esteem and healthy narcissism can be ensured.

NOTES TO THE TEXT

[1] Cullberg, J, *Kris och utveckling*, Natur o Kultur, Stockholm, 1975.

[2] Bowlby, J, *Attachment and Loss*, Vol. III, Loss, Sadness and Depression, Hogarth Press, London, 1980.

[3] Spitz, R A, *The First Year of Life*, Int. Univ. Press, New York, 1965.

[4] Holmes, T H and Rahe, R H, 'The social readjustment rating scale', J. Psychosomat. Res11, 1967, pp.213–218.

[5] Mahler, M S, Pine, F, and Bergmann, A, *The Psychological Birth of the Human Infant*, Hutchinson, London, 1975.

[6] Winnicott, D W, *Playing and Reality*, Tavistock Publ., London, 1971.

[7] Evang, A, *Utvikling, Personlighet og borderline*, Cappelen, Oslo, 1986.

[8] Kohut, H, *The Restoration of the Self*, Int. Univers. Press., New York, 1977.

[9] Kernberg, O, *Borderline Conditions and Pathological Narcissism*, Jason Aronson, New York, 1975.

[10] Lidz, T *The Origin and Treatment of Schizophrenic Disorders*, Basic Books, New York, 1973.

[11] Lidz, T and Fleck, S, *Schizophrenia and the Family*, Int. Univers. Press, New York, 1985.

[12] Wynne, I C, and Singer, M T, 'Thought disorder and family relations of schizophrenics', II, Arch. Gen. Psychiatr. 9, 1963, p. 199.

[13] Stierlin, H, *Conflict and Reconciliation. A study of human relations and schizophrenia*, Science House, New York, 1969.

[14] Alanen, O Y, 'The family in the patogenesis of schizophrenic and neurotic disorders', Acta. Psychiat. Scand. 42, 1958, p. 189.

[15] Miller, A, *Du sollst nicht merken*, Suhrkamp, Frankfurt, 1981.

[16] Thielst, P, *Narkissos og Ekko*, Hans Reitzels Forlag, København, 1989.

[17] Jørstad, J, 'Narcissism and Leadership: Some differences in male and female leaders', Nord. J. Psychiatry, 1995, 49, pp.409–416.

[18] Kohut, H, op. cit.

[19] Winnicott, D W, *Playing and Reality*, Tavistock Publ., London, 1971.

[20] McDougall, J., *Theaters of the body*, W.W. Norton & Co., New York, 1989.

[21] Kernberg, O.F. *Severe Personality Disorders*, Yale Univers. Press, New Haven and London, 1984.

Chapter XV
WORDS AND LACK OF WORDS – OPPORTUNITIES AND LIMITATIONS
On communication in psychotherapy

Words have so many uses

In psychotherapy, words are indispensable tools for communicating between therapist and patient, even though a great deal takes place without words. In a sense, words are also a balancing act – between speech and emotions, between speaking and silence, theory and life, fantasy and reality, fragments and wholeness, and between our external and internal worlds.

Concepts and theories can serve to create structure, order and system in psychotherapeutic work – to provide a sense of connectedness and meaning to our understanding of the external and internal realities of both patient and therapist, and to the way in which these interact. Words can also be used by both parties to attain opposite goals: to prevent communication, to create distance, to confuse and obscure issues, to separate feelings from words, and as an escape from reality. As therapists, we are aware of that these strategies are part of the patient's defence mechanism and resistance. But even we may sometimes resort to artificial phrases and empty words in order to cover up our uncertainty or ignorance. Words can also be used as weapons in overt or covert power struggles between patient and therapist, as they can in other interpersonal relationships. Sometimes we regard this as an interaction between transference and countertransference.

The fear of words may express our basic fear of the unknown in ourselves, or the fear of facing reality. The Norwegian saying

'Words may awaken the trolls' signifies the magical power of words, and can be traced back to an almost universal fear, a remnant from the magical years of childhood, when we did not distinguish between fantasy, word and action. This fear is enhanced by our experiences while growing up, as well as by cultural influences: in many circles it is often simply not done to say what one means or feels. It may therefore seem dangerous, even catastrophic, to put feelings and fantasies into words. In psychotherapy, the opposite is often the case: the trolls thriving in the darkness of the nether world must be brought up into the light, and when they are, they burst. Indeed, sometimes the right word at the right time may help to sharpen the awareness of both patient and therapist.

One of the challenges in current psychotherapeutic work is the apparently increasing number of patients who have blockages between words and feelings, and who may even partly lack words to describe their feelings (Chapter XIII). Some of these individuals may have been understimulated by their childhood environment, others may have defects or injuries that can be traced back to a wordless period early in their lives. How then can we reach these individuals with our words? Is it possible to impart something to them without words? This is not only a concern regarding our patients. Similar phenomena are also seen in many of us who are the therapists.

Words as communication

While minding three of my grandchildren aged one, three and five, some time ago, I was again reminded of the significance of words on a fundamental level. I was struck by the intense joy expressed by the three year old when using words – words that communicated something she had experienced, something that she could offer her grandfather who would listen to her words and understand them. I listened to her, understood and confirmed to her that I knew what she was telling me. Her eagerness to explain as much as possible in as short a time as possible, her joy about mastering the language and being able to reach me was quite obvious.

This is a recurrent phenomenon in psychotherapeutic dialogues: putting thoughts and feelings into words, finding the right words, getting through to the other person and experiencing that the words are heard and accepted, and that they have an impact on the other person because the answer confirms that one has been understood. It is this type of dialogue between two people that furthers the therapeutic process.

Dialogues, where the cognitive and symbolic content of words is confirmed by the other, can also take place outside therapy – as in the example with my small grandchild. The factors common in these dialogues are time and space, presence, accessibility and responsiveness, and they require a minimum of mutual sympathy in both partners, as well as mutual trust and respect.

In a dialogue of this kind the words cannot be seen as isolated phenomena, they cannot be detached from their context. Moreover, they convey nuances of feelings, attitudes and values by the way in which they are pronounced. Form and content are inextricably connected to external and internal reality in space and time, and to the way in which the words are connected to people and things outside ourselves. Internal reality is revealed through our recognition of the other person's importance to us, and through the emotions, inner images and fantasies which are connected to him or her. It also reveals itself in the extent to which our emotions are contained in the words, and how they influence the non-verbal part of our communication: our breathing, voice, tone of voice, facial expressions and movements. Different intonations of one and the same word can give widely different meanings, for example, recognition or hatred, love or violent dislike.

The psychotherapeutic relationship, however, is unique and different from all other human relationships. In addition to the aspect of shared humanity, mutuality and dialogue, there is also a professional relationship in which the therapist and the patient have different roles. A psychotherapist is a person with a specialised education, training and experience. In psychotherapy, the use of words and feelings are regulated and restricted. The therapist must not tell all he or she thinks and feels unless it is relevant to the therapy situation. And yet a therapist will always communicate something about his or her person, and about his or her conscious and unconscious feelings on a non-verbal level – without words.

The patient is usually a person who has personally applied for help, and who is supposed to cooperate by expressing as directly and as honestly as possible in words whatever comes to his or her mind and what he or she feels. The aim of the treatment is to reduce painful symptoms, and to achieve a measure of personal development and growth. We know that it is this specific difference between psychotherapy and other human relationships that is necessary for a therapy to be successful. This is why the boundaries between the patient and the therapist are so important, since the balance between closeness and distance may have both physical and linguistic consequences. A friendship or a love affair between the therapist and the patient will destroy these boundaries and with it the entire therapy.

Closeness and distance

As a very young and inexperienced physician at the beginning of my career, I once went the rounds at the Furuli ward at Oslo City mental hospital, Dikemark. I saw a newly arrived male patient in his thirties sitting in the room, and in my ignorance I went up to him, sat down on a chair next to him and said a few friendly words. After a few seconds, he rose and firmly planted a clenched fist straight into my face so that blood spurted from my broken nose, and my smashed glasses tinkled across the floor. In a flash I saw a young man with a diagnosis of catatonic schizophrenia, who had been standing immobile on a corner, suddenly come alive and throw himself onto my assailant, enabling me to escape and lock myself into the ward office. The aides who had witnessed this scene hurried away to fetch help. This was the only time I was ever physically attacked by a patient.

This episode taught me several important lessons: firstly, that being physically close to another person may be felt by some patients as an intense provocation and frighten them. This particular man, who was suffering from paranoid psychosis, had experienced my physical closeness as an intrusion – as well as a homosexual provocation, as he later told. My empty words and phrases had at the same time revealed my insecurity, helplessness and ignorance, proving to this man that I did not understand the terror he felt when someone tried to approach him. Secondly, this episode taught me that it can often be useful to be very patient when trying to make contact with severely ill, schizophrenic patients, even if they withhold a verbal answer for a long time. I had tried for several months to make contact with the young man who had come to my aid. Often we only sat silently next to each other. If I said anything, he would more often than not only give a monosyllabic reply. But a silence can also be meaningful. He had noticed my presence and had come to my rescue when I really needed it.

Silence in psychotherapy can convey interest, respect, thoughtfulness and attempts at understanding, thus giving room for important developments in the psychotherapeutic process. On the other hand, silence may also convey distance, rejection, anger or attempts at concealing ignorance.

The language behind the language

Ten years later I returned to Dikemark after having worked at two other hospitals, Ullevål and Lovisenberg. I had become a specialist in psychiatry and held the post of consultant physician at the Lien ward at Dikemark. Meanwhile, the chief physician, Harald Frøshaug, had effected some changes in the ward. He had realised the importance of providing active milieu therapy, and also – if possible – individual psychotherapy, for severely ill schizophrenic patients.

One of the first patients in my care at Lien was a schizophrenic woman in her thirties to whom I began giving systematic psychotherapy. At the time of our initial contact, she was acutely ill with massive delusions of persecution and auditive hallucinations. Before being admitted to the hospital, she had thrown herself in front of a tramcar because an inner voice had commanded her to do so.

This therapy continued for several years, first in the ward, and later, after she had been discharged, in the outpatients' department. Since then we have kept in touch sporadically, mostly by letter or telephone. She is one of the patients who has taught me a great deal about schizophrenia, about the pain, loneliness and anxiety involved, and also that psychotherapy may be of the utmost importance, and even be felt to be life-saving by the patient.

One of the first things she taught me was what she called 'the language behind the language'. In her – at times – strange and incoherent language with unknown words and symbols, there often emerged a deeper meaning which gradually became more intelligible as we continued to explore this form of communication over months and years. In her special language, the apparently meaningless actually contained meanings. Important personal messages were wrapped up and squeezed together into this language: It was a 'language behind the language'. I had to learn to 'listen with my third ear', and try to empathise with her psychotic world.

She taught me the significance of being visible and 'alive' in my role as a physician and therapist by telling me about a doctor outside the hospital whom she had been seeing before being hospitalised. He had been distant, silent and passive, and had gradually become merely a bad projection figure for her. During a session I once impulsively made some very personal and emotional remarks. Afterwards she told me that she had suddenly perceived me as a real person, and not just as someone playing a role. It had been a turning point for her – she could now more easily conceive of me as a helper with whom it was possible to cooperate.

The third lesson I learned from this patient was about the time perspective involved in a psychotherapy with a schizophrenic patient. It is vital for the therapist to persist, to be patient and not to expect results after just a short time. His or her ability to tolerate, contain and persist may be decisive to the outcome. It is particularly important to be able to tolerate the knowledge that there is so much we can neither understand nor explain, at any rate at the beginning.

A few years later this patient moved to a different part of the country and we remained in contact, mostly by letter. It was then that I learned about a fourth perspective in psychotherapy. After many years of working together with a patient, we may be 'incorporated' by the patient, internalised, and thus become an inner helper, independent of our physical presence. For many years, the letters written to me by this patient usually contained an inner dialogue which she had had with me, especially in situations where she had to confront problems and difficulties, or in times of crises. It was then that she had these inner conversations with me which she reported to me in her letters. It was a strange experience to read them; they expressed what I actually would have thought and said if she and I had had a real conversation. As a rule these imaginary dialogues did not contain any repetitions of what I had said to her in previous sessions. My only reply to her could be: 'Yes, that is exactly what I would have thought and said, you were quite right.' This ability to 'incorporate the therapist', to internalise him or her, highlights the importance of the therapeutic dialogue.

Concepts and theories

Studying psychiatry in Oslo introduced me to a great number of new words, most of which were connected to symptoms and diagnoses. The lectures helped to clarify the psychiatric concepts, the patients were divided into categories and systems, and the treatment consisted mostly of drugs, electroconvulsive therapy (ECT), and common sense-dialogues. When interviewing patients, one of our professors displayed a shocking lack of sensitivity. There was obviously a considerable disparity between theory and practice, and between the words in the textbooks and those that were articulated. Needless to say, our teachers did not realise how repulsive their attitudes seemed to the students and how much they contributed to the generally negative image of psychiatry.

After graduating, I set up a practice in the country and discovered that psychic or psychosomatic symptoms were predominant in my patients, even though they would often present only a physical symptom as an alibi. The knowledge I had acquired during my student days was not sufficient to enable me to understand many of these patients, and even less to know what I could do to help them. All these words and diagnoses were not particularly helpful in the real world. I also gradually discovered that many people who came to my office because of physical afflictions, were in reality troubled by problems and stress in their life situations and in their relationships to other people. While trying hard to comprehend, I detected the presence of strong irrational feelings and reactions in my patients and in myself – phenomena which I had never heard about in my student days. Some patients seemed repulsive to me and others were attractive without there being any rational basis for such feelings. Some patients did not seem to improve although I was convinced that I had given them the right treatment, while others seemed to get well even though I knew that I had done nothing except listen to what they told me, and then examine them.

These experiences encouraged me to specialise in psychiatry and learn more about the irrational aspects of the doctor/patient relationship. In my subsequent work with psychiatric patients, this relationship came increasingly into focus, and concepts such as transference and countertransference, resistance and defence mechanisms, regression and repetition compulsion, helped me to understand irrational phenomena. Some of my colleagues and I attended introductory lectures on the theory and concepts of psychoanalyis at the Institute for Psychotherapy.

In subsequent years, annual seminars were held by well known Norwegian and foreign psychotherapists, during spring at Dikemark hospital, and during autumn at Modum Bads Nervesanatorium. These seminars greatly influenced my work with patients who were in psychotherapy with me.[1]

With the years, from studying the writings of Sigmund Freud and some of his successors who further developed his theories, we acquired a great number of new concepts and theories. I have also been fascinated by several neo-Freudian theories – egopsychology and the concepts of existential analysis. Later, object-relation theory and Kohut's self-psychology greatly helped me in my understanding of patients with early injuries and defects.[2,3,4,5,6,7,8,9,10,11,12]

For many of my colleagues and myself, technical terms such as psychic energy, cathexis, id, ego, superego, inner objects, self-objects, defence mechanisms, etc. began imperceptibly to acquire dimensions linking them to reality. In our minds they no longer were mere theoretical concepts and auxiliary constructions, but became genuine phenomena and internal structures. Special fields, such as psychology and psychiatry tend to lead to intellectualising and psychologising. The concepts and theories may then serve as a means of distancing ourselves from personal and emotional relationships, thus preventing a deeper understanding of our inner world and that of others. Diagnoses and theories can also be exploited to demonstrate one's own knowledge and skills, or as an instrument of power compensating for one's uncertainty and impotence.

In his article 'Knowledge, learning and lack of thought', the English psychoanalyst Tom Main describes a phenomenon which terms 'the hierarchical promotion of ideas'.[13] With this he implies that words and knowledge formally linked to personal and poignant experiences will, in time, rise to ever higher levels in our inner world. Finally they will establish themselves on the superego level as cut and dried 'truths'. Words that were once integrated with our feelings and therefore a source of mastering, joy, growth and development, will harden into dogmas with which we can hit others on the head, thus demonstrating our superiority by laying down the law. In psychotherapeutic work this is a manifestation of narcissism, of our need to demonstrate our excellence. It interferes with our ability to listen to the patient's verbal and non-verbal messages, and does not make room for thoughtfulness and a joint exploration of the inner world and outer reality.

Words without feeling

One of the specific unconscious defence mechanisms is isolation, where words are split off – and isolated – from emotions and effects. This phenomenon can often be observed in individuals with compulsion neurosis and psychosomatic illnesses. In a paper on psychoanalysis, the Norwegian psychologist, Professor Bjørn

Killingmo, points out the existence of this particular phenomenon which takes many different forms in all developmental stages. Separating words from feelings is perhaps the earliest strategy we use in order to protect ourselves from intolerably painful emotions.[14]

Killingmo indicates the different meanings given to words: we may use them to protect ourselves, but as they also reflect our identity, they may ensnare and commit us. They may separate us from our inner world as well as expose us to it.

Isolation can therefore function on many levels. We can separate the semantic meaning of words from an effect, for example, by lowering our voice, or by separating the word-sound from the word-image by not pronouncing certain words; also, by saying them in a different language, or by just writing them down. Isolation can also manifest itself in our bodies when we dissociate our self-image from our body-image, as is the case in eating disorders. However, isolation may also have its roots in severe injuries from early childhood, 'narcissistic traumas', when feelings could not yet be expressed in words. This brings us back to the concept of alexithymia (Chapter XIII).

The above may perhaps explain why words – which are fundamental requirements for learning and developing, for coping with our inner and outer world, and for communication and interplay with others, may cause us also to distance ourselves from ourselves and from others.

Our entire Western culture, our school system and our educational science, bear the hallmarks of a biased rationalistic view of mankind which also affects the way words are used. In psychiatric work, we see so much human suffering, anxiety and misery, and are confronted by such violent effects, that we often need to protect ourselves. Intellectualising and psychologising may therefore easily become part of our defence mechanism, on a personal as well as on a professional level. Thus the use of words and theories which create a distance has become an occupational hazard for psychologists and psychiatrists. For this very reason it is of the utmost importance that professional therapists undergo psychoanalysis themselves. Unfortunately most psychiatrists and psychologists lack this essential experience.

My two psychoanalyses

My first psychoanalysis with Professor Harald Schjelderup made a profound impact on me. Above all, it made me aware of the importance of attitude and process, and of the relative value of words used in all psychotherapy and psychoanalysis. Those of us who were analysed by Harald Schjelderup appreciated his personal qualities, his presence, tolerance, respect and patience, as well as his reticence with regard to interpretations. He gave us time and space for aha-experiences in our quest for discovering our inner worlds. During the five years of my psychoanalysis with him, he never confronted me with anything that did not come from me, that was not mine. It also mattered to me that, by turning my head a little, I was able to look at him during the sessions – he sat beside the couch and not out of sight behind the headboard. His friendly face, voice and gestures made as much impression on me as the words he uttered. I can still see him with my inner eye which clearly proves that I have internalised some aspects of his personality.

In my role as a patient it became important to me that I should be the one to give voice to the unspoken, in the presence of one who would listen. Then the dangerous became not so dangerous any more, the special no longer so special, because it had become visible in a universally human perspective. 'The trolls burst' as soon as they are brought out into the light. By pronouncing the words to another person who accepted them and confirmed what I had been saying, at times even without words, a gradually ascending process was initiated. New layers emerged from the mists of oblivion, links were uncovered and emotions re-experienced time and time again, through the transference to the analyst.

Mainly through my own words, the past and the present were linked to my life history, and to my fantasies and feelings towards the analyst in the here and now. These words were not merely theoretical concepts, but were filled with feelings, with effects and experience. Insight did not primarily turn into intellectual, cognitive knowledge, but was transformed into 'corrective emotional experiences', a term used by Franz Alexander. I have since come to the conclusion that insight is more of a consequence than a primary goal in the psychotherapeutic process. In some cases, changes may even occur without prior insight.

It is appropriate here to mention the significance of dreams in psychotherapy and psychoanalysis. Indeed, in my two psychoanalyses, dreams played an important part. I am still fascinated by dreams, this 'royal road to the unconscious', as Freud called it. Dreams can be of great help to us, whatever our problems or afflictions, even if we are not ill at all.[15] Winnicott called the dream an 'intermediate area' where our inner and outer worlds meet. When the dream's imagery, the primary process, is translated into words, the secondary process, it may lead to increased awareness. The therapist's interpretations are not as important here as the patient's own associations to the dream as a whole. It is the dreamer who holds the key to the understanding of his dream. When working with dreams, I have repeatedly registered how patients – often with a feeling of aha – begin to see themselves and their life situations in a new light. They also discover new connections between their past and present, and become aware of new sides to their character, and the way they relate to others, including the therapist.

As described in Chapter VII, it was a dream which made me realise that attitude and process in psychoanalysis are not always enough. The dream in which I dreamed that I was the murderer Raskolnikov, led to my second analysis, this time with a woman, Astri Brun, M.A., whose attitude was totally different from that of Harald Schjelderup. She was more active, calling attention to details, and strongly confronting me which provoked my early, primitive rage. During my analysis with Schjelderup this rage had gone into hiding together with my guilt feelings. It was not easy for me to 'kill' Schjelderup since, in my transference, I experienced him as a man who was as kind and sensitive as my own father. I even believe he actually had some of my father's qualities. However, too much kindness and understanding may sometimes obstruct the therapeutic process.

Silence and inner space in psychotherapy

Analysts know that the absence of words – silence during the sessions – may give room for thoughts and feelings which are pushed away by words. I mentioned earlier that using words to express feelings may create anxiety; but the opposite, silence in the session, may also create anxiety. However, if silence is used wisely and empathetically, then it may further the therapeutic process. Both parties will then have an opportunity to open up, inwardly and outwardly, to 'feel' and to give free rein to their fantasies and emotions. Therapists can use periods of silence to register their own countertransference feelings and fantasies, which will help them to understand the patient's wordless communications. This was what Freud had in mind when, in an article giving advice to psychoanalysts, he wrote that 'the physician's subconscious should receive the patient's subconscious'.[16]

Psychotherapy creates an 'inner room' or an 'intermediary area' between the outer and the inner world. It was Winnicott who first pointed to the importance of 'transitional objects' which the child creates in this intermediary area. With this he meant the thumb, the comforter and the cuddly animal which become symbols of mother's breast and mother's presence and which help the child to tolerate the anxiety aroused by the separation and individuation process (Chapter I). It is in this intermediary area that play and speech are developed. The child's very first words resemble transitional objects.

'Mummy' becomes a magic symbol of mother's presence, a sound that can make her reappear.[17]

When doing psychotherapy with children, this 'intermediary room' is used for play, while in psychotherapy with adult patients, it is the dream images and the free associations which reflect something from our inner and outer worlds. There may be a considerable amount of acting out by patients in this intermediary area; 'acting in' when it occurs in the therapy session, and 'acting out' when it is done outside – the purpose being not to have to express anything in words. However, it may also be a way of experimenting with new modes of conduct, and the acts will then represent a wordless mode of communication.

Many years ago I realised that creative work with clay could be used as a transitional object and a means of communication for patients who initially had no words with which to express their feelings. By means of the figurative language of the shapes created in clay, they were able to express the deprivations they had suffered in early childhood, and their problems and conflicts. Looking at these shapes, I also saw something of the patients' inner world. By expressing in words some of my own thoughts and fantasies about these figures, the patients were gradually helped to use words to express their own feelings. By shaping forms in clay, the inner world found its way into words.[18]

Attempts have been made by different body-oriented and physiotherapeutical methods to build a bridge to the wordless domain but I cannot here elaborate on this exciting and as yet fairly unexplored field. Many early experiences and strong affects, as well as the defence against them, are contained within the body's musculature and inner organs (Chapters Twelve and Thirteen).

No one was there

There are times when we meet patients who, in the course of the therapy, regress to an early and wordless period of their lives where there had been no words; indeed in some cases there had not even been a human being. This type of total abandonment causes, I believe, the most unbearable human pain, and contains an autistic or psychotic core where the world comes to an end and everything dissolves and disappears.

Many years ago I had a female patient who for weeks and months kept silent during most of the sessions, while at the same time staring straight into my eyes with an expressionless face.[19] It made me gradually fantasise about something lonely, sad and wordless which went far back in time. After many sessions, I saw that a few tears were beginning to roll down her cheek and discovered simultaneously that I myself was on the brink of tears. When, after several weeks, I told her about my fantasies, she did not reply at first. In a later session she told me that, by looking into my eyes, it was as though she saw right through me and sank down into herself. It was as though she made contact with something important far back in her childhood which was both painful and good. Little by little she realised that the painful part was connected to extremely painful experiences of loss and separation, dating back to the first two years of her life. She had been abandoned both physically and emotionally, and was left in a state where she felt that there was no one, and that she would perish. She now remembered what her father had told her: that during the first three years of her life, at certain periods, she had been totally unresponsive to contact, lying in bed and banging her head against the wall. This autistic behaviour had also frightened her father.

The good part of the memory had to do with her mother's eyes; it seemed as though she could find her mother again by looking into my eyes. In a way, she could cling to something good out there which had to do with herself, and which turned into something good inside her.

One way of explaining this phase of the therapy is to say that our wordless eye-contact, which became a recurrent feature in the sessions over a period of several months, led to regression in the patient, to a return to the first years of her life. In the space created by the silence, the patient was able to relive some of the severe traumas caused by loss and abandonment, which had become the key to her problems later on in life. And yet, through silence, and by remaining in eye contact, she also came in contact with something that had been good before she was abandoned: her mother's eyes which had been kind when they looked at her. They had been 'incorporated' by her through introjection – and had left behind something good inside her, an inner anchor, a good core with its roots in the symbiotic phase. In this phase of the child's experiential world there exist no boundaries between the child and its mother – they are fused into one unit.

Through this silent eye contact I also came in touch with part of her inner world which was wordless, unbelievably lonely and frightening. By going into my own feelings and registering my countertransference, and by gradually attempting to express my own feelings in words, I was able to convey to her in words, that I understood. Perhaps this enabled her later to put a name to the wordless and the frightening. It transmitted to me several shades of meaning and perspectives from the inner and outer dramas in her life – the past dramas and the current ones in her daily life.

This story illustrates what I have earlier described as projective identification. It may be more correct to call it an interplay between projection and introjection – between pushing something out and taking something in. The patient projected something from her inner world onto me without words, made perhaps especially powerful through our silent eye-contact. The eyes are rightly called 'the mirror of the soul'. Unconsciously I took this 'something' into me, 'introjected' it, which caused me to have feelings and fantasies which again provoked physiological reactions in the form of tears. Perhaps I recognised something I myself had experienced; something I could identify with and understand on a cognitive level which enabled me to put into words what I was feeling. By identifying empathetically with her, I used these words to convey to her my feelings and fantasies. After several sessions she was able to confirm in her own words that what I had felt and said, had been partly correct. Possibly she had recognised something in my voice or in my words that bridged the gap between her inner world and her use of language. Together we were now able to understand a great deal more, and to see how some of the material that had emerged from her childhood was connected to her present adult life.

During a later phase of the eye contact, she was able to express in words the grandiose fantasies she had about absorbing me into herself by staring at me, partly as a conscious wish to hold on to an inner image of me, but also connected to fantasies about having me within her power and gaining full control over me. These wishes may express projective and introjective fantasies, as a defence against intense separation anxiety. They also had an impact on me. At times they would make me feel 'sucked dry' or caught in a 'deadlock'; this I also told her.

Summary

I have here sought to demonstrate that words are key elements in psychodynamic psychotherapy and in psychoanalysis. However, if we only use words acquired by study and they do not spring from the heart, then they will be empty and isolated from our inner being, and thus have no effect. The same applies to all theories and abstract concepts in our field. They can only be of value as auxiliary constructions helping us to understand partly what goes on inside us and between people.

Spoken words may transmit more than a cognitive content. They often convey a message about a person's inner world and outer reality, about feelings and effects, and about the relationship to the person we are in communication with. In the psychotherapeutic relationship this goes both ways.

Through wordless communication we may sometimes share, and reflect, our understanding of emotional traumas and experiences dating back to the patient's earliest developmental phases – the time when there were no words. Here, however, we find ourselves in one of the most complex areas, one which has been very little researched and where words alone do not suffice to establish communication. 'Transitional objects' may here be helpful in furthering communication.

How often do we who work as therapists succeed in creating this inner space in the therapy for the wordless and often frightening world of the early developmental stages? How often do we drown the wordless with our own words, satisfying our own need for being active, instead of just 'being' with the patient? Perhaps we become apprehensive about coming close to the patient's psychotic core, and becoming involved in the immense loneliness, anxiety, destruction or hopelessness that may lurk there.

It may be natural for the reader to ask at this point: what exactly is psychotherapy? Since I am not in a position to give an exhaustive answer, I have endeavoured to describe a few aspects of this process, including my own experience of two psychoanalyses.

The matter presented in this book may perhaps make us realise the importance of dialectic interplay and balance between the therapist's attitude conveying a mode of being, of being an individual, being together, being present and accessible to the other – and a mode of doing something, conveying something active, also using words to confirm, clarify, confront and possibly interpret. This may lead to gradual development and integration, through different forms of internalisations – from the introjection of the therapist's person to identification with certain aspects of him or her. Through the unique interaction taking place in psychotherapy or psychoanalysis, many patients will learn a great deal about themselves, and about what it means to be a human being in interaction with others. Aha-experiences will often stimulate a liberating process. But it is hard work, and we know that structural changes often require a great deal of time, often even many years.

I agree with Winnicott when he connects 'being' with the female element in both women and men, and being active, 'doing', with the male element in both men and women.[20] This is also in accordance with modern brain research.[21] My training analyst, Harald Schjelderup, had more of 'being', while Astri Brun had more of active 'doing'. I am glad to have had both these experiences in my analyses in that order, first of 'being' and then of 'doing'.

A third perspective concerns the question about what happens to the primitive rage which many people keep well concealed (Chapter VII). This rage must be allowed to vent itself through words and feelings in the transference to the psychotherapist. Fundamental changes may take place when the patient realises that he or she is neither punished nor rejected, and that the therapist 'survives' and is still there, alive and accessible. Using my example from Chapter VII, the patient will then discover that: 'I am no murderer after all! I am not evil and I do not deserve to be punished! I am free!' Without this, in the deepest sense, the good cannot triumph over the evil, and the split between good and evil cannot be removed. Rage will then no longer be self-destructive. It may be at this moment that I first discover that I am not alone in the world, that there are other people who may be of help indeed, there may even be others apart from the therapist. And most importantly: I will discover my own resources!

NOTES TO THE TEXT

[1] Jørstad, J, Psykoterapiens plass og utvikling I norsk psykiatri In: *Psykiatrisk Vidsyn, Festskrift til O.W. Steenfeldt-Foss på hans 60-års dag*, Eds. Gude, Albretsen, Lund og Retterstøl, Oslo University Publ. Co., 1991, pp.97–104.

[2] Winnicott, D W, *Playing and Reality*, Tavistock Publ., London, 1971.

[3] Guntrip, H, *Schizoid Phenomena, Object-relations and the Self*, The Hogarth Press, London, 1974.

[4] Kohut, H, *The Restoration of the Self*, Int. Univers. Press., New York, 1977.

[5] Sullivan, H S, *The Interpersonal Theory of Psychiatry*, W.W. Norton & Co. Inc., New York, 1953.

[6] Horney, K, *The Neurotic Personality in our Time*, Northon, New York, 1937.

[7] ——*New Ways in Psychoanalysis*, Norton, New York, 1939.

[8] ——*Neurosis and Human Growth*, Norton, New York, 1950.

[9] Hartmann, H, *Ego psychology and the problem of adaptation*, Int. Univers. Press, New York, 1958.

[10] Hartmann, H, Kris, E and Loewenstein, R M, *Papers on psychoanalytic psychology*, Int. Univers. Press, New York, 1964.

[11] Cyvin, K, *Eksistensialistick seminar*, Stensil, Oslo, 1964.

[12] ——*Sigmund Freud og Matrin Heidegger*, Stensil, Oslo, 1965.

[13] Main, T F, 'Knowledge, learning and lack of thought', The Austral. and New Zeal. J. Psychiat., 2, 1967, pp.64–71.

[14] Killingmo, B, 'Beyond semantics: A clinical and theoretical study of isolation', Int. J. of Psychoanal., 71, 1, 1990, pp.113–126.

[15] Jørstad, J, Drømmer – er de fortsatt knogeveien til det ubevisste? I: *Psykoanalyse idag*, Eds., Anti, Auestad, Haugsgjerd, Holter, Jørstad and Vaglum, Tano, Oslo, 1986, pp.33–63.

[16] Freud, S, (1912*), Recommendations to Physicians practising Psychoanalysis*, S.E. Vol. XII, The Hogarth Press, London, 1958.

[17] Winnicott, D W, *An Anthology of Papers from D.W.W.*, (Swedish Edition), The Winnicott Trust, London, 1993.

[18] Jørstad, J, 'Clay forming in psychotherapy, a possible remedy to communication and insight', Acta Psychiatr. Scand., 41, 4, 1965, pp.491–526.

[19] Jørstad, J, 'Aspects of Transference and Countertransference in Relation to Gaze and mutual Gaze during Psychoanalysis', Scand. Psychoanal. Rev. 1988, 11, pp.117–140.

[20] Winnicott, D W, op. cit.

[21] Moir, A and Jessel, D, *Brain Sex*, Michael Joseph Ltd, London, 1989.

Epilogue

This is not a book for specialists, nor is it a scientific treatise or a psychiatry text book. And it is not an autobiography with my personal life as the main topic. As mentioned in the foreword, I have attempted to convey to the readers some of the most important experiences in my own life, and in my work with people. My life and work has been rich in events and full of diversities. Because my experiences touch the basic areas of life, common and so important to most people, I have felt it my duty to relate and share these experiences. I hope that readers will identify with them, and recognise something from their own lives, and that this recognition will prove to be helpful in life's eternal voyage between Scylla and Charybdis.

There lies more in this hope than mere cognition. We know that increased knowledge does not always lead to change. It is therefore my hope – even though it may be expecting too much – that the reader will gain more than knowledge, but rather an expanded awareness, as I would call it. With this I mean recognition that reaches deeper levels than conscious and cognitive levels, which will have consequences for life and the choices we make. It was in critical moments when I was anxious and under great stress that I was shaken out of my habitual way of thinking and taking conventional courses of action. At other times this happened through being in contact with people who were close or important to me.

I have experienced both these aspects of life in psychotherapy and psychoanalysis. It has been a privilege, through my two training analyses, to take part in a process which leads to greater awareness and freedom. It has also been a privilege to be able to continue working with people in a way which has been meaningful to my patients and myself.

In times when intellectual knowledge, technology and economic considerations dominate the public and private world, it is important not to forget humanistic values, the individual's situation in society, and how relationships between people evolve. Most important is the interaction between parents and children, and between men and women. This is one of my concerns in this book. Another basic theme is being aware of the power of the unconscious, both in individuals and collectively. If we take this seriously, it will have great consequences in our lives and in the society we live in.

I would like to say in the words of the Norwegian poet Arne Garborg: 'I would rather see with my eyes, than walk blindly and deafly through the world, not recognising the truth.'